MOST REQUESTED

Taste of Home

Weeknight Favorites

TASTE OF HOME BOOKS • RDA ENTHUSIAST BRANDS, LLC • MILWAUKEE, WI

MOST REQUESTED

Taste of Home

Weeknight Favorites

OUR MOST CONVENIENT,
MOST TREASURED AND
MOST REQUESTED RECIPES!

THE BEST RECIPES FOR YOUR BUSIEST WEEKNIGHTS

Short on time doesn't mean short on flavor— and fast to the table doesn't mean resorting to fast food! For the tightest schedules and the busiest evenings, you'll find everything you need in this new collection of ultra convenient family recipes.

Talented home cooks around the country have shared their recipes with us, and we're sharing the best of them with you. ***Taste of Home Most Requested Weeknight Favorites*** showcases 374 of our most-loved dishes so you can create convenient, timesaving meals that will satisfy everyone at your table.

Each recipe was approved by the experts in the *Taste of Home* Test Kitchen, so you can be sure they'll all work the first time. Full-color photos of finished dishes on every page and helpful kitchen tips scattered throughout the book make it even easier to cook with confidence.

Refer to these handy at-a-glance icons to make the most of your time in the kitchen.

5i These dishes require no more than five items (not counting water, oil, salt, pepper and optional ingredients). What could be easier?

❄ To boost the convenience factor even higher, these freezer-friendly recipes are perfect for nights when you don't have time to cook.

🍎 Looking for healthier recipe choices? This icon identifies healthy and calorie-conscious options.

🍲 If you're a fan of prepping in the morning and eating when you get home, look for our slow-cooker icon.

🍲 Instant Pot™ recipes make the most of the newest sensational kitchen gadget.

Dive in, and soon the recipes in ***Most Requested Weeknight Favorites*** will be among the most requested in your house. Don't wait for the weekend—now every night is the right time for a scrumptious home-cooked meal!

© 2019 RDA Enthusiast Brands, LLC.
1610 N. 2nd St., Suite 102, Milwaukee WI 53212-3906
All rights reserved. Taste of Home is a registered trademark of RDA Enthusiast Brands, LLC.
Visit *tasteofhome.com* for other *Taste of Home* books and products.

International Standard Book Number:
978-1-61765-906-5
Library of Congress Control Number: 2019946410
Component Number:
119200038H

Executive Editor: Mark Hagen
Senior Art Director:
Raeann Thompson
Editor: Hazel Wheaton

Designer: Arielle Jardine
Copy Editor: Ann Walter

Cover Photography
Photographer: Dan Roberts
Set Stylist: Melissa Franco
Food Stylist: Shannon Norris

Pictured on front cover:
Garlic Beef Enchiladas, p. 142

Pictured on title pages:
Meatball Pizza, p. 48; Easy Ground Beef Taco Salad, p. 101

Pictured on back cover:
Jalapeno Swiss Burgers, p. 85; Spinach & Tortellini Soup, p. 125; Pumpkin Mousse, p. 232

Printed in China
1 3 5 7 9 10 8 6 4 2

TABLE OF
CONTENTS

To find a recipe: *tasteofhome.com*
To submit a recipe: *tasteofhome.com/submit*
To find out about other *Taste of Home* products:
  shoptasteofhome.com

f LIKE US facebook.com/tasteofhome

🐦 TWEET US twitter.com/tasteofhome

📷 FOLLOW US @tasteofhome

📌 PIN US pinterest.com/taste_of_home

STOVETOP & SKILLET

Don't bother to turn on the oven! From sizzling stir-frys to skillet all-in-ones to pan-cooked chops with tasty sauces, these come together on top of the stove, right before your eyes!

TENDERLOIN WITH HERB SAUCE

Tender pork is treated to a rich and creamy sauce with a slight red-pepper kick. This hearty dish is simple to prepare and always a dinnertime winner.
—*Monica Shipley, Tulare, CA*

Takes: 25 min. • **Makes:** 6 servings

- 2 pork tenderloins (1 lb. each)
- ½ tsp. salt
- 4 tsp. butter
- ⅔ cup half-and-half cream
- 2 Tbsp. minced fresh parsley
- 2 tsp. herbes de Provence
- 2 tsp. reduced-sodium soy sauce
- 1 tsp. beef bouillon granules
- ½ to ¾ tsp. crushed red pepper flakes

1. Cut each tenderloin into 12 slices; sprinkle with salt. In a large nonstick skillet, melt butter over medium heat; brown pork in batches, 3-4 minutes per side. Return all pork to pan.
2. Mix the remaining ingredients; pour over pork. Cook, uncovered, over low heat until the sauce is thickened and a thermometer inserted in the pork reads 145°, 2-3 minutes, stirring occasionally. Let stand 5 minutes before serving.

4 OZ. COOKED PORK: 238 cal., 10g fat (5g sat. fat), 104mg chol., 495mg sod., 2g carb. (1g sugars, 0.29g fiber), 31g pro. **DIABETIC EXCHANGES:** 4 lean meat, 1 fat

READER REVIEW

"This was incredible! The easiest and tastiest pork loin I have ever had—I wouldn't change a single thing about it. I loved it, my kids loved it (and they don't even *like* pork!), and my husband liked it so much he asked if we could have it again later this week!"

JENNB76, TASTEOFHOME.COM

WEEKNIGHT CABBAGE KIELBASA SKILLET

I like the challenge of cooking lower-fat meals that pack big flavor. This recipe, from a dear friend, fits the bill. My son rates it a 10 out of 10!
—*Beverly Batty, Forest Lake, MN*

Takes: 30 min. • **Makes:** 4 servings

- 1½ tsp. cornstarch
- ¼ cup cider vinegar
- 1 Tbsp. honey
- 1 tsp. Dijon mustard
- ¼ tsp. salt
- ¼ tsp. pepper
- 1 Tbsp. canola oil
- 1 pkg. (14 oz.) smoked turkey kielbasa, cut into ¼-in. slices
- 2 medium red potatoes (about 8 oz.), cut into ½-in. cubes
- ½ cup sliced sweet onion
- ½ cup chopped sweet red pepper
- 4 bacon strips, cooked and crumbled
- ½ cup water
- 1 tsp. beef bouillon granules
- 1 pkg. (14 oz.) coleslaw mix

1. In a small bowl, whisk the first 6 ingredients until smooth.

2. In a large skillet, heat oil over medium-high heat. Add the kielbasa, potatoes, onion, red pepper and bacon; cook and stir 3-5 minutes or until the kielbasa is lightly browned.

3. Add water and bouillon; bring to a boil. Reduce heat; simmer, covered, 6-8 minutes or until the potatoes are almost tender. Add the coleslaw mix; cook, covered, 4-6 minutes longer or until tender, stirring occasionally.

4. Stir the cornstarch mixture and add it to pan. Bring to a boil; cook and stir 1-2 minutes or until the sauce is thickened.

1¼ CUPS: 305 cal., 12g fat (3g sat. fat), 70mg chol., 1529mg sod., 25g carb. (12g sugars, 4g fiber), 21g pro.

DINNER IN A BAG

I get a head start on this family-pleasing dinner by assembling a pantry kit that I can grab in an instant. I measure dry macaroni and the spice mixture into separate plastic bags, then store them in a paper bag with canned tomatoes.
—*Darlene Brenden, Salem, OR*

Prep: 5 min. • **Cook:** 25 min.
Makes: 4 servings

- 1 lb. ground beef
- 2 cans (14½ oz. each) stewed tomatoes
- ¼ cup dried minced onion
- 1 tsp. salt
- 1 tsp. chili powder
- ¼ to ½ tsp. pepper
- ¼ tsp. sugar
- 1 cup uncooked elbow macaroni

1. In a large skillet, cook beef over medium heat until no longer pink; drain. Add the tomatoes, seasonings and sugar; bring to a boil. Reduce heat and simmer for 5 minutes.

2. Stir in macaroni; cover and simmer for 15 minutes. Uncover; simmer until macaroni is tender and the sauce is thickened.

1 CUP: 289 cal., 11g fat (5g sat. fat), 56mg chol., 858mg sod., 25g carb. (8g sugars, 2g fiber), 24g pro.

READER REVIEW

"We've made this for years, and call it 'easy goulash'—it's a great go-to meal. I love the idea of having all the ingredients together, ready to go!"

TAMI, TASTEOFHOME.COM

SPICED PORK WITH BOURBON SAUCE

I don't remember where I found this recipe, but it's become one of my favorite entrees to serve to company. I usually prepare it with a side of roasted vegetables.

—*Kathy Kantrud, Fenton, MI*

Takes: 25 min. • **Makes:** 4 servings

- ½ cup bourbon or reduced-sodium chicken broth
- ¼ cup packed dark brown sugar
- 3 Tbsp. white vinegar
- 3 Tbsp. reduced-sodium soy sauce
- 2 garlic cloves, minced
- ½ tsp. pepper
- ½ tsp. chili powder
- ¼ tsp. ground cinnamon
- ⅛ tsp. salt
- ⅛ tsp. ground allspice
- 1 pork tenderloin (1 lb.), cut into 12 slices

1. In a small saucepan, combine the bourbon, brown sugar, vinegar, soy sauce, garlic and pepper. Bring to a boil; cook until the liquid is reduced to about ½ cup, stirring occasionally.
2. Meanwhile, combine the chili powder, cinnamon, salt and allspice; rub over the pork slices.
3. In a large skillet coated with cooking spray, cook pork over medium heat for 2-4 minutes on each side or until tender. Serve with sauce.

3 OZ. COOKED PORK: 221 cal., 4g fat (1g sat. fat), 63mg chol., 581mg sod., 15g carb. (13g sugars, 0 fiber), 23g pro. **DIABETIC EXCHANGES:** 3 lean meat, 1 starch.

> **TEST KITCHEN TIP**
> Pork tenderloin thaws and cooks quickly, so it's great to have in the freezer for last-minute meals. Thaw the tenderloin using the "defrost" cycle of your microwave according to the manufacturer's directions.

BLACK BEAN & CORN QUINOA

My daughter's college asked parents for a favorite healthy recipe to use in the dining halls. This quinoa fits the bill—and the students loved it!

—*Lindsay McSweeney, Winchester, MA*

Takes: 30 min. • **Makes:** 4 servings

- 2 Tbsp. canola oil
- 1 medium onion, finely chopped
- 1 medium sweet red pepper, finely chopped
- 1 celery rib, finely chopped
- 2 tsp. chili powder
- ¼ tsp. salt
- ¼ tsp. pepper
- 2 cups vegetable stock
- 1 cup frozen corn
- 1 cup quinoa, rinsed
- 1 can (15 oz.) black beans, rinsed and drained
- ⅓ cup plus 2 Tbsp. minced fresh cilantro, divided

1. In a large skillet, heat oil over medium-high heat. Add the onion, red pepper, celery and seasonings; cook and stir 5-7 minutes or until vegetables are tender.
2. Stir in vegetable stock and corn; bring to a boil. Stir in quinoa. Reduce heat; simmer, covered, 12-15 minutes or until the liquid is absorbed.
3. Add beans and ⅓ cup of the cilantro; heat through, stirring occasionally. Sprinkle with the remaining cilantro.

1¼ CUPS: 375 cal., 10g fat (1g sat. fat), 0 chol., 668mg sod., 60g carb. (5g sugars, 10g fiber), 13g pro.

HERBED LEMON PORK CHOPS

You'll receive plenty of compliments on these tender and juicy pork chops. Mixed herbs and a final squeeze of lemon pack on the flavor in just 20 minutes!
—*Billi Jo Sylvester, New Smyrna Beach, FL*

Takes: 20 min. • **Makes:** 2 servings

- 1 tsp. salt-free garlic seasoning blend
- ½ tsp. dried basil
- ½ tsp. dried oregano
- ½ tsp. dried parsley flakes
- ¼ tsp. salt
- ¼ tsp. garlic powder
- ¼ tsp. dried rosemary, crushed
- 2 bone-in pork loin chops (6 oz. each)
- 1 tsp. olive oil
- 1 Tbsp. lemon juice

1. Mix seasonings; rub over both sides of the chops. In a large nonstick skillet, heat oil over medium-high heat. Add the pork; cook until a thermometer reads 145°, 5-8 minutes per side.

2. Remove from heat; drizzle with lemon juice. Let stand, covered, 5 minutes before serving.

1 PORK CHOP: 200 cal., 10g fat (3g sat. fat), 74mg chol., 350mg sod., 1g carb. (0 sugars, 0 fiber), 26g pro. **DIABETIC EXCHANGES:** 4 lean meat, ½ fat.

READER REVIEW

"This recipe is delicious and easy to make. I was looking for a healthy pork chop recipe and this one is a keeper! They were very tender and flavorful!"

GUNSLINGER, TASTEOFHOME.COM

PARMESAN-CRUSTED TILAPIA

I usually serve this crispy fish with tartar sauce and seasoned steamed veggies. It's like a Friday night fish fry without all the calories!
—*Christi McElroy, Neenah, WI*

Takes: 25 min. • **Makes:** 4 servings

- ½ cup all-purpose flour
- 1 large egg, beaten
- ½ cup crushed Ritz crackers (about 10 crackers)
- ¼ cup grated Parmesan cheese
- ½ tsp. salt
- 4 tilapia fillets (5 oz. each)
- 2 Tbsp. olive oil
  Lemon wedges

1. Place the flour and egg in separate shallow bowls. In another shallow bowl, combine the crackers, cheese and salt. Dip the fillets in the flour, then the egg, then the cracker mixture; turn until coated.

2. In a large cast-iron or other heavy skillet, cook fillets in oil over medium heat until the tilapia just begins to flake easily with a fork. Serve with lemon wedges.

1 FILLET: 287 cal., 13g fat (3g sat. fat), 125mg chol., 440mg sod., 12g carb. (1g sugars, 0 fiber), 31g pro.

SONALI RUDER
New York, NY

FETA SHRIMP SKILLET

My husband and I tried a dish similar to this one on our honeymoon in Greece. I re-created the flavors with this recipe when we got home. When I make it now, it brings back wonderful memories of our time overseas!
—Sonali Ruder, New York, NY

- -

Takes: 30 min. • **Makes:** 4 servings

- 1 Tbsp. olive oil
- 1 medium onion, finely chopped
- 3 garlic cloves, minced
- 1 tsp. dried oregano
- ½ tsp. pepper
- ¼ tsp. salt
- 2 cans (14½ oz. each) diced tomatoes, undrained
- ¼ cup white wine, optional

- 1 lb. uncooked medium shrimp, peeled and deveined
- 2 Tbsp. minced fresh parsley
- ¾ cup crumbled feta cheese

1. In a large nonstick skillet, heat the oil over medium-high heat. Add onion; cook and stir 4-6 minutes or until tender. Add garlic and seasonings; cook 1 minute longer. Stir in the tomatoes and, if desired, wine. Bring to a boil. Reduce heat; simmer, uncovered, 5-7 minutes or until the sauce is slightly thickened.
2. Add shrimp and parsley; cook 5-6 minutes or until shrimp turn pink, stirring occasionally. Remove from heat; sprinkle with cheese. Let stand, covered, until the cheese is softened.
1¼ CUPS: 240 cal., 8g fat (3g sat. fat), 149mg chol., 748mg sod., 16g carb. (9g sugars, 5g fiber), 25g pro. **DIABETIC EXCHANGES:** 3 lean meat, 1 starch, 1 fat.

TEST KITCHEN TIP
For even more Mediterranean flavor, try adding ¼ cup of chopped kalamata olives to the pan along with the tomatoes. Like it spicy? Try adding a pinch of crushed red pepper with your other seasonings.

SMOTHERED CHICKEN

I top tender chicken breasts with mushrooms, bacon, green onions and cheese for a quick, comforting meal that has become a family favorite in our house.
—Penny Walton, Westerville, OH

Takes: 20 min. • **Makes:** 4 servings

- 4 boneless skinless chicken breast halves (5 oz. each)
- ¼ tsp. seasoned salt
- ¼ tsp. garlic powder
- 3 tsp. canola oil, divided
- 1 cup sliced fresh mushrooms
- 1 cup shredded Mexican cheese blend
- 4 green onions, chopped
- 6 bacon strips, cooked and chopped

1. Pound chicken breasts to ¼-in. thickness. Sprinkle with seasonings.

2. In a large nonstick skillet, heat 1 tsp. oil over medium-high heat; saute mushrooms until tender, 2-3 minutes. Remove from pan.

3. In same pan, cook chicken in remaining oil until bottom is browned, about 4 minutes. Turn chicken; top with the mushrooms and remaining ingredients. Cook, covered, until chicken is no longer pink, 4-5 minutes.

1 CHICKEN BREAST HALF: 363 cal., 21g fat (7g sat. fat), 116mg chol., 555mg sod., 3g carb. (1g sugars, 1g fiber), 40g pro.

BACON & ROSEMARY CHICKEN

Simple ingredients add up to simply fantastic flavor in this fast recipe that everyone will rave about. You'll almost certainly add this to your roster of go-to meals.
—Yvonne Starlin, Westmoreland, TN

Takes: 30 min. • **Makes:** 4 servings

- 4 boneless skinless chicken breast halves (5 oz. each)
- ½ tsp. salt
- ¼ tsp. pepper
- ¼ cup all-purpose flour
- 5 bacon strips, chopped
- 1 Tbsp. butter
- 4 garlic cloves, thinly sliced
- 1 Tbsp. minced fresh rosemary or 1 tsp. dried rosemary, crushed
- ⅛ tsp. crushed red pepper flakes
- 1 cup reduced-sodium chicken broth
- 2 Tbsp. lemon juice

1. Pound chicken breasts slightly with a meat mallet to uniform thickness; sprinkle with salt and pepper. Place flour in a shallow bowl. Dip the chicken in flour to coat both sides; shake off excess.

2. In a large skillet, cook bacon over medium heat until crisp, stirring occasionally. Remove with a slotted spoon; drain on paper towels. Discard drippings, reserving 2 Tbsp. in pan. Cook the chicken in butter and reserved drippings 4-6 minutes on each side or until a thermometer reads 165°. Remove chicken and keep warm.

3. Add garlic, rosemary and pepper flakes to skillet; cook and stir 1 minute. Add broth and lemon juice; bring to a boil. Cook until liquid is reduced by half. Return chicken and bacon to skillet; heat through.

1 CHICKEN BREAST HALF: 304 cal., 16g fat (6g sat. fat), 101mg chol., 719mg sod., 5g carb. (1g sugars, 0 fiber), 33g pro.

HONEY CHICKEN STIR-FRY

I'm a busy mom, and my schedule is very dependent upon my son. So I like meals that can be ready in as little time as possible. This all-in-one stir-fry with a hint of sweetness from honey is a big timesaver.
—*Caroline Sperry, Allentown, MI*

Takes: 30 min. • **Makes:** 4 servings

- 2 tsp. cornstarch
- 1 Tbsp. cold water
- 3 tsp. olive oil, divided
- 1 lb. boneless skinless chicken breasts, cut into 1-in. pieces
- 1 garlic clove, minced
- 3 Tbsp. honey
- 2 Tbsp. reduced-sodium soy sauce
- ⅛ tsp. salt
- ⅛ tsp. pepper
- 1 pkg. (16 oz.) frozen broccoli stir-fry vegetable blend
   Hot cooked rice, optional

1. Mix cornstarch and water until smooth. In a large nonstick skillet, heat 2 tsp. oil over medium-high heat; stir-fry chicken and garlic for 1 minute. Add honey, soy sauce, salt and pepper; cook and stir until chicken is no longer pink, 2-3 minutes. Remove from pan.
2. In the same pan, stir-fry vegetable blend in the remaining oil just until tender, 4-5 minutes. Return chicken to pan. Stir cornstarch mixture and add to pan; bring to a boil. Cook and stir until thickened, about 1 minute. Serve with rice if desired.
1 CUP STIR-FRY: 249 cal., 6g fat (1g sat. fat), 63mg chol., 455mg sod., 21g carb. (15g sugars, 3g fiber), 25g pro. **DIABETIC EXCHANGES:** 3 lean meat, 2 vegetable, ½ starch.

CHICKEN THIGHS WITH SHALLOTS & SPINACH

What could be better than an entree that comes with its own creamy vegetable side? It makes an eye-catching presentation and goes together in no time flat for a healthy supper.
—*Genna Johannes, Wrightstown, WI*

Takes: 30 min. • **Makes:** 6 servings

- 6 boneless skinless chicken thighs (about 1½ lbs.)
- ½ tsp. seasoned salt
- ½ tsp. pepper
- 1½ tsp. olive oil
- 4 shallots, thinly sliced
- ⅓ cup white wine or reduced-sodium chicken broth
- 1 pkg. (10 oz.) fresh spinach, trimmed
- ¼ tsp. salt
- ¼ cup reduced-fat sour cream

1. Sprinkle chicken with seasoned salt and pepper. In a large nonstick skillet, heat oil over medium heat. Add chicken; cook until a thermometer reads 170°, about 6 minutes on each side. Remove from pan; keep warm.
2. In the same pan, cook and stir shallots until tender. Add wine; bring to a boil. Cook until wine is reduced by half. Add spinach and salt; cook and stir just until the spinach is wilted. Stir in sour cream; serve with chicken.
FREEZE OPTION: Before adding sour cream, cool chicken and the spinach mixture. Freeze in freezer containers. To use, partially thaw in refrigerator overnight. Heat through slowly in a covered skillet until a thermometer inserted in the chicken reads 170°, stirring occasionally. Stir in sour cream.
1 CHICKEN THIGH WITH ¼ CUP SPINACH MIXTURE: 223 cal., 10g fat (3g sat. fat), 77mg chol., 360mg sod., 7g carb. (2g sugars, 1g fiber), 23g pro. **DIABETIC EXCHANGES:** 3 lean meat, 1½ fat, 1 vegetable.

CURRY CHICKEN & RICE

I updated this chicken and rice dish by adding veggies and cashews to give it fresh and crunchy appeal. The green chiles in the tomatoes give it just a little kick, but if you really like spice, add fresh diced jalapeno.
—*Denise Klibert, Shreveport, LA*

Takes: 30 min. • **Makes:** 4 servings

- 1¾ cups water
- 1 Tbsp. olive oil
- 1 pkg. (7.2 oz.) rice pilaf mix
- 1 tsp. curry powder
- 2 cups shredded rotisserie chicken
- 1 can (14½ oz.) diced tomatoes with mild green chiles, undrained
- 1 cup frozen peas (about 4 oz.)
- ½ cup chopped lightly salted cashews

1. In a large saucepan, bring water and oil to a boil. Stir in the pilaf mix, the contents of its seasoning packet, and curry powder. Return to a boil. Reduce heat; simmer, covered, for 15 minutes.

2. Stir in chicken, tomatoes and peas. Cook, covered, 8-10 minutes longer or until liquid is almost absorbed and the rice is tender. Sprinkle with cashews.

1⅓ CUPS: 500 cal., 18g fat (4g sat. fat), 62mg chol., 1162mg sod., 53g carb.(6g sugars, 5g fiber), 32g pro.

SKILLET BEEF & POTATOES

Sirloin strips with red potatoes and fresh rosemary are seriously amazing and ready in a flash. The key is precooking the potatoes in the microwave to speed the process.
—*Taste of Home Test Kitchen*

Takes: 25 min. • **Makes:** 4 servings

- 1½ lbs. red potatoes (about 5 medium), halved and cut into ¼-in. slices
- ⅓ cup water
- ½ tsp. salt
- 1 lb. beef top sirloin steak, cut into thin strips
- ½ cup chopped onion
- 3 Tbsp. olive oil, divided
- 2 tsp. garlic pepper blend
- 1½ tsp. minced fresh rosemary

1. Place the potatoes, water and salt in a microwave-safe dish; microwave, covered, on high until the potatoes are tender, 7-9 minutes. Drain.

2. Meanwhile, toss beef with onion, 2 Tbsp. of oil and the pepper blend. In a large skillet over medium-high heat, cook and stir half of the beef mixture until beef is browned, 1-2 minutes. Remove from pan; repeat with remaining beef mixture.

3. In a clean skillet, heat the remaining oil over medium-high heat. Add potatoes; cook until lightly browned, 4-5 minutes, turning occasionally. Stir in the beef mixture; heat through. Sprinkle with rosemary.

1½ CUPS: 320 cal., 16g fat (4g sat. fat), 63mg chol., 487mg sod., 20g carb. (2g sugars, 2g fiber), 23g pro. **DIABETIC EXCHANGES:** 3 lean meat, 2 fat, 1 starch.

TILAPIA WITH JASMINE RICE

This tender, full-flavored tilapia with fragrant jasmine rice is absolutely to die for. And it gets better: Each serving has only 5 grams of fat!
—*Shirl Parsons, Cape Carteret, NC*

- -

Takes: 25 min. • **Makes:** 2 servings

¾	cup water
½	cup uncooked jasmine rice
1½	tsp. butter
¼	tsp. ground cumin
¼	tsp. seafood seasoning
¼	tsp. pepper
⅛	tsp. salt
2	tilapia fillets (6 oz. each)
¼	cup fat-free Italian salad dressing

1. In a small saucepan, combine water, rice and butter; bring to a boil. Reduce the heat; simmer, covered, until the liquid is absorbed and rice is tender, 15-20 minutes.
2. Meanwhile, mix seasonings; sprinkle over tilapia. In a large skillet, heat salad dressing over medium heat until hot. Add fillets; cook until the fish just begins to flake easily with a fork, 3-4 minutes per side. Serve with rice.
1 FILLET WITH ¾ CUP RICE: 356 cal., 5g fat (3g sat. fat), 91mg chol., 743mg sod., 41g carb. (2g sugars, 1g fiber), 35g pro. **DIABETIC EXCHANGES:** 4 lean meat, 3 starch, ½ fat.

BARBARA PLETZKE
Herndon, VA

HEALTH TIP

Tilapia is low in calories, rich in high-quality protein and a good source of many B vitamins. You can substitute any thin, delicate white fish, such as red snapper, sole, trout or catfish for the tilapia, if you'd like.

PORK & RAMEN STIR-FRY

I put a bit of a spin on a traditional stir-fry. Ramen noodles are quick to substitute for the expected rice, and bagged coleslaw mix gives the dish a good crisp-tender bite along with fresh broccoli.
—*Barbara Pletzke, Herndon, VA*

- -

Takes: 30 min. • **Makes:** 4 servings

¼	cup reduced-sodium soy sauce
2	Tbsp. ketchup
2	Tbsp. Worcestershire sauce
2	tsp. sugar
¼	tsp. crushed red pepper flakes
3	tsp. canola oil, divided
1	lb. boneless pork loin chops, cut into ½-in. strips
1	cup fresh broccoli florets
4	cups coleslaw mix
1	can (8 oz.) bamboo shoots, drained
4	garlic cloves, minced
2	pkg. (3 oz. each) ramen noodles

1. In a small bowl, whisk the first 5 ingredients until blended. In a large skillet, heat 2 tsp. oil over medium-high heat. Add pork; stir-fry 2-3 minutes or until pork is no longer pink. Remove from pan.
2. In the same pan, stir-fry the broccoli in the remaining oil for 3 minutes. Add coleslaw mix, bamboo shoots and garlic; stir-fry 3-4 minutes longer or until the broccoli is crisp-tender. Stir in the soy sauce mixture and pork; heat through.
3. Meanwhile, cook noodles according to package directions, discarding or saving seasoning packets for another use. Drain noodles; add to the pork mixture and toss to combine.
1¾ CUPS: 354 cal., 14g fat (5g sat. fat), 44mg chol., 794mg sod., 32g carb. (6g sugars, 3g fiber), 23g pro.

KOREAN BEEF & RICE

A friend raved about Korean bulgogi—beef cooked in soy sauce and ginger—so I tried it. It's delicious! Dazzle the table with this tasty version of beef and rice.
—Elizabeth King, Duluth, MN

Takes: 15 min. • **Makes:** 4 servings

- 1 lb. lean ground beef (90% lean)
- 3 garlic cloves, minced
- ¼ cup packed brown sugar
- ¼ cup reduced-sodium soy sauce
- 2 tsp. sesame oil
- ¼ tsp. ground ginger
- ¼ tsp. crushed red pepper flakes
- ¼ tsp. pepper
- 2⅔ cups hot cooked brown rice
- 3 green onions, thinly sliced

1. In a large skillet, cook beef and garlic over medium heat for 6-8 minutes or until the beef is no longer pink, breaking up beef into crumbles. In a small bowl, mix brown sugar, soy sauce, oil and seasonings.

2. Stir sauce into beef; heat through. Serve with rice. Sprinkle with green onions.

FREEZE OPTION: Freeze cooled meat mixture in freezer containers. To use, partially thaw in refrigerator overnight. Heat through in a saucepan, stirring occasionally.

½ CUP BEEF MIXTURE WITH ⅔ CUP RICE: 413 cal., 13g fat (4g sat. fat), 71mg chol., 647mg sod., 46g carb. (14g sugars, 3g fiber), 27g pro. **DIABETIC EXCHANGES:** 3 starch, 3 lean meat, ½ fat.

HEALTH TIP
Using lean ground beef instead of beef that's 80% lean saves 45 calories per 4-oz. serving of beef. Lean ground beef is also 29% lower in saturated fat.

QUICK CHICKEN PICCATA

Laced with lemon and simmered in white wine, this stovetop entree is super easy and elegant. Just add sides of bread and veggies to make it into a great meal.
—*Cynthia Heil, Augusta, GA*

Takes: 30 min. • **Makes:** 4 servings

- ¼ cup all-purpose flour
- ½ tsp. salt
- ½ tsp. pepper
- 4 boneless skinless chicken breast halves (4 oz. each)
- ¼ cup butter, cubed
- ¼ cup white wine or chicken broth
- 1 Tbsp. lemon juice
  Minced fresh parsley, optional

1. In a shallow bowl, mix flour, salt and pepper. Pound the chicken breasts with a meat mallet to ½-in. thickness. Dip the chicken in the flour mixture to coat both sides; shake off excess.
2. In a large skillet, heat butter over medium heat. Brown chicken on both sides. Add the wine; bring to a boil. Reduce heat; simmer, uncovered, until the chicken is no longer pink, 12-15 minutes. Drizzle with lemon juice. If desired, sprinkle with parsley.

1 CHICKEN BREAST HALF WITH ABOUT 1 TBSP. SAUCE: 265 cal., 14g fat (8g sat. fat), 93mg chol., 442mg sod., 7g carb. (0 sugars, 0 fiber), 24g pro.

SKILLET LASAGNA

My husband loves my simple stovetop lasagna. Loaded with ground beef and cheeses, this easy version makes a super supper.
—*Lucinda Walker, Somerset, PA*

Prep: 25 min. • **Cook:** 40 min. + standing
Makes: 8 servings

- 1½ lbs. lean ground beef (90% lean)
- 1 small onion, chopped
- 1 medium green pepper, chopped
- 1 jar (24 oz.) spaghetti sauce with mushrooms
- 1 tsp. dried oregano
- 1 tsp. dried basil
- 6 lasagna noodles, cooked and rinsed
- 3 cups shredded mozzarella cheese
- ½ cup grated Parmesan cheese
  Torn fresh basil leaves, optional

1. In a Dutch oven, brown the beef, onion and pepper; drain if necessary. Stir in the spaghetti sauce, oregano and basil. Simmer, uncovered, for 10-15 minutes.
2. Spread ¼ cup of the meat sauce into a 10-in. cast-iron or other heavy skillet. Top with 3 noodles, cutting to fit as needed. Layer with half of the remaining sauce and half of the mozzarella and Parmesan cheeses. Top with the remaining noodles, meat sauce and Parmesan cheese.
3. Cover and heat on medium for 3 minutes. Reduce heat to low; cook for 35 minutes. Sprinkle with the remaining mozzarella cheese; let stand for 10 minutes with the cover ajar. If desired, sprinkle with torn fresh basil leaves.

1 PIECE: 395 cal., 18g fat (9g sat. fat), 78mg chol., 842mg sod., 29g carb. (10g sugars, 3g fiber), 31g pro.

GINGER PORK STIR-FRY

An easy homemade stir-fry sauce is the perfect base for this weeknight dish. It comes together quickly, but tastes impressive.
—*Adeline Russell, Hartford, WI*

- -

Takes: 20 min. • **Makes:** 4 servings

- 2   Tbsp. cornstarch
- 1   cup beef broth
- 3   Tbsp. soy sauce
- 1   Tbsp. sugar
- 1½ tsp. ground ginger
- ½   tsp. garlic powder
- ½   tsp. crushed red pepper flakes
- 1   pork tenderloin (1 lb.),
       cut into 2-in. strips
- 2   Tbsp. canola oil, divided
- 1   pkg. (16 oz.) frozen sugar snap
       stir-fry vegetable blend, thawed
       Hot cooked rice
       Minced fresh cilantro, optional

1. In a small bowl, combine cornstarch and broth until smooth. Stir in the soy sauce, sugar, ginger, garlic powder and pepper flakes; set aside.

2. In a wok or large skillet, stir-fry the pork in 1 Tbsp. oil until juices run clear. Remove and keep warm. In the same pan, stir-fry the vegetables in remaining oil until crisp-tender.

3. Stir the broth mixture and add to the vegetables. Bring to a boil; cook and stir for 1 minute or until thickened. Return pork to the pan; heat through. Serve with rice and, if desired, sprinkle with cilantro.

1 CUP: 278 cal., 11g fat (2g sat. fat), 63mg chol., 958mg sod., 16g carb. (7g sugars, 4g fiber), 27g pro.

GINGER-ORANGE PORK STIR-FRY: Omit the first 7 ingredients. Combine 1 Tbsp. cornstarch with 1 cup orange juice and 2 Tbsp. soy sauce until smooth. Stir in 2 minced garlic cloves and ¾ tsp. ground ginger. Proceed as the recipe directs.

DID YOU KNOW?
To prevent food from sticking, season your wok every time you use it. Put some oil in the wok and heat to smoking hot while swirling it (carefully!) around the surface. Pour off the oil and add fresh oil for cooking.

EASY SAUSAGE & VEGETABLE SKILLET

This recipe has been passed down in our family through my sister-in-law. When I was a child, she did most of the cooking in our house, and this was my favorite meal. The variety of vegetables makes this an attractive dish, and the cooking time is minimal.
—*Ruby Williams, Bogalusa, LA*

- -

Takes: 25 min. • **Makes:** 2 servings

- ½   lb. Italian sausage links
- 1   Tbsp. canola oil
- 1   cup cubed yellow summer squash
       (¾-in. pieces)
- ½   cup chopped green onions
- 2   garlic cloves, minced
- 1½ cups chopped fresh tomatoes
- 2   tsp. Worcestershire sauce
- ⅛   tsp. cayenne pepper

1. In a large skillet, cook the sausage over medium heat in oil until a thermometer reads 160°; drain.

2. Cut sausage into ½-in. slices. Add sausage, squash and onions to the skillet; cook for 3-4 minutes or until the vegetables are tender. Add garlic; cook for 1 minute longer. Stir in the tomatoes, Worcestershire sauce and cayenne pepper; heat through.

1 SERVING: 304 cal., 22g fat (6g sat. fat), 45mg chol., 607mg sod., 14g carb. (7g sugars, 3g fiber), 14g pro.

MEDITERRANEAN CHICKPEAS

Add this to your meatless Monday lineup—it's great with feta cheese on top. We serve this with couscous; you could also spoon it over egg noodles or into a pita pocket.
—*Elaine Ober, Brookline, MA*

- -

Takes: 25 min. • **Makes:** 4 servings

- 1   cup water
- ¾   cup uncooked whole wheat couscous
- 1   Tbsp. olive oil
- 1   medium onion, chopped
- 2   garlic cloves, minced
- 1   can (15 oz.) chickpeas or garbanzo beans, rinsed and drained
- 1   can (14½ oz.) no-salt-added stewed tomatoes, cut up
- 1   can (14 oz.) water-packed artichoke hearts, rinsed, drained and chopped
- ½   cup pitted Greek olives, coarsely chopped
- 1   Tbsp. lemon juice
- ½   tsp. dried oregano
      Dash pepper
      Dash cayenne pepper

1. In a small saucepan, bring water to a boil. Stir in couscous. Remove from heat; let stand, covered, 5-10 minutes or until the water is absorbed. Fluff with a fork.
2. Meanwhile, in a large nonstick skillet, heat oil over medium-high heat. Add the onion; cook and stir until tender. Add garlic; cook 1 minute longer. Sir in remaining ingredients; heat through, stirring occasionally. Serve with the couscous.

1 CUP CHICKPEA MIXTURE WITH ⅔ CUP COUSCOUS: 340 cal., 10g fat (1g sat. fat), 0 chol., 677mg sod., 51g carb. (9g sugars, 9g fiber), 11g pro.

GARLIC CHICKEN WITH HERBS

Pan-roasting garlic cloves turns them into rich, creamy deliciousness. This chicken is fantastic with crusty Italian bread or mashed potatoes on the side.
—*Kathy Fleming, Lisle, IL*

- -

Takes: 30 min. • **Makes:** 4 servings

- 4   boneless skinless chicken thighs (about 1 lb.)
- ½   tsp. salt
- ¼   tsp. pepper
- 1   Tbsp. butter
- 10   garlic cloves, peeled and halved
- ¼   cup white wine or chicken broth
- 1½   tsp. minced fresh rosemary
- ½   tsp. minced fresh sage
- 1   cup chicken broth
      Hot cooked rice of your choice

1. Sprinkle chicken with salt and pepper. In a large skillet, heat butter over medium-high heat; brown chicken on both sides. Remove from pan, reserving drippings.
2. In same skillet, saute garlic in drippings over medium-high heat until light golden brown. Add wine and herbs; bring to a boil, stirring to loosen browned bits from pan. Cook until mixture is almost evaporated. Add broth and chicken; bring to a boil. Reduce heat; simmer, covered, until a thermometer inserted in chicken reads at least 170°, 10-12 minutes.
3. To serve, spoon pan juices over chicken. Serve with rice.

1 SERVING: 214 cal., 12g fat (3g sat. fat), 76mg chol., 487mg sod., 3g carb. (0 sugars, 0 fiber), 22g pro. **DIABETIC EXCHANGES:** 3 lean meat, ½ fat.

TURKEY BREAST TENDERLOINS WITH RASPBERRY SAUCE

Sweet and tangy raspberry sauce is a perfect complement to versatile turkey tenderloins. In fact, the sauce is so good, you'll be tempted to eat it with a spoon.

—*Deirdre Cox, Kansas City, MO*

- -

Takes: 30 min. • **Makes:** 2 servings

- 2 **turkey breast tenderloins (5 oz. each)**
- ⅛ **tsp. salt**
- ⅛ **tsp. pepper**
- 2 **tsp. olive oil**
- 1 **tsp. cornstarch**
- ¼ **cup cranberry-raspberry juice**
- 2 **Tbsp. Heinz 57 steak sauce**
- 2 **Tbsp. red raspberry preserves**
- ½ **tsp. lemon juice**

1. Sprinkle turkey with salt and pepper. In a large nonstick skillet over medium heat, brown turkey in oil on all sides. Cover and cook until a thermometer reads 165°, 10-12 minutes. Remove and keep warm.

2. Combine cornstarch and juice until smooth; add to the pan. Stir in steak sauce, preserves and lemon juice. Bring to a boil; cook and stir until thickened, about 1 minute. Slice turkey; serve with sauce.

1 TENDERLOIN WITH ¼ CUP SAUCE: 275 cal., 6g fat (1g sat. fat), 69mg chol., 425mg sod., 22g carb. (19g sugars, 0 fiber), 33g pro.

TEST KITCHEN TIP
This recipe calls for turkey, but the sauce also would be delicious with other meats and cuts, including chicken breasts, pork chops and pork tenderloin medallions.

SWEET CHILI & ORANGE CHICKEN

My husband loves this simple chicken dish so much he often requests it when he comes home from deployment. The sweet chili sauce adds just the right amount of heat to the bright, citrusy flavors.

—*Jessica Eastman, Bremerton, WA*

- -

Takes: 20 min. • **Makes:** 4 servings

- 1 **lb. boneless skinless chicken breasts, cut into 1-in. pieces**
- ¼ **tsp. salt**
- ¼ **tsp. pepper**
- 2 **Tbsp. butter**
- ¾ **cup sweet chili sauce**
- ⅓ **cup thawed orange juice concentrate**
  Hot cooked jasmine or other rice
  Minced fresh basil

1. Toss chicken with salt and pepper. In a large skillet, heat butter over medium-high heat; stir-fry chicken until no longer pink, 5-7 minutes. Remove chicken from pan; keep warm.

2. Add the chili sauce and juice concentrate to skillet; cook and stir until heated through. Stir in chicken. Serve with rice; sprinkle with basil.

½ CUP CHICKEN MIXTURE: 309 cal., 9g fat (4g sat. fat), 78mg chol., 1014mg sod., 33g carb. (31g sugars, 1g fiber), 24g pro.

AMY DONG
Woodbury, MN

EASY ASIAN GLAZED MEATBALLS

As a writer and a busy mom of three boys, I need tasty meals on the quick. We serve these glazed meatballs over a steaming bed of rice.
—Amy Dong, Woodbury, MN

- -

Takes: 20 min. • **Makes:** 4 servings

- ½   cup hoisin sauce
- 2   Tbsp. rice vinegar
- 4   tsp. brown sugar
- 1   tsp. garlic powder
- 1   tsp. Sriracha chili sauce
- ½   tsp. ground ginger
- 1   pkg. (12 oz.) frozen fully cooked homestyle or Italian meatballs, thawed
      Optional: Thinly sliced green onions and toasted sesame seeds
      Hot cooked rice

1. In a large saucepan, mix first 6 ingredients until blended. Add the homestyle meatballs, stirring to coat; cook, covered, over medium-low heat until heated through, 12-15 minutes, stirring occasionally.
2. If desired, sprinkle with green onions and sesame seeds. Serve with rice.
1 SERVING: 376 cal., 23g fat (10g sat. fat), 36mg chol., 1296mg sod., 29g carb. (17g sugars, 2g fiber), 13g pro.

SUPER QUICK CHICKEN FRIED RICE

After my first child was born, I no longer had a lot of time to spend cooking, and I needed meals that were satisfying and fast. This fried rice is now part of our routine dinners.
—Alicia Gower, Auburn, NY

- -

Takes: 30 min. • **Makes:** 6 servings

- 1   pkg. (12 oz.) frozen mixed vegetables
- 2   Tbsp. olive oil, divided
- 2   large eggs, lightly beaten
- 4   Tbsp. sesame oil, divided
- 3   pkg. (8.8 oz. each) ready-to-serve garden vegetable rice
- 1   rotisserie chicken, skin removed, shredded
- ¼   tsp. salt
- ¼   tsp. pepper

1. Prepare the frozen vegetables according to package directions. Meanwhile, in a large skillet, heat 1 Tbsp. olive oil over medium-high heat. Pour in eggs; cook and stir until the eggs are thickened and no liquid egg remains. Remove from pan.
2. In the same skillet, heat 2 Tbsp. sesame oil and the remaining olive oil over medium-high heat. Add rice; cook and stir until the rice begins to brown, 10-12 minutes.
3. Stir in chicken, salt and pepper. Add the eggs and vegetables; heat through, breaking eggs into small pieces and stirring to combine. Drizzle with the remaining sesame oil.
1½ CUPS: 548 cal., 25g fat (5g sat. fat), 163mg chol., 934mg sod., 43g carb. (3g sugars, 3g fiber), 38g pro.

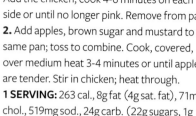

APPLE-MUSTARD CHICKEN TENDERS

My husband says this dish is sweet and a little bit sassy, just like me. I like to use Granny Smith apples for a bit of tartness. Winesaps are great for this dish, too.
—*Linda Cifuentes, Mahomet, IL*

Takes: 30 min. • **Makes:** 6 servings

- 1½ lbs. chicken tenderloins
- ½ tsp. salt
- ¼ tsp. pepper
- 3 Tbsp. butter
- 2 small Granny Smith apples, thinly sliced
- ½ cup packed brown sugar
- ¼ cup stone-ground mustard

1. Sprinkle chicken with salt and pepper. In a large skillet, heat butter over medium heat. Add the chicken; cook 4-6 minutes on each side or until no longer pink. Remove from pan.
2. Add apples, brown sugar and mustard to same pan; toss to combine. Cook, covered, over medium heat 3-4 minutes or until apples are tender. Stir in chicken; heat through.

1 SERVING: 263 cal., 8g fat (4g sat. fat), 71mg chol., 519mg sod., 24g carb. (22g sugars, 1g fiber), 27g pro.

READER REVIEW

"This recipe was very easy and tasty. We really enjoyed the sweet flavor of the apples with the chicken. Great recipe for a work day."

GREATWITHOUTGLUTEN, TASTEOFHOME.COM

SAUCY PORK CHOP SKILLET

Skillet pork chops make easy comfort food. We serve these up with a salad and fruit. If you have fresh green beans or steamed broccoli, go for it!
—*Donna Roberts, Manhattan, KS*

Takes: 30 min. • **Makes:** 6 servings

- 3 cups uncooked instant brown rice
- 2 tsp. canola oil
- 6 boneless pork loin chops (6 oz. each)
- 1 small onion, sliced
- 1 cup canned diced tomatoes
- 1 cup reduced-sodium beef broth
- 1 Tbsp. dried parsley flakes
- ½ tsp. salt
- ¼ tsp. pepper
- ⅛ tsp. dried basil
- ⅛ tsp. dried oregano
- 2 Tbsp. all-purpose flour
- ½ cup water

1. Cook rice according to package directions. Meanwhile, in a large nonstick skillet, heat oil over medium-high heat. Brown pork chops on both sides; remove from pan.
2. Add onion to the drippings; cook and stir until tender. Stir in tomatoes, broth, parsley and seasonings; bring to a boil. Return pork to the pan. Reduce heat; simmer, covered, for 6-8 minutes or until a thermometer inserted in the pork reads 145°.
3. Remove pork to a serving plate; keep warm. In a small bowl, mix the flour and water until smooth; stir into the sauce. Bring to a boil, stirring constantly; cook and stir for 2 minutes or until thickened. Spoon over the pork; serve with brown rice.

1 PORK CHOP WITH ⅔ CUP COOKED RICE AND ⅓ CUP SAUCE: 436 cal., 13g fat (4g sat. fat), 83mg chol., 382mg sod., 39g carb. (2g sugars, 3g fiber), 38g pro. **DIABETIC EXCHANGES:** 5 lean meat, 2½ starch.

CHICKEN WITH TARRAGON SAUCE

This is comfort food at its finest. I cook it at least once a week and usually serve it with homemade mashed potatoes and sauteed fresh green beans.
—*Cher Schwartz, Ellisville, MO*

- -

Takes: 30 min. • **Makes:** 4 servings

- 4 boneless skinless chicken breast halves (5 oz. each)
- ¾ tsp. salt, divided
- ¼ tsp. pepper
- 1 Tbsp. butter
- 1 Tbsp. olive oil
- 1 shallot, chopped
- ¾ cup heavy whipping cream
- 3 tsp. minced fresh tarragon, divided
- 2 tsp. lemon juice

1. Pound the chicken breasts with a meat mallet to ½-in. thickness. Sprinkle the chicken with ½ tsp. salt and pepper.
2. In a large skillet, heat butter and oil over medium heat. Add the chicken; cook for 4-5 minutes on each side or until no longer pink. Remove chicken from pan; keep warm.
3. Add shallot to same pan; cook and stir over medium heat until tender. Add cream, stirring to loosen browned bits from pan. Increase heat to medium-high; cook until slightly thickened. Stir in 2 tsp. tarragon, lemon juice and remaining salt. Serve with chicken. Sprinkle with remaining tarragon.
1 CHICKEN BREAST HALF WITH 2 TBSP. SAUCE: 370 cal., 26g fat (14g sat. fat), 137mg chol., 547mg sod., 3g carb. (2g sugars, 0 fiber), 30g pro.

CASHEW CHICKEN WITH NOODLES

I tried this recipe with some friends one night when we were doing freezer meals. I was smitten! It's quick, easy and so delicious!
—*Anita Beachy, Bealeton, VA*

- -

Takes: 20 min. • **Makes:** 4 servings

- 8 oz. uncooked thick rice noodles
- ¼ cup reduced-sodium soy sauce
- 2 Tbsp. cornstarch
- 3 garlic cloves, minced
- 1 lb. boneless skinless chicken breasts, cubed
- 1 Tbsp. peanut oil
- 1 Tbsp. sesame oil
- 6 green onions, cut into 2-in. pieces
- 1 cup unsalted cashews
- 2 Tbsp. sweet chili sauce
  Toasted sesame seeds, optional

1. Cook the rice noodles according to the package directions.
2. Meanwhile, in a small bowl, combine soy sauce, cornstarch and garlic. Add chicken. In a large cast-iron or other heavy skillet, saute the chicken mixture in the peanut and sesame oils until no longer pink. Add onions; cook for 1 minute longer.
3. Drain noodles; stir into skillet. Add cashews and chili sauce and heat through. If desired, top with toasted sesame seeds.
1½ CUPS: 638 cal., 26g fat (5g sat. fat), 63mg chol., 870mg sod., 68g carb. (6g sugars, 3g fiber), 33g pro.

CHIPOTLE CHICKEN WITH SPANISH RICE

Here in Texas, we just love southwestern cooking. Chipotle pepper adds smoky heat to this zesty chicken and rice dish. It's so quick and easy.
—*Carolyn Collins, Freeport, TX*

Takes: 25 min. • **Makes:** 4 servings

- 4 boneless skinless chicken thighs (about 1 lb.)
- ½ tsp. garlic salt
- 2 Tbsp. canola oil
- 1 can (15 oz.) black beans, rinsed and drained
- 1 cup chunky salsa
- 1 chipotle pepper in adobo sauce, finely chopped
- 2 pkg. (8.8 oz. each) ready-to-serve Spanish rice
- ½ cup shredded Mexican cheese blend or Monterey Jack cheese
- 2 Tbsp. minced fresh cilantro or parsley

1. Sprinkle chicken with garlic salt. In a large skillet, heat oil over medium-high heat. Brown chicken on both sides. Stir in beans, salsa and chipotle pepper; bring to a boil. Reduce the heat; simmer, covered, 6-8 minutes or until a thermometer inserted into chicken thighs reads 170°.

2. Meanwhile, prepare rice according to package directions. Serve chicken with beans and rice; sprinkle with cheese and cilantro.

1 SERVING: 578 cal., 23g fat (5g sat. fat), 88mg chol., 1638mg sod., 57g carb. (5g sugars, 5g fiber), 32g pro.

SHRIMP WITH TOMATOES & FETA

Any recipe that's special enough for company but easy enough for a weeknight meal is a favorite in my book. All you need to finish off the meal is a side salad and crusty French bread to sop up the delicious tomato and wine juices.
—*Susan Seymour, Valatie, NY*

Takes: 30 min. • **Makes:** 6 servings

- 3 Tbsp. olive oil
- 2 shallots, finely chopped
- 2 garlic cloves, minced
- 6 plum tomatoes, chopped
- ½ cup white wine or chicken broth
- 1 Tbsp. dried oregano
- ½ tsp. salt
- ½ tsp. crushed red pepper flakes
- ¼ tsp. sweet paprika
- 2 lbs. uncooked large shrimp, peeled and deveined
- ⅔ cup crumbled feta cheese
- 2 tsp. minced fresh mint
  Hot cooked rice

1. In a large skillet, heat oil over medium-high heat. Add shallots and garlic; cook and stir until tender. Add tomatoes, wine, oregano, salt, pepper flakes and paprika; bring to a boil. Reduce heat; simmer, uncovered, 5 minutes.

2. Stir in shrimp and cheese; cook 5-6 minutes or until the shrimp turn pink. Stir in the mint. Serve with rice.

1 CUP: 261 cal., 11g fat (3g sat. fat), 191mg chol., 502mg sod., 8g carb. (2g sugars, 2g fiber), 28g pro. **DIABETIC EXCHANGES:** 4 lean meat, 1 vegetable, 1 fat.

LEMON SHRIMP WITH PARMESAN RICE

I grew up in Biloxi, Mississippi, where rice, garlic and seafood are staples of Gulf Coast cuisine. This easy shrimp and rice dish is a longtime family favorite that's ready in minutes.
—Amie Overby, Reno, NV

Takes: 20 min. • **Makes:** 4 servings

  2   cups chicken broth
  2   cups uncooked instant rice
  1   lb. uncooked medium shrimp, peeled and deveined
  ½   cup chopped green onions
  2   Tbsp. butter
  2   Tbsp. olive oil
  2   tsp. minced garlic
  3   Tbsp. lemon juice
  ¼   tsp. pepper
  ½   cup grated Parmesan cheese
  2   Tbsp. minced fresh parsley

1. In a small saucepan, bring broth to a boil. Stir in rice; cover and remove from the heat. Let stand for 5 minutes.
2. Meanwhile, in a large cast-iron or other heavy skillet, cook shrimp and onions in butter and oil over medium heat until shrimp turn pink, 4-5 minutes. Add garlic; cook 1 minute longer. Stir in lemon juice and pepper.
3. Stir cheese and parsley into rice; serve with the shrimp.
1 CUP SHRIMP WITH ¾ CUP RICE: 438 cal., 17g fat (7g sat. fat), 191mg chol., 908mg sod., 43g carb. (2g sugars, 1g fiber), 27g pro.

DID YOU KNOW?
If you want to grate your own fresh Parmesan cheese, you can use a food processor. Cut the cheese into 1-in. cubes and process no more than 1 cup of cubes at a time on high until finely grated.

PIEROGI BEEF SKILLET

Hearty and thick with beef, veggies and potatoes, this is a complete meal in one.
—Taste of Home *Test Kitchen*

Takes: 25 min. • **Makes:** 4 servings

  1   lb. ground beef
  ½   cup chopped onion
  ¼   cup all-purpose flour
  ½   tsp. Italian seasoning
  ½   tsp. pepper
  ⅛   tsp. salt
  1   can (14½ oz.) beef broth
  1   pkg. (16 oz.) frozen cheese and potato pierogi, thawed
  2   cups frozen mixed vegetables (about 10 oz.), thawed and drained
  ½   cup shredded cheddar cheese

1. In a large cast-iron or other heavy skillet, cook and crumble the beef with onion over medium heat until the meat is no longer pink, 5-7 minutes; drain, reserving 3 Tbsp. of the drippings. Stir in flour and seasonings until blended. Gradually stir in broth; bring to a boil. Cook and stir until thickened, 1-2 minutes.
2. Stir in pierogi and vegetables. Cook, uncovered, until heated through, about 5 minutes, stirring occasionally. Sprinkle with cheese.
1¾ CUPS: 654 cal., 31g fat (12g sat. fat), 102mg chol., 1157mg sod., 57g carb. (12g sugars, 7g fiber), 34g pro.

SWEET & SPICY CHICKEN

My husband and children love this tender chicken with its spicy sauce. Peach preserves add just a touch of sweetness, while taco seasoning and salsa give this dish some kick.
—*Sheri White, Higley, AZ*

Takes: 20 min. • **Makes:** 4 servings

- 3 Tbsp. taco seasoning
- 1 lb. boneless skinless chicken breasts, cut into ½-in. cubes
- 1 to 2 Tbsp. canola oil
- 1⅔ cups chunky salsa
- ½ cup peach preserves
  Hot cooked rice

1. Place taco seasoning in a large shallow dish; add chicken and turn to coat.

2. In a large skillet, brown chicken in oil until no longer pink. Combine salsa and preserves; stir into skillet. Bring to a boil. Reduce heat; cover and simmer for 2-3 minutes or until heated through. Serve with rice.

1 CUP: 301 cal., 6g fat (1g sat. fat), 63mg chol., 985mg sod., 37g carb. (27g sugars, 0 fiber), 23g pro.

SPAGHETTI SQUASH & SAUSAGE EASY MEAL

I first created my son's favorite dish using homegrown squash, kielbasa and salsa. This variation uses only a few ingredients. What could be easier?
—*Pam Mascarenas, Taylorsville, UT*

Takes: 30 min. • **Makes:** 6 servings

- 1 medium spaghetti squash
- 1 Tbsp. olive oil
- 1 pkg. (14 oz.) smoked sausage, halved lengthwise and sliced
- 1 cup pico de gallo
- ¼ tsp. salt
- ⅛ tsp. pepper

1. Cut squash lengthwise in half; discard the seeds. Place halves on a microwave-safe plate, cut side down. Microwave, uncovered, on high 15-20 minutes or until tender.

2. Meanwhile, in a large skillet, heat oil over medium heat. Add sausage; cook and stir 4-5 minutes or until lightly browned.

3. When squash is cool enough to handle, use a fork to separate the strands. Add squash, pico de gallo, salt and pepper to sausage; heat through, tossing to combine.

1 CUPS: 326 cal., 22g fat (8g sat. fat), 44mg chol., 901mg sod., 24g carb. (2g sugars, 5g fiber), 12g pro.

HEALTH TIP
Eating lower-carb, but still want a satisfying dinner? One cup of cooked spaghetti squash has about 10 grams of carbohydrates versus 45 grams for regular spaghetti.

SWISS MUSHROOM CHICKEN

Everyone enjoys these golden chicken breasts topped with ham, melted Swiss cheese and fresh mushrooms. It's easy to prepare but looks and tastes special enough for company.
—*Jan Baxter, Humarock, MA*

- -

Takes: 30 min. • **Makes:** 4 servings

- 4 **boneless skinless chicken breast halves (4 oz. each)**
- 1 **large egg**
- 1 **cup crushed butter-flavored crackers (about 25 crackers)**
- ¾ **tsp. salt**
- ½ **lb. fresh mushrooms, sliced**
- 2 **Tbsp. butter, divided**
- 4 **slices deli ham or thinly sliced hard salami**
- 4 **slices Swiss cheese**

1. Preheat broiler. Flatten chicken to ¼-in. thickness. In a shallow bowl, lightly beat the egg. Combine cracker crumbs and salt in another shallow bowl. Dip chicken in egg, then in crumbs; set aside.

2. In a large ovenproof skillet, saute the mushrooms in 1 Tbsp. butter until tender; remove and set aside. In the same skillet, cook chicken over medium heat in the remaining butter for 3-4 minutes on each side or until no longer pink.

3. Top each chicken breast half with a ham slice, mushrooms and a cheese slice. Broil 4-6 in. from the heat for 1-2 minutes or until the cheese is melted.

1 CHICKEN BREAST HALF: 343 cal., 21g fat (10g sat. fat), 119mg chol., 956mg sod., 18g carb. (3g sugars, 1g fiber), 20g pro.

PORK CHOPS IN A HONEY-MUSTARD SAUCE

Pork chops are a great economical cut and cook up quickly, making them ideal for busy weeknight meals. But turning out tender chops can be tricky. Browning them, then finishing them in this tangy, slightly sweet sauce results in perfectly cooked chops every time.
—*Susan Bentley, Burlington, NJ*

- -

Takes: 30 min. • **Makes:** 4 servings

- ¾ **tsp. garlic powder, divided**
- ½ **tsp. salt**
- ¼ **tsp. pepper**
- 4 **boneless pork loin chops (6 oz. each)**
- 1 **Tbsp. olive oil**
- ½ **cup white wine or chicken broth**
- ¼ **cup chicken broth**
- 2 **Tbsp. Dijon mustard**
- 1 **Tbsp. honey**
- ½ **cup heavy whipping cream**

1. Combine ½ tsp. garlic powder, the salt and pepper; sprinkle over pork chops. In a large skillet over medium heat, brown pork chops in oil. Remove and keep warm.

2. Remove skillet from heat; add wine, stirring to loosen browned bits from pan. Bring to a boil over medium-high heat; cook until liquid is reduced by half. Reduce heat to medium. Whisk in the broth, mustard, honey and the remaining garlic powder; cook and stir for 1 minute. Whisk in cream; cook and stir for 4-6 minutes or until thickened.

3. Return pork chops and juices to the skillet. Cover and cook for 3-5 minutes or until a thermometer inserted in pork reads 145°. Let stand 5 minutes before serving.

1 PORK CHOP WITH 2 TBSP. SAUCE: 411 cal., 24g fat (11g sat. fat), 123mg chol., 597mg sod., 8g carb. (6g sugars, 0 fiber), 33g pro.

PIZZA & PASTA

Quick and easy and always a hit with the family—there's a reason pizza and pasta are the ultimate busy-night meals. Try these great recipes to elevate those favorites into homemade masterpieces that are just as quick. You may never eat frozen pizza again!

LORRAINE CALAND
Shuniah, ON

MUSHROOM CAPRESE PIZZA

When my tomatoes ripen all at once, I use them up in simple and delicious recipes like this one. Cheesy baguette pizzas, served with a salad, are ideal for lunch or a light dinner.
—*Lorraine Caland, Shuniah, ON*

- -

Prep: 25 min. • **Bake:** 10 min.
Makes: 6 servings

2	tsp. olive oil
8	oz. sliced fresh mushrooms
2	medium onions, halved and sliced
2	garlic cloves, minced
½	tsp. Italian seasoning
¼	tsp. salt
	Dash pepper
1	French bread baguette (10½ oz.), halved lengthwise
1½	cups shredded part-skim mozzarella cheese
¾	cup thinly sliced fresh basil leaves, divided
3	medium tomatoes, sliced

1. Preheat oven to 400°. In a large skillet, heat oil over medium-high heat; saute mushrooms and onions until tender. Add the garlic and seasonings; cook and stir for 1 minute.
2. Place baguette halves on a baking sheet, cut side up; sprinkle with half the cheese and ½ cup basil. Top with the mushroom mixture, tomatoes and the remaining cheese.
3. Bake until cheese is melted, 10-15 minutes. Sprinkle with the remaining basil. Cut each half into 3 portions.
1 PIECE: 260 cal., 7g fat (4g sat. fat), 18mg chol., 614mg sod., 36g carb. (5g sugars, 3g fiber), 13g pro. **DIABETIC EXCHANGES:** 2 starch, 1 vegetable, 1 medium-fat meat.

STACKED VEGETABLES & RAVIOLI

Yellow squash, zucchini and basil meet ricotta and ravioli in this crowd-pleasing entree with delicious summer flavors. One bite and you'll know—this is what summer fresh tastes like!
—Taste of Home *Test Kitchen*

- -

Prep: 20 min. • **Bake:** 30 min. + standing
Makes: 6 servings

- 2 yellow summer squash
- 2 medium zucchini
- 1 pkg. (9 oz.) refrigerated cheese ravioli
- 1 cup ricotta cheese
- 1 large egg
- ½ tsp. garlic salt
- 1 jar (24 oz.) marinara or spaghetti sauce
- 10 fresh basil leaves, divided
- ¾ cup shredded Parmesan cheese

1. Preheat oven to 350°. Using a vegetable peeler, cut squash and zucchini lengthwise into very thin strips. In a Dutch oven, cook ravioli according to package directions, adding the vegetable strips during the last 3 minutes of cooking.
2. Meanwhile, in a small bowl, combine ricotta cheese, egg and garlic salt; set aside. Drain the ravioli and vegetables.
3. Spread ½ cup of marinara sauce into a greased 11x7-in. baking dish. Layer with half the ravioli and vegetables, half the ricotta mixture, 7 basil leaves and 1 cup of the marinara sauce. Layer with the remaining ravioli, vegetables and marinara sauce. Dollop the remaining ricotta mixture over top; sprinkle with Parmesan cheese.
4. Cover and bake 25 minutes. Uncover and bake 5-10 minutes longer or until cheese is melted. Let stand 10 minutes before cutting. Thinly slice remaining basil; sprinkle over top.
1 PIECE: 323 cal., 11g fat (6g sat. fat), 76mg chol., 779mg sod., 39g carb. (15g sugars, 4g fiber), 19g pro. **DIABETIC EXCHANGES:** 2 starch, 2 medium-fat meat, 1 vegetable.

LINGUINE WITH BROCCOLI RABE & PEPPERS

Broccoli rabe is one of my favorite veggies. Since it cooks right with the pasta, you can multitask. Before you know it, dinner is served.
—*Gilda Lester, Millsboro, DE*

- -

Takes: 25 min. • **Makes:** 6 servings

- 1 lb. broccoli rabe
- 1 pkg. (16 oz.) linguine
- 3 Tbsp. olive oil
- 2 anchovy fillets, finely chopped, optional
- 3 garlic cloves, minced
- ½ cup sliced roasted sweet red peppers
- ½ cup pitted Greek olives, halved
- ½ tsp. crushed red pepper flakes
- ¼ tsp. pepper
- ⅛ tsp. salt
- ½ cup grated Romano cheese

1. Cut ½ in. off the ends of the broccoli rabe; trim woody stems. Cut the stems and leaves into 2-in. pieces. Cook linguine according to package directions, adding the broccoli rabe during the last 5 minutes of cooking. Drain, reserving ½ cup of the pasta water.
2. Meanwhile, in a large skillet, heat oil over medium-high heat. Add anchovies and garlic; cook and stir 1 minute. Stir in red peppers, olives, pepper flakes, pepper and salt.
3. Add the linguine and broccoli rabe to the skillet; toss to combine, adding the reserved pasta water as desired to moisten. Serve with cheese.
1¼ CUPS: 429 cal., 15g fat (4g sat. fat), 2mg chol., 487mg sod., 60g carb. (4g sugars, 5g fiber), 17g pro.

THAI BEEF STIR-FRY

A distinctive peanut sauce is a knockout complement to this colorful combination of tender sirloin strips, cauliflower, carrots, broccoli and mushrooms. I like to dish this up over spaghetti, but you could use fried noodles instead.
—*Janice Fehr, Austin, MB*

- -

Prep: 20 min. • **Cook:** 20 min.
Makes: 6 servings

½	cup packed brown sugar
2	Tbsp. cornstarch
2	cups beef broth
⅓	cup reduced-sodium soy sauce
1	tsp. onion powder
1	tsp. garlic powder
1	tsp. ground ginger
¼	tsp. hot pepper sauce

2	lbs. boneless beef sirloin steak, cut into thin strips
6	Tbsp. olive oil, divided
4	cups fresh broccoli florets
	2 cups fresh cauliflowerets
1½	cups julienned carrots
2	cups sliced fresh mushrooms
¼	cup peanut butter
	Hot cooked spaghetti
½	cup chopped peanuts

1. In a small bowl, combine first 8 ingredients until smooth; set aside. In a large cast-iron skillet or wok, stir-fry beef in 3 Tbsp. of oil until the meat is no longer pink. Remove and keep warm.

2. In the same skillet, stir-fry broccoli florets, cauliflower and carrots in the remaining oil for 5 minutes. Add the sliced mushrooms; stir-fry until the vegetables are crisp-tender, 3-5 minutes.

3. Stir the broth mixture and add it to the pan. Bring to a boil; cook and stir until thickened, about 2 minutes. Reduce heat; add the beef and peanut butter. Cook and stir over medium heat until the peanut butter is blended. Serve with spaghetti. Sprinkle with peanuts.

FREEZE OPTION: Do not cook spaghetti. Freeze cooled beef mixture in freezer containers. To use, partially thaw in refrigerator overnight. Cook spaghetti according to package directions. Place beef mixture in a large skillet and heat through, stirring occasionally; add a little broth if necessary. Serve with spaghetti and sprinkle with peanuts.

1 CUP: 586 cal., 32g fat (6g sat. fat), 61mg chol., 974mg sod., 35g carb. (22g sugars, 5g fiber), 42g pro.

❄ BUFFALO CHICKEN PIZZA

If your family likes spicy Buffalo chicken wings, they'll love this rendition that turns their favorite flavors into pizza. Serve it up with blue cheese dressing and crisp celery, just like the tasty original.
—*Shari DiGirolamo, Newton, PA*

Prep: 20 min. • **Bake:** 20 min. • **Makes:** 8 pieces

- 1 tube (13.8 oz.) refrigerated pizza crust
- 1 cup Buffalo wing sauce, divided
- 1½ cups shredded cheddar cheese
- 1½ cups part-skim shredded mozzarella cheese
- 2 lbs. boneless skinless chicken breasts, cubed
- ½ tsp. each garlic salt, pepper and chili powder
- 2 Tbsp. butter
- ½ tsp. dried oregano
    Celery sticks and blue cheese salad dressing

1. Preheat oven to 400°. Unroll pizza crust into a lightly greased 15x10x1-in. baking pan; flatten dough and build up edges slightly. Bake for 7 minutes. Brush dough with 3 Tbsp. Buffalo wing sauce. Combine the cheddar and mozzarella cheeses; sprinkle a third over the crust. Set aside.

2. In a large skillet, cook the chicken, garlic salt, pepper and chili powder in butter until the chicken is no longer pink. Add the remaining wing sauce; cook and stir over medium heat 5 minutes longer.

3. Spoon chicken mixture over pizza. Sprinkle with oregano and remaining cheese.

4. Bake until the crust is golden brown and the cheese is melted, 18-20 minutes. Serve with celery and blue cheese dressing.

FREEZE OPTION: Bake pizza crust as directed; cool. Top with all the ingredients as directed; securely wrap and freeze unbaked pizza. To use, unwrap pizza and bake as directed, increasing time as necessary.

NOTE: This recipe was tested with Frank's Red Hot Buffalo Wing Sauce.

1 PIECE: 427 cal., 19g fat (9g sat. fat), 105mg chol., 1675mg sod., 27g carb. (4g sugars, 1g fiber), 37g pro.

CREAMY SALMON LINGUINE

The taste and texture of this creamy pasta toss is downright luxurious. We love it as is, but you could easily substitute any veggies you have on hand for the broccoli.

—Jacob Kitzman, Seattle, WA

- -

Takes: 25 min. • **Makes:** 5 servings

- 8 oz. uncooked linguine
- 1 bunch broccoli, cut into florets
- 2 Tbsp. butter
- 2 garlic cloves, minced
- 2 cups heavy whipping cream
- 2 Tbsp. lemon juice
- 1 lb. fully cooked salmon, flaked
- ¼ tsp. salt
- ¼ tsp. pepper
- 1 cup shredded Parmesan cheese
- 3 Tbsp. minced fresh basil or 1 Tbsp. dried basil
- 2 Tbsp. capers, drained
- 2 tsp. grated lemon zest

1. Cook linguine according to the package directions, adding broccoli during the last 5 minutes of cooking.

2. Meanwhile, in a large skillet, heat butter over medium heat. Add minced garlic; cook and stir 1 minute. Stir in cream and lemon juice. Bring to a boil. Reduce heat; simmer, uncovered, 2-3 minutes or until slightly thickened, stirring constantly.

3. Add salmon, salt and pepper; heat through. Drain the linguine and broccoli; add to skillet. Stir in cheese, basil, capers and lemon zest.

1⅓ CUPS: 802 cal., 55g fat (30g sat. fat), 207mg chol., 649mg sod., 44g carb. (4g sugars, 6g fiber), 36g pro.

READER REVIEW

"I cut this recipe in half for just my husband and me. It was so easy and good, I wish I'd made it all!"

PRPLMONKY5, TASTEOFHOME.COM

FOUR-CHEESE PIZZA

This ooey-gooey pizza doesn't have sauce, but it gets unforgettable flavor from a blend of cheeses, vegetables and garlic. Using frozen bread dough makes it ultra convenient.

—Doris Johns, Hurst, TX

- -

Prep: 15 min. • **Bake:** 25 min. • **Makes:** 8 slices

- 1 loaf (16 oz.) frozen bread dough, thawed
- 1 large sweet red pepper, chopped
- 1 large green pepper, chopped
- 1 cup shredded part-skim mozzarella cheese
- ¾ cup shredded Swiss cheese
- ½ cup grated Parmesan cheese
- ½ cup crumbled feta cheese
- 2 Tbsp. minced fresh parsley
- 1 Tbsp. minced fresh basil or 1 tsp. dried basil
- 3 plum tomatoes, thinly sliced
- 1 Tbsp. olive oil
- 2 garlic cloves, minced

1. Preheat oven to 400°. On a lightly floured surface, roll dough into a 15-in. circle. Transfer to a greased 14-in. pizza pan; build up edges slightly. Prick dough several times with a fork.

2. Bake 8-10 minutes or until lightly browned. Remove from the oven.

3. Reduce heat to 375°. Sprinkle the chopped peppers, cheeses, parsley and basil over crust. Arrange tomato slices over top. Combine oil and garlic; brush over the tomatoes.

4. Bake for 15-20 minutes or until the cheese is melted. Let stand for 5 minutes before cutting.

1 SLICE: 307 cal., 13g fat (6g sat. fat), 28mg chol., 559mg sod., 34g carb. (5g sugars, 3g fiber), 16g pro.

MAKE-AHEAD SPINACH MANICOTTI

Many of the people I invite to dinner have started requesting this pasta bake—it's that good! The manicotti is stuffed before it's cooked, making it easy on the cook, too.
—*Christy Freeman, Central Point, OR*

- -

Prep: 20 min. + chilling • **Bake:** 40 min.
Makes: 7 servings

- 1   carton (15 oz.) whole-milk ricotta cheese
- 1   pkg. (10 oz.) frozen chopped spinach, thawed and squeezed dry
- 1½ cups shredded part-skim mozzarella cheese, divided
- ¾   cup shredded Parmesan cheese, divided
- 1   large egg, lightly beaten
- 2   tsp. minced fresh parsley
- ½   tsp. onion powder
- ½   tsp. pepper
- ⅛   tsp. garlic powder
- 3   jars (24 oz. each) spaghetti sauce
- 1   cup water
- 1   pkg. (8 oz.) manicotti shells

1. In a large bowl, mix ricotta, spinach, 1 cup mozzarella cheese, ¼ cup Parmesan cheese, egg, parsley and seasonings. In a large bowl, mix spaghetti sauce and water; spread 1 cup of the sauce mixture into a greased 13x9-in. baking dish.

2. Fill uncooked manicotti shells with the ricotta mixture; arrange over the sauce. Pour the remaining spaghetti sauce mixture over top. Sprinkle with the remaining mozzarella cheese and Parmesan cheese. Refrigerate, covered, overnight.

3. Remove from refrigerator 30 minutes before baking. Preheat oven to 350°. Bake, uncovered, 40-50 minutes or until manicotti is tender.

FREEZE OPTION: Cover and freeze unbaked casserole. To use, partially thaw in refrigerator overnight. Remove from the refrigerator 30 minutes before baking. Bake as directed, increasing time as necessary to heat through and for a thermometer inserted in center to read 165°.

2 STUFFED MANICOTTI SHELLS: 363 cal., 16g fat (8g sat. fat), 68mg chol., 822mg sod., 35g carb. (11g sugars, 4g fiber), 22g pro.

SAUSAGE MANICOTTI: Combine 1 lb. each bulk pork sausage (uncooked) and 4% cottage cheese. Use in place of spinach filling. Bake as directed until a thermometer inserted into the center of a shell reads 160°.

BEEF MANICOTTI: Combine 1½ lbs. ground beef, cooked and drained, with 1 cup shredded mozzarella cheese, 1 cup spaghetti sauce, 1 Tbsp. onion powder, 1 tsp. salt and ½ tsp. pepper. Use in place of spinach filling. Bake as directed.

PIZZA MANICOTTI: For each manicotti shell, layer a thin slice of deli ham with a basil leaf, a piece of string cheese and 3 slices pepperoni; roll up. Instead of spinach filling, insert the rolls into the shells; bake as directed.

ARTICHOKE BLUE CHEESE FETTUCCINE

When I'm in a rush, I use store-bought Alfredo sauce to speed along my blue-cheesy noodles with mushrooms. Fresh refrigerated fettuccine gets it done even faster.
—*Jolanthe Erb, Harrisonburg, VA*

- -

Takes: 20 min. • **Makes:** 4 servings

- 1   pkg. (12 oz.) fettuccine
- 1   cup sliced fresh mushrooms
- 1   can (14 oz.) water-packed artichoke hearts, drained and chopped
- 1½ cups Alfredo sauce
- ¼   cup crumbled blue cheese

1. Cook the fettuccine according to package directions.

2. Meanwhile, place a lightly oiled large nonstick skillet over medium-high heat. Add mushrooms and artichoke hearts; cook and stir until the mushrooms are tender. Stir in Alfredo sauce; bring to a boil over medium heat. Reduce heat; simmer, uncovered, for 5 minutes, stirring occasionally.

3. Drain fettuccine, reserving ⅓ cup pasta water. Add the fettuccine to the artichoke mixture; toss to combine, adding reserved pasta water as necessary for consistency. Sprinkle with blue cheese.

1 CUP: 499 cal., 14g fat (9g sat. fat), 33mg chol., 770mg sod., 74g carb. (6g sugars, 4g fiber), 21g pro.

STEAK & BLUE CHEESE PIZZA

Even my hubby, who doesn't normally like blue cheese, adores this scrumptious pizza! If time allows, cook the onion until it's rich and caramelized for an unbeatable flavor.
—*Kadija Bridgewater, Boca Raton, FL*

Takes: 30 min. • **Makes:** 6 servings

- ½ lb. beef top sirloin steak, thinly sliced
- ¼ tsp. salt
- ¼ tsp. pepper
- 2 Tbsp. olive oil, divided
- 2 cups sliced baby portobello mushrooms
- 1 large onion, sliced
- ½ cup heavy whipping cream
- ¼ cup crumbled blue cheese
- 1 prebaked 12-in. pizza crust
- 2 tsp. minced fresh parsley

1. Preheat oven to 450°. Sprinkle beef with salt and pepper. In a large skillet, heat 1 Tbsp. olive oil over medium heat. Add the beef and mushrooms; cook until beef is no longer pink, 3-4 minutes. Remove from pan.
2. Cook sliced onion in the remaining olive oil until tender, 2-3 minutes. Add the cream and blue cheese; cook until slightly thickened, 3-5 minutes longer.
3. Place crust on a 12-in. pizza pan or baking sheet. Spread with the cream mixture; top with the beef mixture. Sprinkle with parsley. Bake until sauce is bubbly and crust is lightly browned, 10-12 minutes.
1 SLICE: 365 cal., 19g fat (8g sat. fat), 47mg chol., 535mg sod., 33g carb. (3g sugars, 2g fiber), 18g pro.

PORK PANCIT

A dear friend gave me a pork recipe that's so tempting, we never have leftovers. Try it with other meats, like chicken or sausage.
—*Priscilla Gilbert, Indian Harbour Beach, FL*

Takes: 30 min. • **Makes:** 6 servings

- 8 oz. uncooked vermicelli or angel hair pasta
- 1 lb. boneless pork loin chops (½ in. thick), cut into thin strips
- 3 Tbsp. canola oil, divided
- 4 garlic cloves, minced
- 1½ tsp. salt, divided
- 1 medium onion, halved and thinly sliced
- 2½ cups shredded cabbage
- 1 medium carrot, julienned
- 1 cup fresh snow peas
- ¼ tsp. pepper

1. Break vermicelli in half; cook according to package directions. Drain.
2. Meanwhile, in a bowl, toss pork with 2 Tbsp. oil, the garlic and ½ tsp. salt. In a large skillet over medium-high heat, stir-fry half of the pork mixture for 2-3 minutes or until browned. Remove from pan. Repeat with the remaining pork mixture.
3. In the same skillet, heat the remaining oil over medium-high heat. Add onion; stir-fry 1-2 minutes or until tender. Add the remaining vegetables; stir-fry for 3-5 minutes or until crisp-tender. Stir in pepper and the remaining salt. Return pork to pan. Add vermicelli; heat through, tossing to combine.
1⅓ CUPS: 326 cal., 12g fat (2g sat. fat), 36mg chol., 627mg sod., 34g carb. (3g sugars, 3g fiber), 21g pro. **DIABETIC EXCHANGES:** 2 starch, 2 lean meat, 1 vegetable, 1 fat.

KADIJA BRIDGEWATER
Boca Raton, FL

STUFFED-CRUST PIZZA

String cheese is the secret to this popular stuffed-crust pizza. Prebaking the crust before you add the toppings ensures the cheese inside will melt completely.
—*Terri Gonzalez, Roswell, NM*

- -

Prep: 25 min. • **Bake:** 25 min.
Makes: 8 slices

- 2 to 2½ cups all-purpose flour
- 1 pkg. (¼ oz.) quick-rise yeast
- 1 tsp. salt
- 1 cup water
- 2 Tbsp. canola oil
- 8 pieces string cheese
- ½ lb. bulk Italian sausage
- 1 medium green pepper, diced
- 1 cup tomato sauce
- 1 tsp. dried oregano
- ¼ tsp. pepper
- ⅛ tsp. garlic powder
- 1 jar (4½ oz.) sliced mushrooms, drained
- 1½ cups shredded part-skim mozzarella cheese

1. Preheat oven to 425°. In a large bowl, combine 2 cups flour, the yeast and salt. In a saucepan, heat water and oil to 120°-130°. Add to the dry ingredients; beat just until moistened. Stir in enough of the remaining flour to form a soft dough. Let dough rest for 5 minutes.
2. On a lightly floured surface, roll into a 14-in. circle. Transfer to a greased 12-in. pizza pan, letting dough drape 2 in. over the edge.
3. Place string cheese around the edge of the pan, on top of the dough; fold dough over cheese and pinch to seal. Prick dough thoroughly with a fork. Bake for 10 minutes.
4. Meanwhile, in a large skillet, cook sausage and green pepper over medium heat until the meat is no longer pink; drain. In a small bowl, combine the tomato sauce, oregano, pepper and garlic powder; spread over the crust. Sprinkle with the meat mixture, mushrooms and mozzarella.
5. Bake for 15-20 minutes or until the cheese is melted and the crust is golden brown.
1 SLICE: 343 cal., 17g fat (8g sat. fat), 44mg chol., 976mg sod., 28g carb. (2g sugars, 2g fiber), 20g pro.

ASPARAGUS & SHRIMP WITH ANGEL HAIR PASTA

We've all heard the way to a man's heart is through his stomach, so when I plan a romantic dinner, I like to serve this dish. It's easy on the budget and turns out perfectly for two.
—*Shari Neff, Takoma Park, MD*

- -

Takes: 30 min. • **Makes:** 2 servings

- 3 oz. uncooked angel hair pasta
- ½ lb. uncooked shrimp (16-20 per lb.), peeled and deveined
- ¼ tsp. salt
- ⅛ tsp. crushed red pepper flakes
- 2 Tbsp. olive oil, divided
- 8 fresh asparagus spears, trimmed and cut into 2-in. pieces
- ½ cup sliced fresh mushrooms
- ¼ cup chopped seeded tomato, peeled
- 4 garlic cloves, minced
- 2 tsp. chopped green onion
- ½ cup white wine or chicken broth
- 1½ tsp. minced fresh basil
- 1½ tsp. minced fresh oregano
- 1½ tsp. minced fresh parsley
- 1½ tsp. minced fresh thyme
- ¼ cup grated Parmesan cheese
  Lemon wedges

1. Cook pasta according to the package directions. Meanwhile, sprinkle shrimp with salt and pepper flakes. In a large skillet or wok over medium-high, heat 1 Tbsp. oil. Add shrimp; stir-fry until pink, 2-3 minutes. Remove; keep warm.
2. In the same pan, stir-fry next 5 ingredients in the remaining oil until the vegetables are crisp-tender, about 5 minutes. Add wine and seasonings. Return shrimp to pan.
3. Drain pasta; add to the shrimp mixture and toss gently. Cook and stir until heated through, 1-2 minutes. Sprinkle with Parmesan cheese. Serve with lemon wedges.
1¾ CUPS: 488 cal., 19g fat (4g sat. fat), 132mg chol., 584mg sod., 41g carb. (4g sugars, 3g fiber), 29g pro.

TEST KITCHEN TIP
To keep pasta from sticking, use a large pot with lots of water and stir periodically. Adding a little cooking oil works, but may keep sauce from clinging to the cooked pasta.

SPICY SHRIMP & PENNE PASTA

I created this creamy pasta dish when I needed to use up some marinara. Red pepper flakes give it a little heat, which my family loves. It's super versatile, so try it with chicken or stir in some fresh basil.

—Lorri Stout, Gaithersburg, MD

Takes: 30 min. • Makes: 6 servings

- 3 cups uncooked penne pasta (about 12 oz.)
- 1 Tbsp. butter, divided
- 1 Tbsp. olive oil, divided
- 2 lbs. uncooked shrimp (31-40 per lb.), peeled and deveined, divided
- ½ tsp. crushed red pepper flakes, divided
- 1 jar (24 oz.) marinara sauce
- ¾ cup half-and-half cream
- 4 cups chopped fresh spinach

1. In a 6-qt. stockpot, cook pasta according to package directions; drain and return to pot.
2. In a large skillet, heat half the butter and half the oil over medium-high heat. Saute half the shrimp with ¼ tsp. pepper flakes until the shrimp turn pink, 3-5 minutes; remove from the pan. Repeat.
3. In the same pan, heat marinara sauce and cream just to a boil over medium heat, stirring to blend. Stir in spinach until wilted; add to pasta. Stir in shrimp; heat through.

1⅔ CUPS: 395 cal., 12g fat (4g sat. fat), 206mg chol., 702mg sod., 38g carb. (9g sugars, 4g fiber), 33g pro. DIABETIC EXCHANGES: 4 lean meat, 2 starch, 1 vegetable, 1 fat.

READER REVIEW

"Made as directed except added salt, pepper and a shake of Parmesan. We absolutely loved this!"

LYNN, TASTEOFHOME.COM

CHEESY BOW TIE CHICKEN

This super simple dish tastes like it's straight from a nice Italian restaurant. Spinach-artichoke dip is usually available in a store's frozen foods section; you might also find it at the deli counter.

—Sally Sibthorpe, Shelby Township, MI

Takes: 30 min. • Makes: 4 servings

- 2 pkg. (8 oz. each) frozen spinach and artichoke cheese dip
- 3 cups uncooked bow tie pasta
- 3 cups cubed rotisserie chicken
- 1 cup chopped roasted sweet red peppers
- ⅓ cup pitted Greek olives, halved
- ½ tsp. salt
- ¼ tsp. pepper

1. Heat the dip according to the package directions. Meanwhile, in a Dutch oven, cook pasta according to the package directions; drain, reserving ½ cup of the pasta water. Return pasta to pot.
2. Stir in chicken, dip, peppers, olives, salt and pepper, adding enough of the reserved pasta water to reach a creamy consistency; heat through.

1½ CUPS: 453 cal., 12g fat (3g sat. fat), 93mg chol., 795mg sod., 44g carb. (4g sugars, 2g fiber), 38g pro.

GREEK-STYLE RAVIOLI

I gave an Italian dish a Greek twist by adding spinach, olives and feta. I like serving this easy weeknight ravioli with garlic cheese toast.
—*Hetti Williams, Rapid City, SD*

- -

Takes: 25 min. • **Makes:** 2 servings

- 12 frozen cheese ravioli
- ⅓ lb. lean ground beef (90% lean)
- 1 cup canned diced tomatoes with basil, oregano and garlic
- 1 cup fresh baby spinach
- ¼ cup sliced ripe olives
- ¼ cup crumbled feta cheese

1. Cook the ravioli according to package directions; drain. Meanwhile, in a skillet, cook beef over medium heat for 4-6 minutes or until no longer pink; drain. Stir in tomatoes; bring to a boil. Reduce the heat; simmer, uncovered, 10 minutes, stirring occasionally.
2. Add ravioli, spinach and olives to skillet; heat through, stirring gently to combine. Sprinkle with cheese.
1¼ CUPS: 333 cal., 12g fat (5g sat. fat), 61mg chol., 851mg sod., 28g carb. (5g sugars, 4g fiber), 23g pro. **DIABETIC EXCHANGES:** 3 lean meat, 2 starch, ½ fat.

DEEP-DISH PIZZA

My family devours this crusty pan pizza with easy-to-swap toppings. For extra color, use a combination of green, red and yellow peppers.
—*Patricia Howson, Carstairs, AB*

- -

Prep: 15 min. + standing • **Bake:** 20 min.
Makes: 8 servings

- 1 pkg. (¼ oz.) active dry yeast
- 1 cup warm water (110° to 115°)
- 1 tsp. sugar
- 1 tsp. salt
- 2 Tbsp. canola oil
- 2½ cups all-purpose flour
- 1 lb. ground beef, cooked and drained
- 1 can (10¾ oz.) condensed tomato soup, undiluted
- 1 tsp. each dried basil, oregano and thyme
- 1 tsp. dried rosemary, crushed
- ¼ tsp. garlic powder
- 1 small green pepper, julienned
- 1 can (8 oz.) mushroom stems and pieces, drained
- 1 cup shredded part-skim mozzarella cheese

1. In a large bowl, dissolve yeast in warm water. Add the sugar, salt, oil and 2 cups of flour. Beat until smooth. Stir in enough of the remaining flour to form a soft dough. Cover and let rest for 20 minutes.
2. Preheat oven to 425°. On a floured surface, roll dough into a 13x9-in. rectangle. Transfer to a greased 13x9-in. baking pan. Sprinkle with ground beef.
3. In a small bowl, combine the soup and seasonings; spoon over the beef. Top with the green pepper, mushrooms and cheese.
4. Bake for 20-25 minutes or until the crust and cheese are lightly browned.
FREEZE OPTION: Cover and freeze unbaked pizza. To use, partially thaw in refrigerator overnight. Remove from the refrigerator 30 minutes before baking. Preheat oven to 425°. Bake pizza as directed, increasing time as necessary.
1 SLICE: 364 cal., 14g fat (5g sat. fat), 49mg chol., 704mg sod., 39g carb. (5g sugars, 3g fiber), 20g pro.

❄

MEXICAN CHICKEN ALFREDO

One family member likes Italian, another likes Mexican. They never have to argue when this rich and creamy sensation is on the menu!
—*Tia Woodley, Stockbridge, GA*

- -

Prep: 25 min. • **Bake:** 30 min.
Makes: 2 casseroles (4 servings each)

- 1 pkg. (16 oz.) gemelli or spiral pasta
- 2 lbs. boneless skinless chicken breasts, cubed
- 1 medium onion, chopped
- ¼ tsp. salt
- ¼ tsp. pepper
- 1 Tbsp. canola oil
- 2 jars (15 oz. each) Alfredo sauce
- 1 cup grated Parmesan cheese
- 1 cup medium salsa
- ¼ cup 2% milk
- 2 tsp. taco seasoning

1. Preheat oven to 350°. Cook pasta according to package directions.
2. Meanwhile, in a large skillet over medium heat, cook chicken, onion, salt and pepper in oil until chicken is no longer pink. Stir in Alfredo sauce; bring to a boil. Stir in cheese, salsa, milk and taco seasoning.
3. Drain pasta; toss with chicken mixture. Divide mixture between 2 greased 8-in. square baking dishes. Cover and bake until bubbly, 30-35 minutes.
FREEZE OPTION: Cover and freeze unbaked casserole up to 3 months. To use, thaw in refrigerator overnight. Remove from refrigerator 30 minutes before baking. Preheat oven to 350°. Bake casserole, covered, until bubbly, 50-60 minutes.
1½ CUPS: 559 cal., 20g fat (11g sat. fat), 102mg chol., 899mg sod., 55g carb. (4g sugars, 3g fiber), 40g pro.

GRILLED FLATBREAD VEGGIE PIZZA

We pile veggies onto flatbread for a fun way to eat healthier. Our go-to recipe for weeknights easily changes with different veggies or meats.
—*Darla Andrews, Schertz, TX*

- -

Takes: 25 min. • **Makes:** 4 servings

- 1 Tbsp. butter
- ½ lb. sliced baby portobello mushrooms
- 1 large green pepper, julienned
- 4 cups fresh baby spinach (about 4 oz.)
- ¼ tsp. salt
- ⅛ tsp. pepper
- 2 naan flatbreads or 4 whole pita breads
- 2 Tbsp. olive oil
- ¼ cup prepared pesto
- 2 plum tomatoes, sliced
- 2 cups shredded part-skim mozzarella cheese

1. In a large skillet, heat butter over medium-high heat. Add mushrooms and green pepper; cook and stir 5-7 minutes or until tender. Add spinach, salt and pepper; cook and stir for 2-3 minutes or until spinach is wilted.
2. Brush both sides of the flatbreads with oil. Grill flatbreads, covered, over medium heat for 2-3 minutes on one side or until lightly browned.
3. Remove from grill. Spread the grilled sides with pesto; top with the vegetable mixture, tomatoes and cheese. Return to grill; cook, covered, 2-3 minutes longer or until cheese is melted. Cut pizzas in half before serving.
½ PIZZA: 426 cal., 28g fat (11g sat. fat), 47mg chol., 1005mg sod., 25g carb. (6g sugars, 3g fiber), 20g pro.

DARLA ANDREWS
Schertz, TX

PEPPERONI PENNE CARBONARA

Sun-dried tomatoes and turkey pepperoni lend fantastic flavor to this creamy, hearty pasta dish. It's a great change of pace from everyday spaghetti.
—Taste of Home *Test Kitchen*

Takes: 30 min. • **Makes:** 6 servings

- 3   cups uncooked penne pasta
- 2   cups chopped sun-dried tomatoes (not packed in oil)
- 3   cups boiling water
- ¼   cup butter
- ½   tsp. minced garlic
- 1   cup chopped turkey pepperoni
- 1   cup shredded Parmesan cheese
- 1   cup heavy whipping cream
- 3   Tbsp. minced fresh basil
- ½   tsp. salt
- ¼   tsp. pepper

1. Cook pasta according to package directions. Meanwhile, soak tomatoes in boiling water for 10 minutes; drain well.
2. In a large skillet, saute tomatoes in butter for 3 minutes. Add garlic; cook 1 minute longer.
3. Stir in the pepperoni, cheese, cream, basil, salt and pepper. Cook over low heat until heated through. Drain pasta; toss with sauce.
1½ CUPS: 483 cal., 29g fat (17g sat. fat), 108mg chol., 1245mg sod., 39g carb. (7g sugars, 4g fiber), 19g pro.

TEST KITCHEN TIP
To quickly chop a lot of basil, stack several leaves and roll them into a tight tube. Slice the leaves widthwise; you'll have long thin strips called a chiffonade. For smaller pieces, like the minced basil in this recipe, chop the basil again without loosening it.

EASY-TO-STUFF MANICOTTI

It's so easy to make my simplified version of manicotti. I fill each pasta shell with a piece of string cheese for a deliciously gooey center, then I top the shells with a beefy tomato sauce.
—*Suzanne Runtz, Mount Pleasant, SC*

Prep: 20 min. • **Bake:** 30 min.
Makes: 7 servings

- 1   pkg. (8 oz.) manicotti shells
- 1   lb. ground beef
- ½   cup chopped onion
- 1   jar (24 oz.) spaghetti sauce
- 14 pieces string cheese
- 1½ cups shredded part-skim mozzarella cheese

1. Cook manicotti according to package directions. Meanwhile, in a large skillet, cook beef and onion over medium heat until meat is no longer pink; drain. Stir in spaghetti sauce. Spread half of the meat sauce into a greased 13x9-in. baking dish.
2. Drain manicotti; stuff each shell with a piece of string cheese. Place over meat sauce; top with remaining sauce. Cover and bake at 350° until heated through, 25-30 minutes.
3. Sprinkle with mozzarella cheese. Bake until the cheese is melted, 5-10 minutes longer.
2 PIECES: 558 cal., 29g fat (14g sat. fat), 93mg chol., 1059mg sod., 36g carb. (10g sugars, 4g fiber), 42g pro.

CREAMY SPINACH & RIGATONI BAKE

Macaroni and cheese is one of the ultimate comfort foods. Go ahead and give it an Italian twist—it's mac and cheese a whole new way!
—*Tammy Rex, New Tripoli, PA*

Prep: 25 min. • **Bake:** 20 min.
Makes: 10 servings

- 1 pkg. (16 oz.) rigatoni
- 8 oz. sliced pancetta, chopped
- ¾ cup butter, cubed
- ½ cup chopped onion
- ¾ cup all-purpose flour
- 1½ tsp. salt
- ¾ tsp. pepper
- 5¼ cups 2% milk
- 4 cups shredded Italian cheese blend
- 1 can (14 oz.) water-packed artichoke hearts, rinsed, drained and chopped
- 1 pkg. (10 oz.) frozen chopped spinach, thawed and squeezed dry
- ¼ cup shredded Parmesan cheese

1. Preheat oven to 375°. Cook the rigatoni according to package directions.
2. Meanwhile, in a large skillet over medium heat, cook pancetta until crisp, stirring occasionally. Remove with a slotted spoon; drain on paper towels. Discard the drippings; wipe the skillet clean.
3. In the same pan, heat butter over medium-high heat. Add onion; cook and stir until tender. Stir in flour, salt and pepper until blended; gradually whisk in milk. Bring to a boil, stirring constantly; cook and stir until thickened, 2-3 minutes. Remove from heat. Stir in cheese blend until melted.
4. Stir in artichokes, spinach and the pancetta. Drain the rigatoni; add to the cheese sauce. Transfer to a greased 13x9-in. baking dish; sprinkle with Parmesan cheese.
5. Bake, uncovered, until golden brown and bubbly, 20-25 minutes.
1¼ CUPS: 643 cal., 35g fat (20g sat. fat), 99mg chol., 1438mg sod., 53g carb. (8g sugars, 3g fiber), 28g pro.

EFFORTLESS ALFREDO PIZZA

Here's a lighter, scrumptious twist for pizza night. I often use collard greens instead of spinach. The recipe makes good use of leftovers and convenience items, so I don't have to spend much time in the kitchen.
—*Brittney House, Lockport, IL*

Takes: 20 min. • **Makes:** 6 slices

- 1 pkg. (10 oz.) frozen chopped spinach, thawed and squeezed dry
- 1 cup shredded cooked turkey breast
- 2 tsp. lemon juice
- ¼ tsp. salt
- ¼ tsp. pepper
- 1 prebaked 12-in. pizza crust
- 1 garlic clove, peeled and halved
- ½ cup reduced-fat Alfredo sauce
- ¾ cup shredded fontina cheese
- ½ tsp. crushed red pepper flakes

1. Preheat oven to 450°. In a large bowl, mix the first 5 ingredients until blended.
2. Place crust on an ungreased 12-in. pizza pan; rub with cut sides of garlic. Discard the garlic. Spread Alfredo sauce over crust. Top with the spinach mixture, cheese and pepper flakes. Bake until crust is lightly browned, 8-12 minutes.
1 SLICE: 302 cal., 10g fat (4g sat. fat), 45mg chol., 756mg sod., 33g carb. (1g sugars, 1g fiber), 20g pro. **DIABETIC EXCHANGES:** 2 starch, 2 lean meat, ½ fat.

CHICKEN GARDEN MEDLEY

After my family sampled this cozy casserole at a friend's house, it quickly became a favorite—especially with our teenage daughters, who now request it at least once a week.
—*Dohreen Winkler, Howell, MI*

- -

Prep: 25 min. • **Bake:** 20 min.
Makes: 4 servings

1	lb. boneless skinless chicken breasts, cut into strips
1	garlic clove, minced
¼	cup butter, divided
1	small yellow squash, halved lengthwise and sliced
1	small zucchini, halved lengthwise and sliced
½	cup julienned sweet red pepper
½	cup julienned green pepper
¼	cup thinly sliced onion
2	Tbsp. all-purpose flour
½	tsp. salt
¼	tsp. pepper
¾	cup chicken broth
½	cup half-and-half cream
8	oz. angel hair pasta, cooked and drained
2	Tbsp. shredded Parmesan cheese

1. Preheat oven to 350°. In a large skillet, saute chicken and garlic in 2 Tbsp. butter for 10-12 minutes or until the chicken juices run clear. Add vegetables. Cook until crisp-tender; remove from skillet and set aside.

2. In the same skillet, melt the remaining butter. Add flour, salt and pepper; stir to form a smooth paste. Gradually add broth. Bring to a boil; cook and stir for 2 minutes or until thickened. Stir in cream and heat through. Add the chicken and vegetables; stir until well mixed.

3. Place pasta in a greased 2-qt. baking dish. Pour chicken mixture over top. Sprinkle with Parmesan cheese. Cover and bake for 15 minutes; uncover and bake 5 minutes longer.

1½ CUPS: 404 cal., 19g fat (11g sat. fat), 111mg chol., 690mg sod., 26g carb. (4g sugars, 2g fiber), 30g pro.

MEATBALL PIZZA

I always keep meatballs and pizza crusts in the freezer to make this specialty at the spur of the moment. Add a tossed salad and you have a delicious dinner.
—*Mary Humeniuk-Smith, Perry Hall, MD*

Takes: 25 min. • **Makes:** 8 servings

- 1 prebaked 12-in. pizza crust
- 1 can (8 oz.) pizza sauce
- 1 tsp. garlic powder
- 1 tsp. Italian seasoning
- ¼ cup grated Parmesan cheese
- 1 small onion, halved and sliced
- 12 frozen fully cooked Italian meatballs (½ oz. each), thawed and halved
- 1 cup shredded part-skim mozzarella cheese
- 1 cup shredded cheddar cheese

Preheat oven to 350°. Place the crust on an ungreased 12-in. pizza pan or baking sheet. Spread sauce over crust; sprinkle with garlic powder, Italian seasoning and Parmesan cheese. Top with onion and meatballs; sprinkle with remaining cheeses. Bake 12-17 minutes or until cheese is melted.

1 SERVING: 321 cal., 16g fat (8g sat. fat), 36mg chol., 755mg sod., 28g carb. (3g sugars, 2g fiber), 17g pro.

RAVIOLI WITH CREAMY SQUASH SAUCE

Store-bought ravioli speeds assembly of this cozy, restaurant-quality dish that tastes so good, your family won't notice it's meatless.
—*Taste of Home Test Kitchen*

Takes: 20 min. • **Makes:** 4 servings

- 1 pkg. (9 oz.) refrigerated cheese ravioli
- 3 garlic cloves, minced
- 2 Tbsp. butter
- 1 pkg. (12 oz.) frozen cooked winter squash, thawed
- 1 pkg. (6 oz.) fresh baby spinach
- 1 cup heavy whipping cream
- ⅓ cup vegetable broth
- ¼ tsp. salt
- 1 cup chopped walnuts, toasted

1. Cook ravioli according to the package directions. Meanwhile, in a Dutch oven, saute garlic in butter for 1 minute. Add squash and spinach; cook 2-3 minutes longer or until spinach is wilted. Stir in cream, broth and salt. Bring to a gentle boil; cook for 6-8 minutes or until slightly thickened.

2. Drain ravioli; add to squash mixture. Toss to coat. Sprinkle with walnuts.

1¼ CUPS: 671 cal., 51g fat (22g sat. fat), 122mg chol., 578mg sod., 42g carb. (2g sugars, 7g fiber), 18g pro.

CONFETTI SPAGHETTI

It's not uncommon for folks to go back for second helpings of this hearty main dish when I share it at church suppers. The combination of ground beef, noodles, cheese and a zippy tomato sauce is a real people-pleaser.
—*Katherine Moss, Gaffney, SC*

- -

Prep: 20 min. • **Bake:** 35 min.
Makes: 12 servings

- 1 pkg. (16 oz.) spaghetti
- 1½ lbs. ground beef
- 1 medium green pepper, chopped
- 1 medium onion, chopped
- 1 can (14½ oz.) diced tomatoes, undrained
- 1 can (8 oz.) tomato sauce
- 1 Tbsp. brown sugar
- 1 tsp. salt
- 1 tsp. chili powder
- ½ tsp. pepper
- ¼ tsp. garlic powder
- ⅛ tsp. cayenne pepper
- ¾ cup shredded cheddar cheese

1. Preheat oven to 350°. Cook the spaghetti according to package directions.
2. Meanwhile, in a large skillet, cook beef, green pepper and onion over medium heat until meat is no longer pink; drain. Stir in the next 8 ingredients. Drain spaghetti; add to the beef mixture.
3. Transfer to a greased 13x9-in. baking dish. Cover and bake for 30 minutes. Uncover; sprinkle with cheese. Bake until cheese is melted, about 5 minutes longer.
1 CUP: 259 cal., 10g fat (4g sat. fat), 42mg chol., 424mg sod., 27g carb. (4g sugars, 2g fiber), 16g pro.

PEAR & TURKEY SAUSAGE RIGATONI

Sweet pear, salty sausage and creamy blue cheese make an elegant combination that's worthy of an expensive restaurant!
—*Debby Harden, Lansing, MI*

- -

Takes: 30 min. • **Makes:** 6 servings

- 8 oz. uncooked rigatoni or large tube pasta
- 2 Italian turkey sausage links (4 oz. each), casings removed
- 2 medium pears, sliced
- 2 cups fresh baby spinach
- ½ cup half-and-half cream
- ½ cup crumbled blue cheese, divided
  Toasted sliced almonds, optional

1. Cook rigatoni according to package directions.
2. Meanwhile, in a Dutch oven, cook sausage over medium heat until no longer pink, 6-8 minutes, breaking into large crumbles. Add pears; cook and stir until lightly browned, 3-5 minutes.
3. Drain rigatoni; add to sausage mixture. Add spinach, cream and ¼ cup cheese; cook until spinach is wilted, 3-4 minutes, stirring occasionally. Top with remaining cheese. If desired, sprinkle with almonds.
NOTE: To toast nuts, bake in a shallow pan in a 350° oven for 5-10 minutes or cook in a skillet over low heat until lightly browned, stirring occasionally.
1⅓ CUPS: 273 cal., 9g fat (4g sat. fat), 32mg chol., 333mg sod., 37g carb. (7g sugars, 3g fiber), 13g pro. **DIABETIC EXCHANGES:** 2½ starch, 2 medium-fat meat.

LEMON CHICKEN WITH ORZO

Here's a dish that's light and summery but still filling. My kids love all the veggies—for real! If you like a lot of lemon, stir in an extra splash of lemon juice just before serving.
—*Shannon Humphrey, Hampton, VA*

Prep: 20 min. • **Cook:** 20 min.
Makes: 4 servings

- ⅓ cup all-purpose flour
- 1 tsp. garlic powder
- 1 lb. boneless skinless chicken breasts
- ¾ tsp. salt, divided
- ½ tsp. pepper
- 2 Tbsp. olive oil
- 1 can (14½ oz.) reduced-sodium chicken broth
- 1¼ cups uncooked whole wheat orzo pasta
- 2 cups chopped fresh spinach
- 1 cup grape tomatoes, halved
- 3 Tbsp. lemon juice
- 2 Tbsp. minced fresh basil
  Lemon wedges, optional

1. In a shallow bowl, mix flour and garlic powder. Cut chicken into 1½-in. pieces; pound each with a meat mallet to ¼-in. thickness. Sprinkle with ½ tsp. salt and pepper. Dip both sides of the chicken in the flour mixture to coat lightly; shake off excess.

2. In a large skillet, heat oil over medium heat. Add chicken; cook 3-4 minutes on each side or until coating is golden brown and chicken is no longer pink. Remove from pan; keep warm. Wipe skillet clean.

3. In same pan, bring broth to a boil; stir in orzo. Return to a boil. Reduce heat; simmer, covered, 8-10 minutes or until tender. Stir in spinach, tomatoes, lemon juice, basil and remaining salt; remove from heat. Return chicken to the pan. If desired, serve with lemon wedges.

1¼ CUPS: 399 cal., 11g fat (2g sat. fat), 63mg chol., 807mg sod., 43g carb. (2g sugars, 9g fiber), 32g pro. **DIABETIC EXCHANGES:** 3 lean meat, 2 starch, 1½ fat, 1 vegetable.

SHRIMP SCAMPI

This shrimp scampi recipe looks elegant enough to serve to company, but it's easy to prepare. The bright flavors of lemon and herbs enhance the shrimp. Serve it over pasta and wait for the compliments.
—*Lori Packer, Omaha, NE*

Takes: 20 min. • **Makes:** 4 servings

- 3 to 4 garlic cloves, minced
- ¼ cup butter, cubed
- ¼ cup olive oil
- 1 lb. uncooked medium shrimp, peeled and deveined
- ¼ cup lemon juice
- ½ tsp. pepper
- ¼ tsp. dried oregano
- ½ cup grated Parmesan cheese
- ¼ cup dry bread crumbs
- ¼ cup minced fresh parsley
  Hot cooked angel hair pasta

1. In a 10-in. ovenproof skillet, saute garlic in butter and oil until fragrant. Add the shrimp, lemon juice, pepper and oregano; cook and stir until shrimp turn pink. Sprinkle with cheese, bread crumbs and parsley.

2. Broil 6 in. from the heat for 2-3 minutes or until topping is golden brown. Serve with pasta.

1 CUP: 395 cal., 30g fat (11g sat. fat), 177mg chol., 420mg sod., 9g carb. (1g sugars, 1g fiber), 24g pro.

GRILLED SHRIMP SCAMPI: Omit the butter, oregano, Parmesan, bread crumbs and pasta. Substitute jumbo shrimp for the medium shrimp. In a large bowl, whisk the garlic, oil, lemon juice and pepper. Add shrimp; toss to coat. Refrigerate, covered, 30 minutes. Thread the shrimp onto 4 metal or soaked wooden skewers. Grill, covered, over medium heat or broil 4 in. from heat 6-8 minutes or until the shrimp turn pink, turning once. Serve with hot cooked rice; sprinkle with parsley.

GARLIC LEMON SHRIMP: Omit the butter, pepper, oregano, Parmesan and bread crumbs. In a large skillet, saute shrimp in 2 Tbsp. oil for 3 minutes. Add the garlic, 1 Tbsp. lemon juice, 1 tsp. cumin and ¼ tsp. salt; cook and stir until shrimp turn pink. Stir in 2 Tbsp. minced fresh parsley. Serve with pasta.

SPINACH-PESTO WHITE PIZZA

When my kids were small, they tried to avoid veggies, so I had to get creative. I figured that because pesto is already green, it would be the perfect place to add some spinach. The recipe gained a following right away.

—*Janet Burbach, North Platte, NE*

- -

Takes: 30 min. • **Makes:** 6 slices

- 1 tsp. olive oil
- 3 cups fresh baby spinach
- ¼ cup plus 1 Tbsp. prepared pesto, divided
- 1 pkg. (6 oz.) ready-to-use grilled chicken breast strips
- 1 prebaked 12-in. pizza crust
- 2 cups shredded part-skim mozzarella cheese
- 5 bacon strips, cooked and crumbled
- ½ cup part-skim ricotta cheese
- ¼ cup shredded Parmesan cheese

1. Preheat oven to 450°. In a large skillet, heat oil over medium-high heat. Add spinach; cook and stir just until wilted. Remove from heat; stir in ¼ cup of the pesto. In a small bowl, toss chicken with the remaining pesto.

2. Place crust on an ungreased baking sheet. Spread with spinach mixture; top with chicken, mozzarella cheese and bacon. Drop ricotta cheese by rounded teaspoonfuls over top; sprinkle with Parmesan cheese. Bake for 8-10 minutes or until cheese is melted.

1 SLICE: 453 cal., 22g fat (8g sat. fat), 52mg chol., 956mg sod., 35g carb. (3g sugars, 2g fiber), 30g pro.

> **TEST KITCHEN TIP**
> If you shred your own mozzarella instead of buying it bagged, try putting the cheese in the freezer for about 30 minutes before you shred it. This will keep the cheese from sticking to the grater.

SAUSAGE SPAGHETTI SPIRALS

My family loves this pasta casserole with hearty chunks of sausage and green pepper. The recipe makes a big pan, so it's especially nice for gatherings.

—*Carol Carolton, Wheaton, IL*

- -

Prep: 15 min. • **Bake:** 30 min.
Makes: 6 servings

- 1 lb. bulk Italian sausage
- 1 medium green pepper, chopped
- 5 cups spiral pasta, cooked and drained
- 1 jar (24 oz.) spaghetti sauce
- 1½ cups shredded part-skim mozzarella cheese

1. Preheat oven to 350°. In a large skillet, cook sausage and green pepper over medium heat until meat is no longer pink; drain. Stir in pasta and spaghetti sauce.

2. Transfer to a greased 13x9-in. baking dish. Cover and bake for 25 minutes. Uncover; sprinkle with cheese. Bake 5-10 minutes longer or until cheese is melted.

1 SERVING: 592 cal., 24g fat (9g sat. fat), 59mg chol., 1071mg sod., 67g carb. (12g sugars, 5g fiber), 26g pro.

5i
TACO PIZZA SQUARES

This dish is always popular at our house. I top a convenient refrigerated pizza dough with leftover taco meat, tomatoes and cheese, bringing a full-flavored fiesta to the table.
—*Sarah Vovos, Middleton, WI*

- -

Takes: 25 min. • **Makes:** 10 servings

- 1 tube (13.8 oz.) refrigerated pizza crust
- 1 can (8 oz.) pizza sauce
- 2 cups seasoned taco meat
- 2 medium tomatoes, seeded and chopped
- 2 cups shredded mozzarella cheese
  Shredded lettuce or sour cream, optional

Preheat oven to 400°. Unroll pizza dough and place in a 15x10x1-in. baking pan. Spread with pizza sauce; sprinkle with the taco meat, tomatoes and cheese. Bake until crust is golden brown, 15-20 minutes. Top with shredded lettuce and sour cream if desired.
1 PIECE: 259 cal., 11g fat (5g sat. fat), 40mg chol., 660mg sod., 23g carb. (4g sugars, 2g fiber), 17g pro.

SAUCY CHICKEN & TORTELLINI

This heartwarming dish is something I threw together years ago for my oldest daughter. When she's having a rough day, I pull out the slow cooker and prepare this special recipe.
—*Mary Morgan, Dallas, TX*

- -

Prep: 10 min. • **Cook:** 6¼ hours
Makes: 8 servings

- 1½ lbs. boneless skinless chicken breasts, cut into 1-in. cubes
- ½ lb. sliced fresh mushrooms
- 1 large onion, chopped
- 1 medium sweet red pepper, cut into ½-in. pieces
- 1 medium green pepper, cut into ½-in. pieces
- 1 can (2¼ oz.) sliced ripe olives, drained
- 1 jar (24 oz.) marinara sauce
- 1 jar (15 oz.) Alfredo sauce
- 2 pkg. (9 oz. each) refrigerated cheese tortellini
  Grated Parmesan cheese, optional
  Torn fresh basil, optional

1. In a 5-qt. slow cooker, combine the first 7 ingredients. Cook, covered, on low until the chicken is tender, 6-8 hours.
2. Stir in Alfredo sauce and tortellini. Cook, covered, until the tortellini is tender, 15-20 minutes. If desired, top with Parmesan cheese and basil.
FREEZE OPTION: Freeze cooled, cooked mixture in freezer containers. To use, partially thaw in refrigerator overnight. Microwave, covered, on high, in a microwave-safe dish until heated through, stirring gently; add water if necessary.
1¼ CUPS: 437 cal., 15g fat (7g sat. fat), 91mg chol., 922mg sod., 44g carb. (8g sugars, 5g fiber), 31g pro.

CREAMY PESTO PENNE WITH VEGETABLE RIBBONS

This beautiful dish will wow guests. It's not just the bright colors; they'll really be amazed by the fresh and indulgent taste.
—Taste of Home *Test Kitchen*

Takes: 30 min. • **Makes:** 4 servings

- 2 cups uncooked penne pasta
- 1 cup frozen shelled edamame, thawed
- 4 medium carrots
- 2 yellow summer squash
- 1 medium onion, halved and thinly sliced
- 2 Tbsp. butter, divided
- 1 garlic clove, minced
- ¾ cup heavy whipping cream
- 2 Tbsp. prepared pesto
- ¼ tsp. salt
- ¼ cup chopped walnuts, toasted

1. In a large saucepan, cook pasta according to package directions, adding the edamame during the last 5 minutes of cooking.
2. Meanwhile, using a vegetable peeler or metal cheese slicer, cut carrots and squash into very thin lengthwise strips.
3. In a large skillet, saute onion in 1 Tbsp. butter until tender. Add the vegetable strips and garlic; saute 2-3 minutes longer or until crisp-tender. Stir in the cream, pesto, salt and remaining butter. Bring to a gentle boil; cook for 2-4 minutes or until the sauce is slightly thickened and the vegetables are tender.
4. Drain pasta and edamame; toss with vegetable mixture. Sprinkle with walnuts.
1½ CUPS: 521 cal., 33g fat (16g sat. fat), 79mg chol., 315mg sod., 45g carb. (9g sugars, 7g fiber), 15g pro.

HAM IT UP PRIMAVERA

I adapted my special primavera from a cookbook my husband and I received when we got married. We love all the veggies, especially the fresh asparagus.
—*Angelia Holland, Plano, TX*

Takes: 30 min. • **Makes:** 12 servings

- 1 pkg. (16 oz.) spaghetti
- 1 lb. fresh asparagus, trimmed and cut into 1-in. pieces
- 2 medium carrots, cut into ¼-in. slices
- ½ cup butter, cubed
- ½ lb. sliced fresh mushrooms
- 2 medium zucchini, halved and cut into ¼-in. slices
- 2 cups cubed fully cooked ham
- 1 pkg. (10 oz.) frozen peas, thawed
- 8 green onions, chopped
- 3 tsp. dried basil
- 1½ tsp. salt
- ¼ tsp. white pepper
- ¼ tsp. ground nutmeg
- 1½ cups heavy whipping cream
- 1 cup grated Parmesan cheese, divided

1. Cook the spaghetti according to the package directions.
2. Meanwhile, in a large skillet, saute the asparagus and carrots in butter for 3 minutes. Add mushrooms and zucchini; saute until crisp-tender.
3. Stir in the ham, peas, onions, basil, salt, pepper and nutmeg. Add cream. Bring to a boil; cook and stir 2 minutes.
4. Drain spaghetti; place in a large bowl. Add the vegetable mixture and ½ cup cheese; toss to combine. Serve with the remaining cheese.
1¼ CUPS: 417 cal., 23g fat (14g sat. fat), 79mg chol., 804mg sod., 38g carb. (4g sugars, 4g fiber), 15g pro.

PENNE BEEF BAKE

I had ground beef and veggies on hand, so I came up with this pizza-flavored casserole. I never expected my family to love it so much. It's a good way to sneak in extra veggies for the kids.

—Jennifer Wise, Selinsgrove, PA

Prep: 20 min. • **Bake:** 25 min.
Makes: 8 servings

- 1 pkg. (12 oz.) whole wheat penne pasta
- 1 lb. lean ground beef (90% lean)
- 2 medium zucchini, finely chopped
- 1 large green pepper, finely chopped
- 1 small onion, finely chopped
- 1 jar (24 oz.) spaghetti sauce
- 1½ cups reduced-fat Alfredo sauce
- 1 cup shredded part-skim mozzarella cheese, divided
- ¼ tsp. garlic powder
  Minced fresh parsley, optional

1. Preheat oven to 375°. Cook the penne according to package directions.
2. Meanwhile, in a Dutch oven, cook the beef, zucchini, pepper and onion over medium heat until the meat is no longer pink; drain. Stir in the spaghetti sauce, Alfredo sauce, ½ cup mozzarella cheese and the garlic powder. Drain penne; stir into the meat mixture.
3. Transfer to a 13x9-in. baking dish coated with cooking spray. Cover; bake 20 minutes. Sprinkle with remaining mozzarella. Bake, uncovered, 3-5 minutes longer or until cheese is melted. If desired, top with parsley.

1⅓ CUPS: 395 cal., 12g fat (6g sat. fat), 62mg chol., 805mg sod., 45g carb. (9g sugars, 7g fiber), 25g pro. **DIABETIC EXCHANGES:** 3 starch, 2 lean meat, 1 fat.

READER REVIEW

"Super easy! It tastes even better the next day! Love the addition of zucchini."

LAURA70, TASTEOFHOME.COM

❄ CHICKEN PIZZA

My fun twist on typical pizza is an excellent way to use up leftover pesto. And since it's loaded with protein-rich chicken and black beans, it's hearty enough to satisfy everyone!
—Taste of Home *Test Kitchen*

Takes: 30 min. • **Makes:** 6 servings

- 1 lb. boneless skinless chicken breasts, cut into 1-in. pieces
- 1 Tbsp. olive oil
- 1 prebaked 12-in. pizza crust
- ¼ cup prepared pesto
- 1 large tomato, chopped
- ½ cup canned black beans, rinsed and drained
- 1 cup shredded part-skim mozzarella cheese
- ½ cup shredded Parmesan cheese

1. Preheat oven to 400°. In a large skillet, cook the chicken in oil over medium heat for 10-15 minutes or until no longer pink.
2. Place the crust on a lightly greased 12-in. pizza pan. Spread with pesto; top with the chicken, tomato, beans and cheeses. Bake for 10-12 minutes or until cheese is melted.
FREEZE OPTION: Securely wrap and freeze unbaked pizza. To use, unwrap pizza; bake as directed, increasing time as necessary.

1 SERVING: 431 cal., 18g fat (6g sat. fat), 65mg chol., 692mg sod., 35g carb. (1g sugars, 1g fiber), 32g pro.

CHICKEN SAUSAGE & GNOCCHI SKILLET

I had a bunch of fresh veggies and combined them with sausage, gnocchi and goat cheese when I needed a quick dinner. Use ingredients you have on hand to give it your own spin.
—*Dahlia Abrams, Detroit, MI*

Takes: 30 min. • **Makes:** 4 servings

- 1 pkg. (16 oz.) potato gnocchi
- 1 Tbsp. butter
- 1 Tbsp. olive oil
- 2 fully cooked Italian chicken sausage links (3 oz. each), sliced
- ½ lb. sliced baby portobello mushrooms
- 1 medium onion, finely chopped
- 1 lb. fresh asparagus, trimmed and cut into ½-in. pieces
- 2 garlic cloves, minced
- 2 Tbsp. white wine or chicken broth
- 2 oz. herbed fresh goat cheese
- 2 Tbsp. minced fresh basil or 2 tsp. dried basil
- 1 Tbsp. lemon juice
- ¼ tsp. salt
- ⅛ tsp. pepper
  Grated Parmesan cheese

1. Cook gnocchi according to the package directions; drain.
2. Meanwhile, in a large skillet, heat butter and oil over medium-high heat. Add sausage, mushrooms and onion; cook and stir until sausage is browned and the vegetables are tender. Add asparagus and garlic; cook and stir 2-3 minutes longer.
3. Stir in wine. Bring to a boil; cook until liquid is almost evaporated. Add goat cheese, basil, lemon juice, salt and pepper. Stir in gnocchi; heat through. Sprinkle with Parmesan cheese.
1½ CUPS: 454 cal., 15g fat (6g sat. fat), 58mg chol., 995mg sod., 56g carb. (11g sugars, 5g fiber), 21g pro.

GRILLED SAUSAGE-BASIL PIZZAS

These easy little pizzas are a wonderful change of pace from the classic cookout menu. Let everybody go crazy with the toppings.
—*Lisa Speer, Palm Beach, FL*

Takes: 30 min. • **Makes:** 4 servings

- 4 Italian sausage links (4 oz. each)
- 4 naan flatbreads or whole pita breads
- ¼ cup olive oil
- 1 cup tomato basil pasta sauce
- 2 cups shredded part-skim mozzarella cheese
- ½ cup grated Parmesan cheese
- ½ cup thinly sliced fresh basil

1. Grill sausages, covered, over medium heat until a thermometer reads 160°, 10-12 minutes, turning occasionally. Cut into ¼-in. slices.
2. Brush both sides of the flatbreads with oil. Grill the flatbreads, covered, over medium heat until bottoms are lightly browned, 2-3 minutes.
3. Remove flatbreads from grill. Layer grilled sides with sauce, sausage, cheeses and basil. Return to grill; cook, covered, until cheese is melted, 2-3 minutes longer.
1 PIZZA: 808 cal., 56g fat (19g sat. fat), 112mg chol., 1996mg sod., 41g carb. (9g sugars, 3g fiber), 34g pro.

CARAMELIZED ONION & GARLIC PASTA

This full-flavored recipe is the result of my mom's love of pasta and our love of cooking together. With heat from the red pepper and smoky flavor from the bacon, the entree is excellent alone or paired with grilled chicken.
—*Lacy Jo Matheson, Sault Sainte Marie, MI*

Prep: 20 min. • **Cook:** 35 min.
Makes: 6 servings

- ¼ cup butter, cubed
- 2 large sweet onions, thinly sliced
- ¼ tsp. crushed red pepper flakes
- ⅛ tsp. salt
- 8 garlic cloves, minced
- 2 cups grape tomatoes, halved
- ¼ cup balsamic vinegar
- ¼ cup olive oil, divided
- 1 pkg. (16 oz.) uncooked angel hair pasta
- 9 bacon strips, cooked and crumbled
- ⅔ cup shredded Parmesan cheese
- ½ tsp. coarsely ground pepper
  Fresh basil leaves, optional

1. In a large skillet over medium-high heat, melt butter. Add the onions, pepper flakes and salt; saute until the onions are tender. Stir in garlic. Reduce heat to medium-low; cook, stirring occasionally, for 30-40 minutes or until onions are deep golden brown.

2. Add the tomatoes, vinegar and 2 Tbsp. of oil to the skillet. Cook the pasta according to package directions. Drain pasta; toss with the onion mixture.

3. Drizzle with the remaining olive oil. Sprinkle with bacon, cheese, and pepper; heat through. Garnish with basil if desired.

1½ CUPS: 574 cal., 24g fat (9g sat. fat), 37mg chol., 495mg sod., 71g carb. (10g sugars, 4g fiber), 18g pro..

BUBBLE PIZZA

Refrigerated biscuits form the easy crust in my recipe. For a jazzed-up version, add your favorite pizza toppings.
—*Jo Groth, Plainfield, IA*

Prep: 15 min. • **Bake:** 25 min.
Makes: 8 servings

- 1½ lbs. lean ground beef (90% lean)
- 1 can (15 oz.) pizza sauce
- 2 tubes (12 oz. each) refrigerated buttermilk biscuits
- 1½ cups shredded part-skim mozzarella cheese
- 1 cup shredded cheddar cheese

1. Preheat oven to 400°. In a large skillet, cook beef over medium heat until no longer pink; drain. Stir in pizza sauce.

2. Cut each biscuit into quarters; place in a greased 13x9-in. baking dish. Top with the beef mixture.

3. Bake, uncovered, at 400° for 20 minutes. Sprinkle with cheeses. Bake until cheese is melted, 5-10 minutes longer. Let stand for 5 minutes before serving.

1 PIECE: 356 cal., 16g fat (8g sat. fat), 73mg chol., 730mg sod., 25g carb. (2g sugars, 1g fiber), 28g pro.

SMOKED SAUSAGE WITH PASTA

Packed with sausage, mushrooms, tomatoes and basil flavor, this quick recipe satisfies the toughest critics. It's one of my husband's favorite dishes, and he has no idea it's lower in fat! Add a green salad for a delicious meal.
—*Ruth Ann Ruddell, Shelby Township, MI*

Takes: 30 min. • **Makes:** 4 servings

- 4 oz. uncooked angel hair pasta
- ½ lb. smoked turkey kielbasa, cut into ½-in. slices
- 2 cups sliced fresh mushrooms
- 2 garlic cloves, minced
- 4½ tsp. minced fresh basil or 1½ tsp. dried basil
- 1 Tbsp. olive oil
- 2 cups julienned seeded plum tomatoes
- ⅛ tsp. salt
- ⅛ tsp. pepper
  Grated Parmesan cheese, optional

1. Cook pasta according to the package directions.

2. Meanwhile, in a large nonstick skillet, saute the sausage, mushrooms, garlic and basil in oil until mushrooms are tender. Drain pasta; add to the sausage mixture. Add the tomatoes, salt and pepper; toss gently. Heat through. If desired, top with additional fresh basil and grated Parmesan cheese.

1 CUP: 232 cal., 7g fat (2g sat. fat), 35mg chol., 639mg sod., 27g carb. (5g sugars, 2g fiber), 15g pro. **DIABETIC EXCHANGES:** 2 lean meat, 1½ starch, 1 vegetable, ½ fat.

DID YOU KNOW?
The name "kielbasa" is used in North America to describe a garlic-heavy, lightly smoked sausage—also often called just Polish sausage. But if you were to go to Poland, you'd have to be a little more specific—there are roughly 100 different varieties of kielbasa!

TANDOORI SPICED CHICKEN PITA PIZZA WITH GREEK YOGURT & CILANTRO

My family and I are big picnickers, and I'm always looking for new dishes to try in the great outdoors. The amazing flavors at our favorite Indian restaurant inspired these mini pizzas.
—*Angela Spengler, Niceville, FL*

Takes: 25 min. • **Makes:** 4 servings

- 1 cup plain Greek yogurt, divided
- 2 Tbsp. chopped fresh cilantro
- ½ tsp. ground coriander
- ½ tsp. ground cumin
- ½ tsp. ground ginger
- ½ tsp. ground turmeric
- ½ tsp. paprika
- ½ tsp. cayenne pepper
- ¾ lb. boneless skinless chicken breasts, cut into ½-in.-thick strips
- 4 whole wheat pita breads (6 in.)
- ⅔ cup crumbled feta cheese
- ⅓ cup chopped seeded tomato
- ⅓ cup chopped fresh Italian parsley

1. For the sauce, mix ½ cup of the yogurt and the cilantro. In a large bowl, mix spices and the remaining yogurt; stir in chicken to coat.

2. Place chicken on an oiled grill rack over medium heat; grill, covered, until no longer pink, 2-3 minutes per side. Grill pita breads until warmed, about 1 minute per side.

3. Spread pitas with sauce. Top with chicken, cheese, tomato and parsley.

1 PIZZA: 380 cal., 12g fat (6g sat. fat), 72mg chol., 598mg sod., 41g carb. (5g sugars, 5g fiber), 29g pro. **DIABETIC EXCHANGES:** 3 lean meat, 2½ starch.

ANGELA SPENGLER
Niceville, FL

BURGERS, WRAPS & SANDWICHES

Dress them up or keep them simple, sandwiches are always popular—especially with kids! Have these on hand for an easy weeknight meal or a fun weekend party.

FETA CHICKEN BURGERS

My friends always request these tasty chicken burgers. I sometimes add olives to punch up the Mediterranean flavor! In the summer, we put them on the grill. Try them with the mayo topping—you won't be disappointed.
—*Angela Robinson, Findlay, OH*

- -

Takes: 30 min. • **Makes:** 6 servings

- ¼ **cup finely chopped cucumber**
- ¼ **cup reduced-fat mayonnaise**

BURGERS
- ½ **cup chopped roasted sweet red pepper**
- 1 **tsp. garlic powder**
- ½ **tsp. Greek seasoning**
- ¼ **tsp. pepper**
- 1½ **lbs. lean ground chicken**
- 1 **cup crumbled feta cheese**
- 6 **whole wheat hamburger buns, split and toasted**
  Lettuce leaves and tomato slices, optional

1. Preheat the broiler. Mix cucumber and mayonnaise; set aside.

2. For burgers, mix chopped red pepper and seasonings. Add chicken and cheese; mix lightly but thoroughly (mixture will be sticky). Shape into six ½-in.-thick patties.

3. Broil burgers 4 in. from the heat until a thermometer reads 165°, 3-4 minutes per side. Serve in buns with cucumber sauce. If desired, top with lettuce and tomato.

FREEZE OPTION: Place uncooked patties on a plastic wrap-lined baking sheet; wrap and freeze until firm. Remove from pan and transfer to an airtight freezer container; return to freezer. To use, broil the frozen patties as directed, increasing time as necessary.

1 BURGER WITH 1 TBSP. SAUCE: 356 cal., 14g fat (5g sat. fat), 95mg chol., 703mg sod., 25g carb. (5g sugars, 4g fiber), 31g pro.
DIABETIC EXCHANGES: 5 lean meat, 2 starch, ½ fat.

ANGELA ROBINSON
Findaly, OH

SHREDDED FRENCH DIP

A chuck roast slow-simmered in beefy broth is delicious when shredded and spooned onto rolls. I serve the cooking juices in individual cups to use for dipping.
—*Carla Kimball, Callaway, NE*

Prep: 5 min. • **Cook:** 6 hours
Makes: 10 servings

- 1 boneless beef chuck roast (3 lbs.), trimmed
- 1 can (10½ oz.) condensed French onion soup, undiluted
- 1 can (10½ oz.) condensed beef consomme, undiluted
- 1 can (10½ oz.) condensed beef broth, undiluted
- 1 tsp. beef bouillon granules
- 8 to 10 French or Italian rolls, split

1. Halve roast and place in a 3-qt. slow cooker. Combine the soup, consomme, broth and bouillon; pour over roast. Cover and cook on low for 6-8 hours or until the meat is tender.
2. Remove meat and shred with 2 forks. Serve on rolls. Skim fat from cooking juices; serve juices on the side for dipping.
1 SANDWICH: 399 cal., 15g fat (5g sat. fat), 91mg chol., 1104mg sod., 30g carb. (2g sugars, 2g fiber), 33g pro.

BARBECUED BURGERS

I can't take all the credit for these winning burgers—my husband's uncle passed down this special barbecue sauce recipe. We love it on, and in, everything, especially burgers with cheese, bacon and the works.
—*Rhoda Troyer, Glenford, OH*

Prep: 25 min. • **Grill:** 15 min.
Makes: 6 servings

SAUCE

- 1 cup ketchup
- ½ cup packed brown sugar
- ⅓ cup sugar
- ¼ cup honey
- ¼ cup molasses
- 2 tsp. prepared mustard
- 1½ tsp. Worcestershire sauce
- ¼ tsp. salt
- ¼ tsp. liquid smoke
- ⅛ tsp. pepper

BURGERS

- 1 large egg, lightly beaten
- ⅓ cup quick-cooking oats
- ¼ tsp. onion salt
- ¼ tsp. garlic salt
- ¼ tsp. pepper
- ⅛ tsp. salt
- 1½ lbs. ground beef
- 6 hamburger buns, split
  Toppings of your choice

1. In a small saucepan, combine the first 10 ingredients. Bring to a boil. Remove from the heat. Set aside 1 cup of barbecue sauce to serve with burgers.
2. In a large bowl, combine the egg, oats, ¼ cup of the remaining barbecue sauce, the onion salt, garlic salt, pepper and salt. Crumble beef over the egg mixture and mix well. Shape into six patties.
3. Grill, covered, over medium heat for 6-8 minutes on each side or until a thermometer reads 160°, basting with ½ cup of barbecue sauce during the last 5 minutes. Serve on buns with toppings of your choice and the reserved barbecue sauce.
1 BURGER: 626 cal., 19g fat (7g sat. fat), 121mg chol., 1146mg sod., 86g carb. (56g sugars, 2g fiber), 30g pro.

INDIAN SPICED CHICKPEA WRAPS WITH PINEAPPLE RAITA

Raita, an Indian condiment made with yogurt, elevates this vegetarian dish into a satisfying gourmet wrap. If you're in the mood to experiment, try subbing diced mango or cucumber for the pineapple, and add fresh herbs like cilantro or mint.
—*Jennifer Beckman, Falls Church, VA*

- -

Takes: 30 min. • **Makes:** 4 servings

- 1 cup (8 oz.) reduced-fat plain yogurt
- ½ cup unsweetened pineapple tidbits
- ¼ tsp. salt
- ¼ tsp. ground cumin

WRAPS

- 2 tsp. canola oil
- 1 small onion, chopped
- 1 Tbsp. minced fresh gingerroot
- 2 garlic cloves, minced
- ½ tsp. curry powder
- ¼ tsp. salt
- ¼ tsp. ground coriander
- ¼ tsp. ground cumin
- ¼ tsp. cayenne pepper, optional
- 1 can (15 oz.) chickpeas, rinsed and drained
- 1 cup canned crushed tomatoes
- 3 cups fresh baby spinach
- 4 whole wheat tortillas (8 in.), warmed

1. For pineapple raita, mix first 4 ingredients. Set aside.

2. In a large nonstick skillet, heat oil over medium-high heat; saute onion until tender. Add ginger, garlic and seasonings; cook and stir until fragrant, about 1 minute. Stir in chickpeas and tomatoes; bring to a boil. Reduce heat; simmer, uncovered, until slightly thickened, 5-8 minutes, stirring occasionally.

3. To serve, place the spinach and chickpea mixture on tortillas. Top with raita and roll up.

1 WRAP: 321 cal., 7g fat (1g sat. fat), 3mg chol., 734mg sod., 55g carb. (15g sugars, 10g fiber), 13g pro.

TEST KITCHEN TIP
To quickly warm tortillas, wrap them in a damp paper towel and heat them in the microwave for a few seconds.

JENNIFER BECKMAN
Falls Church, VA

🍎🍲

STEAK BURRITOS

Slowly simmered all day, the beef is tender and so easy to shred. Just fill flour tortillas and add toppings for a tasty meal.
—Valerie Jones, Portland, ME

- -

Prep: 15 min. • **Cook:** 8 hours
Makes: 10 servings

- 2 beef flank steaks (about 1 lb. each)
- 2 envelopes reduced-sodium taco seasoning
- 1 medium onion, chopped
- 1 can (4 oz.) chopped green chiles
- 1 Tbsp. white vinegar
- 10 flour tortillas (8 in.), warmed
- 1 cup shredded Monterey Jack cheese
- 1½ cups chopped seeded plum tomatoes
- ¾ cup reduced-fat sour cream

1. Cut steaks in half; rub with taco seasoning. Place in a 3-qt. slow cooker coated with cooking spray. Top with onion, chilies and vinegar. Cover and cook on low until meat is tender, 8-9 hours.
2. Remove steaks and cool slightly; shred the meat with 2 forks. Return to slow cooker; heat mixture through.
3. Spoon about ½ cup meat mixture into the center of each tortilla. Top with cheese, tomato and sour cream. Fold bottom and sides of tortilla over filling and roll up.
1 BURRITO: 339 cal., 12g fat (6g sat. fat), 59mg chol., 816mg sod., 33g carb. (5g sugars, 2g fiber), 25g pro. **DIABETIC EXCHANGES:** 3 lean meat, 2 starch.

READER REVIEW

"These were so easy and delicious! I used venison instead of flank steak. My husband takes them to work for lunch and warms them up. Thanks for the great recipe!"
ANGELRYAN75, TASTEOFHOME.COM

SAUSAGE & SPINACH CALZONES

These comforting calzones are perfect for quick meals—or even a midnight snack. My nurse co-workers always ask me to make them when it's my turn to bring in lunch.
—Kourtney Williams, Mechanicsville, VA

- -

Takes: 30 min. • **Makes:** 4 servings

- ½ lb. bulk Italian sausage
- 3 cups fresh baby spinach
- 1 tube (13.8 oz.) refrigerated pizza crust
- ¾ cup shredded part-skim mozzarella cheese
- ½ cup part-skim ricotta cheese
- ¼ tsp. pepper
  Pizza sauce, optional

1. In a large skillet, cook and crumble sausage over medium heat until no longer pink, about 4-6 minutes; drain. Add spinach; cook and stir until wilted. Remove from heat.
2. On a lightly floured surface, unroll and pat dough into a 15x11-in. rectangle. Cut dough into 4 rectangles. Sprinkle mozzarella on half of each rectangle to within 1 in. of edges.
3. Stir ricotta cheese and pepper into sausage mixture; spoon over mozzarella. Fold dough over the filling; press edges with a fork to seal. Place on a greased baking sheet.
4. Bake at 400° until golden brown, 10-15 minutes. If desired, serve with pizza sauce.
FREEZE OPTION: Freeze cooled calzones in an airtight freezer container. To use, microwave on high until heated through.
1 CALZONE: 489 calories, 22g fat (9g saturated fat), 54mg cholesterol, 1242mg sodium, 51g carbohydrate (7g sugars, 2g fiber), 23g protein.

TANGY PULLED PORK SANDWICHES

The slow cooker not only makes this an easy meal, but it keeps the pork tender, moist and loaded with flavor. These sandwiches are real comfort food, and they disappear fast.
—*Beki Kosydar-Krantz, Mayfield, PA*

Prep: 10 min. • **Cook:** 4 hours
Makes: 4 servings

- 1 **pork tenderloin (1 lb.)**
- 1 **cup ketchup**
- 2 **Tbsp. plus 1½ tsp. brown sugar**
- 2 **Tbsp. plus 1½ tsp. cider vinegar**
- 1 **Tbsp. plus 1½ tsp. Worcestershire sauce**
- 1 **Tbsp. spicy brown mustard**
- ¼ **tsp. pepper**
- 4 **rolls or buns, split and toasted Coleslaw, optional**

1. Cut the tenderloin in half; place in a 3-qt. slow cooker. Combine ketchup, brown sugar, vinegar, Worcestershire sauce, mustard and pepper; pour over the pork.

2. Cover and cook on low for 4-5 hours or until the meat is tender. Remove meat; shred with 2 forks. Return to slow cooker; heat through. Serve on toasted rolls or buns, with coleslaw, if desired.
1 SANDWICH: 402 cal., 7g fat (2g sat. fat), 63mg chol., 1181mg sod., 56g carb. (18g sugars, 2g fiber), 29g pro.

PARMESAN CHICKEN SANDWICHES

Coat tender chicken breasts with seasoned bread crumbs and smother them in marinara sauce. Served on a hoagie, they're a real treat!
—*Sue Bosek, Whittier, CA*

Takes: 25 min. • **Makes:** 2 servings

- ½ **cup all-purpose flour**
- 1 **large egg, lightly beaten**
- ¾ **cup seasoned bread crumbs**
- 3 **Tbsp. grated Parmesan cheese**
- 2 **boneless skinless chicken breast halves (5 oz. each)**
- ⅛ **tsp. salt**
- ⅛ **tsp. pepper**
- 2 **Tbsp. olive oil**

- 2 **Italian rolls, split**
- 2 **slices provolone cheese**
- ⅓ **cup marinara or other meatless pasta sauce, warmed**

1. Place flour and egg in separate shallow bowls. In another bowl, toss bread crumbs with Parmesan cheese.
2. Pound chicken with a meat mallet to ½-in. thickness; sprinkle with salt and pepper. Dip chicken in flour to coat both sides; shake off excess. Dip in egg, then in crumb mixture.
3. In a large skillet, heat oil over medium heat. Add chicken; cook until golden brown and the chicken is no longer pink, 4-5 minutes per side. Serve in rolls with provolone cheese and marinara sauce.
1 SANDWICH: 669 cal., 32g fat (10g sat. fat), 198mg chol., 1124mg sod., 45g carb. (3g sugars, 3g fiber), 48g pro.
SOURDOUGH CHICKEN SANDWICHES: Prepare chicken as directed. Spread 4 slices of sourdough bread with mayonnaise (if desired); top 2 slices with a lettuce leaf, a slice of Swiss cheese, tomato slice, 1 bacon strip cooked and cut in half, and the chicken breast. Top with remaining bread.

APPLE CHICKEN QUESADILLAS

My sister came up with this easy recipe that can be served as a main course or an appetizer. People are surprised by the combination of chicken, apples, tomatoes and corn inside the crispy tortillas, but they love it.
—*Stacia Slagle, Maysville, MO*

Takes: 25 min. • **Makes:** 6 servings

- 2 medium tart apples, sliced
- 1 cup diced cooked chicken breast
- ½ cup shredded cheddar cheese
- ½ cup shredded part-skim mozzarella cheese
- ½ cup fresh or frozen corn, thawed
- ½ cup chopped fresh tomatoes
- ½ cup chopped onion
- ¼ tsp. salt
- 6 flour tortillas (8 in.), warmed
  Optional toppings: shredded lettuce, salsa and sour cream

1. Preheat oven to 400°. Toss together the first 8 ingredients. Place ¾ cup of the mixture on half of each tortilla. Fold the tortillas to close; secure with toothpicks.

2. Place on a baking sheet coated with cooking spray. Bake until golden brown, 13-18 minutes, turning halfway through cooking. Discard toothpicks. Serve with toppings as desired.

1 QUESADILLA: 300 cal., 10g fat (4g sat. fat), 33mg chol., 475mg sod., 38g carb. (6g sugars, 3g fiber), 16g pro. **DIABETIC EXCHANGES:** 2½ starch, 2 medium-fat meat.

TEST KITCHEN TIP
You can shred lettuce with a grater or in a food processor, but you risk making the pieces too small and creating lettuce mush. The best method is to remove the core, cut the head into quarters, then slice across each quarter to cut the lettuce into thin strips.

SESAME PULLED PORK SANDWICHES

I wanted to build a better pork sandwich, and this Asian-style filling was a huge hit with my husband and coworkers. Bring on the wasabi mayo!
—*Jennifer Berry, Lexington, OH*

Prep: 15 min. • **Cook:** 4½ hours
Makes: 12 servings

- 3 pork tenderloins (1 lb. each)
- 1¾ cups reduced-fat sesame ginger salad dressing, divided
- ¼ cup packed brown sugar

SLAW

- 1 pkg. (14 oz.) coleslaw mix
- 4 green onions, chopped
- ¼ cup minced fresh cilantro
- 2 Tbsp. reduced-fat sesame ginger salad dressing
- 2 tsp. sesame oil
- 1 tsp. sugar
- 1 tsp. reduced-sodium soy sauce

TO SERVE

- 12 multigrain hamburger buns, split
  Wasabi mayonnaise, optional

1. Place tenderloins in a 5-qt. slow cooker coated with cooking spray; pour ¾ cup salad dressing over the pork, turning to coat. Cook, covered, on low until the meat is tender, for 4-5 hours.

2. Remove pork; cool slightly. Shred the meat into bite-sized pieces; return to slow cooker. Stir in brown sugar and the remaining salad dressing. Cook, covered, until heated through, 30-45 minutes longer.

3. Combine the slaw ingredients. Serve pork on buns with slaw and, if desired, mayonnaise.

NOTE: This recipe was tested with Newman's Own Sesame Ginger Dressing.

1 SANDWICH: 324 cal., 9g fat (2g sat. fat), 64mg chol., 756mg sod., 33g carb. (14g sugars, 3g fiber), 27g pro. **DIABETIC EXCHANGES:** 3 lean meat, 2 starch.

BONNIE HAWKINS
Elkhorn, Wi

GRILLED BEEF & BLUE CHEESE SANDWICHES

Roast beef, red onion and blue cheese really amp up this deluxe grilled sandwich. If you like a little heat, mix some horseradish into the spread.
—*Bonnie Hawkins, Elkhorn, WI*

Takes: 25 min. • **Makes:** 4 servings

- 2 oz. cream cheese, softened
- 2 oz. crumbled blue cheese
- 8 slices sourdough bread
- ¾ lb. thinly sliced deli roast beef
- ½ small red onion, thinly sliced
- ¼ cup olive oil

1. In a small bowl, mix cream cheese and blue cheese until blended. Spread over the bread slices. Layer 4 of the slices with roast beef and onion; top with remaining bread slices.

2. Brush the outsides of the sandwiches with oil. In a large skillet, toast sandwiches over medium heat for 4-5 minutes on each side or until golden brown.

1 SANDWICH: 471 cal., 27g fat (9g sat. fat), 72mg chol., 1021mg sod., 31g carb. (4g sugars, 1g fiber), 27g pro.

FLAVORFUL SLOPPY JOES

This savory all-star recipe makes just enough for two hearty sandwiches. The sauce level is low, making it a neat sloppy Joe.
—*Nancy Collins, Clearfield, PA*

Takes: 25 min. • **Makes:** 2 servings

- ½ lb. lean ground beef (90% lean)
- 2 Tbsp. chopped onion
- 2 Tbsp. chopped green pepper
- ½ cup ketchup
- 1½ tsp. brown sugar
- 1½ tsp. prepared mustard
- 1½ tsp. Worcestershire sauce
- 2 hamburger buns, split

In a small skillet, cook the beef, onion and green pepper over medium heat until the meat is no longer pink; drain. Stir in ketchup, brown sugar, mustard and Worcestershire sauce. Bring to a boil. Reduce heat; simmer, uncovered, for 5 minutes. Serve on buns.

1 SANDWICH: 379 cal., 11g fat (4g sat. fat), 56mg chol., 1112mg sod., 44g carb. (14g sugars, 2g fiber), 27g pro. **DIABETIC EXCHANGES:** 3 lean meat, 2 starch, 2 vegetable.

PEPPERED PORK PITAS

Believe it: Black pepper and garlic are all it takes to give my pork pitas their pop. With these, any weeknight meal is awesome. I like to fill them up with caramelized onions, too.
—*Katherine White, Henderson, NV*

Takes: 20 min. • **Makes:** 4 servings

- 1 lb. boneless pork loin chops, cut into thin strips
- 1 Tbsp. olive oil
- 2 tsp. coarsely ground pepper
- 2 garlic cloves, minced
- 1 jar (12 oz.) roasted sweet red peppers, drained and julienned
- 4 whole pita breads, warmed Garlic mayonnaise and torn leaf lettuce, optional

In a small bowl, combine the pork, oil, pepper and garlic; toss to coat. In a large skillet over medium-high heat, cook and stir pork mixture until no longer pink. Stir in red peppers; heat through. Serve on pita breads. Top pitas with mayonnaise and lettuce if desired.

1 SANDWICH: 380 cal., 11g fat (3g sat. fat), 55mg chol., 665mg sod., 37g carb. (4g sugars, 2g fiber), 27g pro. **DIABETIC EXCHANGES:** 3 lean meat, 2 starch, 1 fat.

TEST KITCHEN TIP
If you're short on time, jarred garlic is a convenient alternative to mincing your own. Typically, ½ teaspoon minced garlic from a jar equals 1 fresh garlic clove, minced. Jarred garlic is slightly milder than fresh...and our Test Kitchen staff prefers fresh.

PESTO CHICKEN TURNOVERS

When it comes to food, I'm all about anything in a pocket—pita bread, bierocks, empanadas and more. These Italian-inspired turnovers are super for dinner. To make appetizer-size turnovers, use 32 single crescent rolls with a tablespoon of filling in each.
—*Greg Munoz, Sacramento, CA*

Takes: 30 min. • **Makes:** 4 servings

- 2 tubes (8 oz. each) refrigerated seamless crescent dough sheets
- 1 pkg. (10 oz.) frozen chopped spinach, thawed and squeezed dry
- 1 pkg. (9 oz.) ready-to-use grilled Italian chicken strips
- 1 cup shredded part-skim mozzarella cheese
- 3 Tbsp. prepared pesto

1. Preheat oven to 375°. Unroll both tubes of crescent dough; cut each into 4 rectangles.
2. In a large bowl, combine spinach, chicken, cheese and pesto; spoon ¾ cup in the center of 4 of the rectangles. Top with the remaining rectangles; pinch seams to seal.
3. Place on greased baking sheets; cut 3 slits in top of each turnover. Bake 18-22 minutes or until golden brown.

FREEZE OPTION: Freeze cooled turnovers in an airtight freezer container. To use, reheat turnovers on a greased baking sheet in a preheated 375° oven until heated through.

1 TURNOVER: 579 cal., 26g fat (10g sat. fat), 54mg chol., 1275mg sod., 57g carb. (11g sugars, 2g fiber), 33g pro.

ITALIAN MEATBALL BURGERS

I just love these burgers! They're a big hit with kids and adults. I serve them with sliced green peppers, tomatoes and onions and a jar of crushed red pepper flakes on the side.

—Priscilla Gilbert, Indian Harbour Beach, FL

- -

Prep: 25 min. • **Grill:** 15 min.
Makes: 8 servings

1	large egg, lightly beaten
⅓	cup seasoned bread crumbs
3	garlic cloves, minced
1	tsp. dried oregano
1	tsp. dried basil
¼	tsp. salt
¼	tsp. dried thyme
1½	lbs. lean ground beef (90% lean)
½	lb. Italian turkey sausage links, casings removed
¾	cup shredded part-skim mozzarella cheese
8	kaiser rolls, split
1	cup roasted garlic Parmesan spaghetti sauce, warmed

1. In a large bowl, combine first 7 ingredients. Crumble beef and sausage over bread crumb mixture and mix well. Shape into 8 burgers.
2. Place burgers on a lightly oiled grill rack over medium heat or in a greased baking pan. Grill burgers, covered, or broil 4 in. from the heat for 5-7 minutes on each side or until a thermometer reads 165° and the juices run clear.
3. Sprinkle burgers with cheese; cook for 2-3 minutes longer or until the cheese is melted. Remove and keep warm.
4. Grill or broil rolls for 1-2 minutes or until toasted. Serve burgers on the rolls with spaghetti sauce.
1 BURGER: 399 cal., 14g fat (5g sat. fat), 102mg chol., 743mg sod., 35g carb. (2g sugars, 2g fiber), 30g pro.

BUFFALO CHICKEN SANDWICHES

I love grilling chicken because it's often a healthier choice. I put my own personal twist on this sandwich with a spicy-sweet marinade and a homemade blue cheese dressing.
—*Joe Slate, Port St Joe, FL*

Prep: 25 min. + marinating • **Grill:** 10 min.
Makes: 4 servings

- 1 cup Louisiana-style hot sauce
- ½ cup packed brown sugar
- 4 Tbsp. butter
- 2 Tbsp. cider vinegar
- 1 tsp. taco seasoning
- 4 boneless skinless chicken breast halves (5 oz. each)
- ¼ cup crumbled blue cheese
- ¼ cup buttermilk
- ¼ cup mayonnaise
- 1 Tbsp. shredded Parmesan cheese
- 1 Tbsp. minced chives
- 1½ tsp. lemon juice
- ½ tsp. balsamic vinegar
- ¼ tsp. minced garlic
- ¼ tsp. pepper
- 4 onion rolls, split and toasted
- 4 cooked bacon strips
- 4 slices Colby cheese (¾ oz. each)
- 4 lettuce leaves
- 4 slices tomato
- 4 slices red onion

1. In a small saucepan over medium heat, bring the first 5 ingredients to a boil and boil, uncovered, for 1 minute. Cool for 10 minutes; set aside ½ cup for basting.
2. Flatten chicken to ½-in. thickness. Pour the remaining marinade into a large shallow container; add chicken, turning to coat. Cover and refrigerate for at least 2 hours.
3. Drain and discard marinade from chicken. Grill chicken, covered, over medium heat or broil 4 in. from heat for 5-6 minutes on each side or until a thermometer reads 170°, basting occasionally with reserved marinade.
4. In a small bowl, combine the blue cheese, buttermilk, mayonnaise, Parmesan cheese, chives, lemon juice, vinegar, garlic and pepper. Spread over the roll bottoms; top with the chicken, bacon, cheese, lettuce, tomato and onion. Replace roll tops.
1 SANDWICH: 720 cal., 35g fat (14g sat. fat), 130mg chol., 2516mg sod., 53g carb. (27g sugars, 3g fiber), 47g pro.

GRILLED PESTO, HAM & PROVOLONE SANDWICHES

These Italian-style sandwiches are loaded with zesty flavors. To lighten them a little, use fat-free mayo. With a cup of minestrone or a crisp salad, they can't be beat.
—*Priscilla Yee, Concord, CA*

Takes: 20 min. • **Makes:** 4 servings

- 2 Tbsp. mayonnaise
- 4 tsp. prepared pesto
- 8 slices sourdough bread
- 8 oz. thinly sliced deli ham
- ½ cup loosely packed basil leaves
- 4 pickled sweet cherry peppers, chopped
- 1 plum tomato, thinly sliced
- ¾ cup shredded provolone cheese
- 2 Tbsp. butter, softened

1. In a small bowl, mix mayonnaise and pesto; spread over 4 slices of bread. Layer with ham, basil, peppers, tomato and cheese. Top with the remaining bread. Spread the outsides of the sandwiches with butter.
2. Using a large cast-iron skillet or electric griddle, toast sandwiches over medium heat until the bread is golden brown and the cheese is melted, 2-3 minutes on each side.
1 SANDWICH: 464 cal., 26g fat (10g sat. fat), 64mg chol., 1701mg sod., 35g carb. (4g sugars, 2g fiber), 24g pro.

BISTRO APPLE PANINI

The bacon, apple and tarragon in this recipe go together so well. If you don't have a panini maker or an indoor grill, you can easily pan-fry or broil these excellent sandwiches.
—*Noelle Myers, Grand Forks, ND*

Prep: 20 min. • **Cook:** 5 min./batch
Makes: 6 servings

- 12 thick-sliced bacon strips, cut in half
- 1 medium apple, thinly sliced
- 1 Tbsp. ginger ale
- 1 tsp. lemon juice
- ¼ cup apple jelly
- 4 tsp. minced fresh tarragon
- 12 slices sourdough bread
- 6 slices Havarti cheese
- 2 Tbsp. Dijon mustard
- 3 Tbsp. butter, softened

1. In a large skillet, cook bacon over medium heat until crisp. Remove to paper towels to drain. In a small bowl, toss apple with ginger ale and lemon juice; set aside.

2. Place jelly in a small microwave-safe bowl; microwave on high for 20-30 seconds or until softened. Stir in tarragon.

3. Spread the jelly mixture over 6 bread slices. Top with cheese, apple and bacon. Spread mustard over the remaining bread; place over bacon. Spread the outsides of the sandwiches with butter.

4. Cook on a panini maker or indoor grill for 3-4 minutes or until the bread is browned and the cheese is melted.

1 PANINI: 512 cal., 25g fat (12g sat. fat), 62mg chol., 1235mg sod., 50g carb. (13g sugars, 2g fiber), 22g pro.

CHICKEN PARMESAN BURGERS

We love chicken Parmesan so we wondered, why not make it into a burger? I like to use fresh mozzarella on these. I've also made the burgers with ground turkey.
—*Charlotte Gehle, Brownstown, MI*

Takes: 30 min. • **Makes:** 4 servings

- ½ cup dry bread crumbs
- ¼ cup grated Parmesan cheese
- 3 garlic cloves, minced
- 1 Tbsp. minced fresh basil
  or 1 tsp. dried basil
- ½ tsp. dried oregano
- 1 lb. lean ground chicken
- 1 cup meatless spaghetti sauce, divided
- 2 slices part-skim mozzarella cheese, cut in half
- 4 slices Italian bread (¾ in. thick)

1. In a large bowl, combine first 5 ingredients. Add the chicken; mix lightly but thoroughly. Shape into four ½-in.-thick oval patties.

2. Grill burgers, covered, over medium heat or broil 4 in. from heat 4-7 minutes on each side or until a thermometer reads 165°. Top the burgers with ½ cup spaghetti sauce and cheese. Cover and grill 30-60 seconds longer or until the cheese is melted.

3. Grill bread, uncovered, over medium heat or broil 4 in. from heat 30-60 seconds on each side or until toasted. Top with the remaining spaghetti sauce. Serve chicken burgers on the toasted bread.

FREEZE OPTION: Place chicken patties on a plastic wrap-lined baking sheet; wrap and freeze until firm. Remove patties from pan and transfer to an airtight freezer container; return to freezer. To use, grill the frozen patties as directed, increasing cooking time as necessary for a thermometer to read 165°.

1 BURGER: 381 cal., 12g fat (5g sat. fat), 93mg chol., 784mg sod., 32g carb. (5g sugars, 3g fiber), 35g pro. **DIABETIC EXCHANGES:** 3 lean meat, 2 starch, 1 fat.

GARDEN TURKEY BURGERS

These juicy burgers get plenty of color and flavor from onion, zucchini and red pepper. It's easy to make the mixture ahead of time and put it in the refrigerator or make and freeze the patties. Later, I can put the burgers on the grill and then whip up a salad or side dish.

—*Sandy Kitzmiller, Unityville, PA*

- -

Takes: 25 min. • **Makes:** 6 servings

- 1 cup old-fashioned oats
- ¾ cup chopped onion
- ¾ cup finely chopped sweet red or green pepper
- ½ cup shredded zucchini
- ¼ cup ketchup
- 2 garlic cloves, minced
- ¼ tsp. salt, optional
- 1 lb. ground turkey
- 6 whole wheat hamburger buns, split and toasted

1. In a large bowl, combine the first seven ingredients. Crumble turkey over mixture and mix well. Shape into six ½-in.-thick patties.

2. Place the burgers on a lightly oiled grill rack over medium heat or in a greased baking pan. Grill burgers, covered, or broil 4 in. from the heat for 4-6 minutes on each side or until a thermometer reads 165° and juices run clear. Serve on buns.

FREEZE OPTION: Place patties on a plastic wrap-lined baking sheet; wrap and freeze until firm. Remove from pan, transfer to an airtight freezer container and return to freezer. To use, cook frozen patties as directed; increase time as necessary for a thermometer to read 165°.

1 BURGER: 188 cal., 7g fat (2g sat. fat), 60mg chol., 201mg sod., 15g carb. (4g sugars, 2g fiber), 16g pro. **DIABETIC EXCHANGES:** 2 lean meat, 1 starch.

ITALIAN TURKEY SANDWICHES

I hope you enjoy these tasty turkey sandwiches as much as our family does. The recipe makes plenty, so it's great for potlucks. And if you have any, the leftovers are just as good.

—*Carol Riley, Ossian, IN*

- -

Prep: 10 min. • **Cook:** 5 hours
Makes: 12 servings

- 1 bone-in turkey breast (6 lbs.), skin removed
- 1 medium onion, chopped
- 1 small green pepper, chopped
- ¼ cup chili sauce
- 3 Tbsp. white vinegar
- 2 Tbsp. dried oregano or Italian seasoning
- 4 tsp. beef bouillon granules
- 12 kaiser or hard rolls, split

1. Place turkey breast in a greased 5-qt. slow cooker. Add onion and green pepper.

2. Combine the chili sauce, vinegar, oregano and bouillon; pour over turkey and vegetables. Cover and cook on low for 5-6 hours or until turkey is tender.

3. Shred turkey with 2 forks and return to the slow cooker; heat through. Spoon ½ cup onto each roll.

FREEZE OPTION: Place cooled meat and juice mixture in freezer containers. To use, partially thaw in refrigerator overnight. Microwave, covered, on high in a microwave-safe dish until heated through, gently stirring and adding a little water if necessary.

1 SANDWICH: 374 cal., 4g fat (1g sat. fat), 118mg chol., 724mg sod., 34g carb. (3g sugars, 2g fiber), 49g pro. **DIABETIC EXCHANGES:** 6 lean meat, 2 starch.

2.
Place hot dogs in buns. Spoon chili over hot dogs. In a small bowl, combine sour cream and salsa; spoon over tops. Sprinkle with cheese and green onions.

1 CHILI DOG: 420 cal., 25g fat (12g sat. fat), 69mg chol., 1096mg sod., 27g carb. (5g sugars, 2g fiber), 20g pro.

ITALIAN SUB SANDWICHES

I serve these sandwiches for a special party treat. The red and green peppers add color along with flavor.

—*Judy Long, Effingham, IL*

- -

Prep: 15 min. • **Cook:** 40 min.
Makes: 8 servings

- 1½ lbs. Italian sausage links, cut into ½-in. pieces
- 2 medium red onions, thinly sliced
- 2 medium sweet red peppers, thinly sliced
- 2 medium green peppers, thinly sliced
- 1 garlic clove, minced
- 3 medium tomatoes, chopped
- 1 tsp. dried oregano
  Salt and pepper to taste
- 8 submarine sandwich buns (about 10 in.), split

1. In a large skillet, cook sausage over medium heat just until no longer pink; drain. Add the onions, peppers and garlic. Cover and cook for 25 minutes or until the vegetables are tender, stirring occasionally. Add tomatoes and oregano. Cover and simmer 5-6 minutes or until the tomatoes are cooked. Season with salt and pepper.

2. Meanwhile, hollow out each roll, leaving a ½-in. shell. (Discard the removed bread or save for another use.) Toast rolls. Fill with the sausage mixture.

FREEZE OPTION: Freeze the cooled meat mixture in freezer containers. To use, partially thaw in refrigerator overnight. Heat through in a saucepan, stirring occasionally and adding a little water if necessary.

1 SANDWICH: 442 cal., 24g fat (7g sat. fat), 46mg chol., 843mg sod., 42g carb. (7g sugars, 4g fiber), 17g pro.

BLUE PLATE OPEN-FACED TURKEY SANDWICH

Turkey with gravy makes divine comfort food that reminds me of old-time diners on the East Coast. Happily, my gravy is not from a can.

—*Christine Schwester, Divide, CO*

- -

Takes: 25 min. • **Makes:** 6 servings

- ⅓ cup butter, cubed
- 1 small onion, chopped
- ⅓ cup all-purpose flour
- 2 tsp. minced fresh parsley
- ¼ tsp. pepper
- ⅛ tsp. garlic powder
- ⅛ tsp. dried thyme
- 3 cups reduced-sodium chicken broth
- 1¼ lbs. sliced deli turkey
- 12 slices white bread

In a large saucepan, heat the butter over medium heat. Add onion; cook and stir for 4-5 minutes or until tender. Stir in the flour, parsley and seasonings until blended; gradually whisk in broth. Bring to a boil, stirring constantly; cook and stir 1-2 minutes or until slightly thickened. Add turkey, one slice at a time; heat through. Serve over bread.

2 OPEN-FACED SANDWICHES: 361 cal., 14g fat (7g sat. fat), 60mg chol., 1462mg sod., 33g carb. (4g sugars, 2g fiber), 25g pro.

CHIPOTLE CHILI DOGS

Long live childhood favorites! I created this recipe for the 125th anniversary celebration for a small town in Minnesota. The chili on these dogs has a medium spice level, and people of all ages love them.

—*Barb Templin, Norwood, MN*

- -

Takes: 25 min. • **Makes:** 6 servings

- 6 hot dogs
- ½ lb. ground beef
- ¼ cup chopped onion
- 1 garlic clove, minced
- 1 can (8 oz.) tomato sauce
- 2½ tsp. minced chipotle peppers in adobo sauce
- ¾ tsp. chili powder
- ¼ tsp. salt
- ⅛ tsp. pepper
- 6 hot dog buns, split
- 3 Tbsp. sour cream
- 3 Tbsp. salsa
- ¾ cup shredded cheddar cheese
- 2 green onions, chopped

1. Cook hot dogs according to the package directions. Meanwhile, in a large skillet, cook the beef, onion and garlic over medium heat until meat is no longer pink; drain. Stir in the tomato sauce, chipotle peppers, chili powder, salt and pepper. Bring to a boil. Reduce heat; simmer, uncovered, for 4-5 minutes or until flavors are blended.

CHUTNEY TURKEY BURGERS

The secret to these burgers is the tangy mango chutney, but the arugula adds a special wow to the plate. I get lots of compliments whenever I serve these at summer or fall cookouts.
—*Jeanne Lueders, Weatherby Lake, MO*

Takes: 25 min. • **Makes:** 4 servings

- ½ cup mango chutney, divided
- 1 Tbsp. Dijon mustard
- 2 tsp. lime juice
- ¼ cup minced fresh parsley
- 2 green onions, chopped
- ½ tsp. salt
- ¼ tsp. pepper
- 1 lb. lean ground turkey
- 4 hamburger buns, split
  Fresh arugula or baby spinach leaves
  Thinly sliced red onion

1. For the sauce, mix ¼ cup chutney, the mustard and lime juice. In a large bowl, combine parsley, green onions, salt, pepper and the remaining chutney. Add turkey; mix lightly but thoroughly. Shape into four ½-in.-thick patties.

2. Place the burgers on a lightly oiled grill rack over medium heat or in a greased 15x10x1-in. pan. Grill, covered, or broil 3-4 in. from heat until a thermometer reads 165°, 5-7 minutes per side. Serve on buns with arugula, onion and sauce.

1 BURGER: 419 cal., 10g fat (3g sat. fat), 78mg chol., 1012mg sod., 51g carb. (21g sugars, 1g fiber), 27g pro.

TEX-MEX SHREDDED BEEF SANDWICHES

You need only a few ingredients to make my delicious shredded beef. While the meat simmers to tender perfection, you will have time to do other things, making it a snap for the busiest nights.
—*Katherine White, Henderson, NV*

Prep: 5 min. • **Cook:** 8 hours
Makes: 8 servings

- 1 boneless beef chuck roast (3 lbs.)
- 1 envelope chili seasoning
- ½ cup barbecue sauce
- 8 onion rolls, split
- 8 slices cheddar cheese

1. Cut the roast in half; place in a 3-qt. slow cooker. Sprinkle with chili seasoning. Pour barbecue sauce over top. Cover and cook on low for 8-10 hours or until the meat is tender.

2. Remove roast; cool slightly. Shred meat with 2 forks. Skim fat from the cooking juices. Return meat to the slow cooker; heat through. Using a slotted spoon, place ½ cup of the meat mixture on each roll bottom; top with cheese. Replace tops.

1 SANDWICH: 573 cal., 29g fat (13g sat. fat), 140mg chol., 955mg sod., 29g carb. (6g sugars, 2g fiber), 47g pro.

CHEESY CHICKEN SUBS

I've been part of the food services staff at a local university for a long time. One summer we created this irresistible sandwich that thousands of students have enjoyed since.
—*Jane Hollar, Vilas, NC*

Takes: 25 min. • **Makes:** 4 servings

- 12 oz. boneless skinless chicken breasts, cut into strips
- 1 envelope Parmesan Italian or Caesar salad dressing mix
- 1 cup sliced fresh mushrooms
- ½ cup sliced red onion
- ¼ cup olive oil
- 4 submarine buns, split and toasted
- 4 slices Swiss cheese

1. Place chicken in a large bowl; sprinkle with salad dressing mix. In a large skillet, saute mushrooms and onion in oil for 3 minutes. Add the chicken; saute for 6 minutes or until chicken is no longer pink.

2. Spoon mixture onto bun bottoms; top with cheese. Broil 4 in. from the heat for 4 minutes or until cheese is melted. Replace tops.

1 SANDWICH: 709 cal., 29g fat (9g sat. fat), 72mg chol., 1478mg sod., 72g carb. (8g sugars, 4g fiber), 35g pro.

HEARTY MEATBALL SUB SANDWICHES

Making these saucy meatballs in advance and reheating them saves me precious time. The satisfying sandwiches are excellent for casual parties.
—*Deena Hubler, Jasper, IN*

Takes: 30 min. • **Makes:** 12 servings

- 2 large eggs, lightly beaten
- 1 cup dry bread crumbs
- 2 Tbsp. grated Parmesan cheese
- 2 Tbsp. finely chopped onion
- 1 tsp. salt
- ½ tsp. pepper
- ½ tsp. garlic powder
- ¼ tsp. Italian seasoning
- 2 lbs. ground beef
- 1 jar (28 oz.) spaghetti sauce
  Optional: Additional Parmesan cheese, sliced onion and green peppers
- 12 sandwich rolls, split

1. In a large bowl, combine first 8 ingredients. Crumble beef over the mixture and mix well. Shape into 1-in. balls. Place in a single layer in a 3-qt. microwave-safe dish.

2. Cover and microwave on high for 3-4 minutes. Turn meatballs; cook 3-4 minutes longer or until no longer pink. Drain. Add spaghetti sauce.

3. Cover and microwave on high until heated through, about 2-4 minutes. If desired, top with additional cheese, sliced onion and green peppers. Serve on rolls.

1 SANDWICH: 464 cal., 18g fat (7g sat. fat), 88mg chol., 1013mg sod., 49g carb. (10g sugars, 3g fiber), 26g pro.

HEARTY BREADED FISH SANDWICHES

Fishing for a burger alternative? Consider it caught. A hint of cayenne is cooled by a creamy yogurt and mayo sauce in this fish sandwich that will put your local drive-thru to shame.
—Taste of Home *Test Kitchen*

Takes: 30 min. • **Makes:** 4 servings

- ½ cup dry bread crumbs
- ½ tsp. garlic powder
- ½ tsp. cayenne pepper
- ½ tsp. dried parsley flakes
- 4 cod fillets (6 oz. each)
- 4 whole wheat hamburger buns, split
- ¼ cup plain yogurt
- ¼ cup fat-free mayonnaise
- 2 tsp. lemon juice
- 2 tsp. sweet pickle relish
- ¼ tsp. dried minced onion
- 4 lettuce leaves
- 4 slices tomato
- 4 slices sweet onion

1. In a shallow bowl, combine the bread crumbs, garlic powder, cayenne and parsley. Coat fillets with bread crumb mixture.
2. Place fish on a lightly oiled grill rack or on a greased baking pan. Grill cod, covered, over medium heat or broil 4 in. from the heat for 4-5 minutes on each side or until fish flakes easily with a fork. Grill buns over medium heat or broil for 30-60 seconds or until toasted.
3. Meanwhile, in a small bowl, combine the yogurt, mayonnaise, lemon juice, relish and minced onion; spread over the bun bottoms. Top with the cod, lettuce, tomato and onion; replace the bun tops.
1 SANDWICH: 292 cal., 4g fat (1g sat. fat), 68mg chol., 483mg sod., 32g carb. (7g sugars, 4g fiber), 32g pro. **DIABETIC EXCHANGES:** 5 lean meat, 2 starch.
SALSA FISH SANDWICHES: Follow method as directed but replace plain yogurt with salsa and omit lemon juice, relish and dried minced onion. Top sandwiches with sliced tomato and fresh cilantro.
1 SANDWICH: 277 cal., 4 g fat (1 g sat. fat), 66mg chol., 512 mg sod., 29 g carb. (6g sugars, 4g fiber), 31 g pro. **DIABETIC EXCHANGES:** 5 lean meat, 2 starch.
SLAW-TOPPED FISH SANDWICHES: Follow method as directed but omit relish, substitute red wine vinegar for lemon juice and stir 1½ cups coleslaw mix into mayonnaise mixture. Omit lettuce, tomato and onion; top cod with slaw mixture.
1 SANDWICH: 292 cal., 4g fat (1g sat. fat), 68mg chol., 483mg sod., 32g carb. (7g sugars, 4g fiber), 32g pro. **DIABETIC EXCHANGES:** 5 lean meat, 2 starch.

BEEF PITAS WITH YOGURT SAUCE

I've always wanted to tour the Mediterranean, but this is as close as I'll get—for now! Top these gyros with a yogurt sauce that doubles as a dip for pita chips.
—Daniel Anderson, Kenosha, WI

Takes: 30 min. • **Makes:** 4 servings

- 1 cup (8 oz.) fat-free plain yogurt
- ¼ cup minced fresh parsley
- 1 garlic clove, minced
- ⅛ tsp. plus ½ tsp. salt, divided
- 1 lb. beef top sirloin steak, cut into thin strips
- 1 tsp. dried oregano
- 1 tsp. minced fresh rosemary
- ¼ tsp. pepper
- 4 tsp. olive oil, divided
- 1 large sweet onion, sliced
- 4 whole pita breads, warmed

1. In a small bowl, mix yogurt, parsley, garlic and ⅛ tsp. salt. Toss beef with herbs, pepper and remaining salt.
2. In a large nonstick skillet, heat 2 tsp. oil over medium-high heat. Add onion; cook and stir 4-6 minutes or until tender. Remove from pan.
3. In same skillet, heat remaining oil over medium-high heat. Add beef; cook and stir 2-3 minutes or until no longer pink. Serve on pitas; top with onion and sauce.
1 FILLED PITA WITH ¼ CUP SAUCE: 405 cal., 10g fat (2g sat. fat), 47mg chol., 784mg sod., 45g carb. (8g sugars, 2g fiber), 33g pro. **DIABETIC EXCHANGES:** 3 starch, 3 lean meat, 1 fat.

PEPPERONI PIZZA LOAF

Because this savory stromboli relies on frozen bread dough, it comes together in no time. The golden loaf is stuffed with cheese, pepperoni, mushrooms, peppers and olives. I often add a few thin slices of ham, too. It's tasty served with warm pizza sauce for dipping.
—*Jenny Brown, West Lafayette, IN*

Prep: 20 min. • **Bake:** 35 min.
Makes: 12 slices

- 1 loaf (1 lb.) frozen bread dough, thawed
- 2 large eggs, separated
- 1 Tbsp. grated Parmesan cheese
- 1 Tbsp. olive oil
- 1 tsp. minced fresh parsley
- 1 tsp. dried oregano
- ½ tsp. garlic powder
- ¼ tsp. pepper
- 8 oz. sliced pepperoni
- 2 cups shredded part-skim mozzarella cheese
- 1 can (4 oz.) mushroom stems and pieces, drained
- ¼ to ½ cup pickled pepper rings
- 1 medium green pepper, diced
- 1 can (2¼ oz.) sliced ripe olives
- 1 can (15 oz.) pizza sauce

1. Preheat the oven to 350°. On a greased baking sheet, roll out dough into a 15x10-in. rectangle. In a small bowl, combine egg yolks, Parmesan cheese, oil, parsley, oregano, garlic powder and pepper. Brush over the dough.

2. Sprinkle with pepperoni, mozzarella cheese, mushrooms, pepper rings, green pepper and olives. Roll up, jelly-roll style, starting with a long side; pinch the seam to seal and tuck the ends under.

3. Position loaf with seam side down; brush with egg whites. Do not let rise. Bake until golden brown and dough is cooked through, 35-40 minutes. Warm the pizza sauce; serve with sliced loaf.

FREEZE OPTION: Freeze cooled unsliced pizza loaf in heavy-duty foil. To use, remove from freezer 30 minutes before reheating. Remove from foil and reheat loaf on a greased baking sheet in a preheated 325° oven until heated through. Serve as directed.

1 SLICE: 296 cal., 17g fat (6g sat. fat), 66mg chol., 827mg sod., 24g carb. (4g sugars, 2g fiber), 13g pro.

TUNA BURGERS

My family was so accustomed to a typical beef burger that they were hesitant to try these when I first made them. Any skepticism disappeared after just one bite.
—*Kim Stoller, Smithville, OH*

Takes: 20 min. • **Makes:** 4 servings

- 1 large egg, lightly beaten
- ½ cup dry bread crumbs
- ½ cup finely chopped celery
- ⅓ cup mayonnaise
- ¼ cup finely chopped onion
- 2 Tbsp. chili sauce
- 1 pouch (6.4 oz.) light tuna in water
- 2 Tbsp. butter
- 4 hamburger buns, split and toasted
  Lettuce leaves and sliced tomato, optional

1. Mix first 6 ingredients; fold in tuna. Shape into 4 patties.
2. In a large cast-iron or other heavy skillet, heat butter over medium heat. Cook patties until lightly browned, 4-5 minutes on each side. Serve on buns. If desired, top with lettuce and tomato.
1 BURGER: 417 cal., 23g fat (7g sat. fat), 79mg chol., 710mg sod., 35g carb. (6g sugars, 2g fiber), 17g pro.

HEALTH TIP
To lighten up this burger, use reduced-fat mayonnaise and brush the patties with 1 Tbsp. butter. Then use your broiler instead of pan-frying. You'll save 75 calories and 10 grams of fat per serving.

HEARTY PITA TACOS

You don't need to skimp on flavor when trying to eat healthy. Our 9-year-old daughter enjoys helping us make these tasty tacos—and enjoys eating them even more.
—*Jamie Valocchi, Mesa, AZ*

Takes: 30 min. • **Makes:** 6 servings

- 1 lb. lean ground beef (90% lean)
- 1 small sweet red pepper, chopped
- 2 green onions, chopped
- 1 can (16 oz.) kidney beans, rinsed and drained
- ¾ cup frozen corn
- ⅔ cup taco sauce
- 1 can (2¼ oz.) sliced ripe olives, drained
- ½ tsp. garlic salt
- ¼ tsp. onion powder
- ¼ tsp. dried oregano
- ¼ tsp. paprika
- ¼ tsp. pepper
- 6 whole wheat pita pocket halves
- 6 Tbsp. shredded reduced-fat cheddar cheese
  Sliced avocado and additional taco sauce, optional

1. In a large skillet, cook the beef, red pepper and onions over medium heat until meat is no longer pink; drain. Stir in the beans, corn, taco sauce, olives and seasonings; heat through.
2. Spoon ¾ cup of the beef mixture into each pita half. Sprinkle with cheese. Serve with avocado and additional taco sauce if desired.
1 PITA POCKET HALF: 339 cal., 10g fat (4g sat. fat), 52mg chol., 787mg sod., 38g carb. (4g sugars, 8g fiber), 26g pro. **DIABETIC EXCHANGES:** 3 lean meat, 2½ starch.

ASIAN STEAK WRAPS

Zesty marinade with a splash of fresh lime juice makes these sesame-flavored wraps a treat. To speed prep time, use a 1-pound package of frozen onion and pepper mix.
—*Trisha Kruse, Eagle, ID*

- -

Prep: 20 min. + marinating • **Cook:** 10 min.
Makes: 4 servings

- ¼ **cup lime juice**
- 3 **Tbsp. honey**
- 1 **Tbsp. reduced-sodium soy sauce**
- 2 **tsp. sesame oil**
- 2 **tsp. minced fresh gingerroot**
- 1½ **tsp. minced fresh cilantro**
- 1 **lb. beef top sirloin steak, cut into thin strips**
- ¼ **tsp. salt**
- ¼ **tsp. pepper**
- 1 **medium onion, halved and thinly sliced**
- 1 **large green pepper, julienned**
- 1 **large sweet red pepper, julienned**
- 4 **flour tortillas (8 in.), warmed**
- 2 **oz. reduced-fat cream cheese**
- 2 **tsp. sesame seeds, toasted**

1. In a small bowl, combine first 6 ingredients. Pour ⅓ cup marinade into a large resealable plastic bag; add the beef. Seal bag and turn to coat; refrigerate for 1 hour. Add salt and pepper to remaining marinade; cover and refrigerate mixture.

2. Drain the beef and discard the marinade. In a large nonstick skillet or wok, lightly oiled, stir-fry beef until no longer pink; remove and keep warm. In the same pan, stir-fry onion and peppers until crisp-tender. Stir in the reserved marinade. Return beef to the pan; heat through.

3. Spread tortillas with cream cheese; top with the beef mixture and sprinkle with sesame seeds. Roll up.

1 WRAP: 402 cal., 14g fat (5g sat. fat), 74mg chol., 575mg sod., 41g carb. (10g sugars, 3g fiber), 29g pro. **DIABETIC EXCHANGES:** 3 lean meat, 2 starch, 1 vegetable, 1 fat.

JOAN HALLFORD
North Richland Hills, TX

TEX-MEX CHEESESTEAK SANDWICHES

We adore cheesesteak sandwiches and anything with southwestern flavor, so I combined the two. If you crave even more firepower, add chopped jalapenos.
—*Joan Hallford, North Richland Hills, TX*

- -

Takes: 25 min. • **Makes:** 4 servings

- 1 **pkg. (15 oz.) refrigerated beef tips with gravy**
- 1 **Tbsp. canola oil**
- 1 **medium onion, halved and thinly sliced**
- 1 **banana pepper, cut into strips**
- ⅛ **tsp. salt**
- ⅛ **tsp. pepper**
- 4 **whole wheat hoagie buns, split**
- ¼ **cup mayonnaise**
- ⅛ **tsp. chili powder, optional**
- 8 **slices pepper jack cheese**

1. Preheat broiler. Heat beef tips with gravy according to package directions. Meanwhile, in a small skillet, heat oil over medium-high heat. Add onion and pepper; cook and stir for 4-6 minutes or until tender. Stir in salt and pepper.

2. Place buns on a baking sheet, cut side up. Mix mayonnaise and, if desired, chili powder; spread on roll bottoms. Layer with beef tips, onion mixture and cheese. Broil 3-4 in. from heat for 1-2 minutes or until the cheese is melted and the buns are toasted.

1 SANDWICH: 600 cal., 36g fat (11g sat. fat), 90mg chol., 1312mg sod., 42g carb. (9g sugars, 7g fiber), 32g pro.

SHREDDED LAMB SLIDERS

These savory sliders feature lamb, which makes even a regular weeknight feel like a special occasion. Once at the Great American Beer Fest, I made about 1,500 sliders in two days, and they went fast—I used every little bit I had to serve the very last customer!
—*Craig Kuczek, Aurora, CO*

Prep: 45 min. • **Cook:** 6 hours
Makes: 2 dozen

- 1 boneless lamb shoulder roast (3½ to 4¼ lbs.)
- 1½ tsp. salt
- ½ tsp. pepper
- 1 Tbsp. olive oil
- 2 medium carrots, chopped
- 4 shallots, chopped
- 6 garlic cloves
- 2 cups beef stock

PESTO
- ¾ cup fresh mint leaves
- ¾ cup loosely packed basil leaves
- ⅓ cup pine nuts
- ¼ tsp. salt
- ¾ cup olive oil
- ¾ cup shredded Parmesan cheese
- ⅓ cup shredded Asiago cheese
- 24 slider buns
- 1 pkg. (4 oz.) crumbled feta cheese

1. Sprinkle roast with salt and pepper. In a large skillet, heat oil over medium-high heat; brown the meat. Transfer to a 6- or 7-qt. slow cooker. In the same skillet, cook and stir carrots, shallots and garlic until crisp-tender, about 4 minutes. Add stock, stirring to loosen the browned bits from the pan. Pour over lamb. Cook, covered, on low until the lamb is tender, 6-8 hours.

2. Meanwhile for the pesto, place mint, basil, pine nuts and salt in a food processor; pulse until chopped. Continue processing while gradually adding oil in a steady stream. Add cheeses; pulse just until blended.

3. When lamb is cool enough to handle, remove meat from bones; discard bones. Shred meat with 2 forks. Strain cooking juices, adding vegetables to shredded meat; skim fat. Return the cooking juices and meat to slow cooker. Heat through. Serve on buns with pesto and feta.

1 SLIDER: 339 cal., 22g fat (7g sat. fat), 56mg chol., 459mg sod., 16g carb. (2g sugars, 1g fiber), 18g pro.

TUNA ARTICHOKE MELTS

After sampling a similar open-faced sandwich at a restaurant, I created my own version of lemon-seasoned tuna salad with artichoke hearts. They make a lovely light meal, especially in the summertime!
—*Evelyn Basinger, Linville, VA*

Takes: 15 min. • **Makes:** 2 servings

- 1 can (6 oz.) light water-packed tuna, drained and flaked
- ⅓ cup coarsely chopped water-packed artichoke hearts, rinsed and drained
- 2 Tbsp. fat-free mayonnaise
- ½ cup shredded reduced-fat Mexican cheese blend, divided
- ¼ tsp. salt-free lemon-pepper seasoning
- ⅛ tsp. dried oregano
- 2 English muffins, split and toasted

1. Preheat the broiler. In a small bowl, combine tuna, artichokes, mayonnaise, ¼ cup cheese, the lemon-pepper seasoning and oregano. Spread over English muffin halves.

2. Place on a baking sheet. Broil 4-6 in. from the heat for 3-5 minutes or until heated through. Sprinkle with the remaining cheese; broil 1-2 minutes longer or until the cheese is melted.

2 MUFFIN HALVES: 335 cal., 8g fat (4g sat. fat), 47mg chol., 989mg sod., 31g carb. (3g sugars, 2g fiber), 34g pro.

JALAPENO SWISS BURGERS

Mexican culture greatly influences our regional cuisine. In this recipe, the mellow flavor of Swiss cheese cuts the heat of the jalapenos.
—*Jeanine Richardson, Floresville, TX*

Takes: 30 min. • **Makes:** 4 servings

- 2 lbs. ground beef
- 4 slices Swiss cheese
- 1 small onion, finely chopped
- 2 to 3 pickled jalapeno peppers, seeded and finely chopped
- 4 hamburger buns, split and toasted Lettuce leaves and ketchup, optional

1. Shape beef into 8 thin patties. Top 4 patties with cheese, onion and jalapenos. Top with remaining patties; press edges firmly to seal.
2. Grill, covered, over medium heat or broil 4 in. from the heat, 8-9 minutes on each side or until a thermometer reads 160° and juices run clear. Serve the burgers on buns with toppings, if desired.
1 BURGER: 665 cal., 37g fat (16g sat. fat), 175mg chol., 423mg sod., 24g carb. (5g sugars, 2g fiber), 55g pro.

FISH STICK SANDWICHES

Make the most of convenient frozen fish sticks with these fun, family-pleasing sandwiches. My mom whipped these up whenever she wanted fish in a hurry.
—*Cherie Durbin, Hickory, NC*

Takes: 25 min. • **Makes:** 6 servings

- ¼ cup butter, melted
- 2 Tbsp. lemon juice
- 1 pkg. (11.4 oz.) frozen breaded fish sticks
- 2 Tbsp. mayonnaise
- 6 hot dog buns, split Shredded lettuce, chopped onion and chopped tomatoes, optional

1. In a shallow bowl, combine the butter and lemon juice. Dip fish in butter mixture. Place in a single layer in an ungreased baking pan.
2. Bake at 400° for 15-18 minutes or until crispy. Spread mayonnaise on bottom of buns; add fish sticks. Top with lettuce, onion and tomato if desired. Replace bun tops.
1 SANDWICH: 355 cal., 20g fat (7g sat. fat), 34mg chol., 572mg sod., 34g carb. (5g sugars, 2g fiber), 9g pro.

TURKEY QUESADILLAS WITH CRANBERRY SALSA

These are kind of a northern variation on southwestern quesadillas. Tortillas stuffed with turkey and cheese get amped up when you add a sweet-tart cranberry salsa.
—*Jodi Kristensen, Macomb, MI*

Takes: 30 min. • **Makes:** 4 servings

- ¾ cup fresh or frozen cranberries
- 2 Tbsp. sugar
- ¼ cup water
- 1 small pear, chopped
- ¼ cup chopped red onion
- 1 jalapeno pepper, seeded and chopped
- 3 Tbsp. chopped celery
- 2 tsp. grated lemon zest
- 1 Tbsp. lemon juice
- ½ tsp. ground cumin
- 4 flour tortillas (6 in.)
- 2 cups cubed cooked turkey breast
- 1 cup shredded reduced-fat white or yellow cheddar cheese

1. In a small saucepan, combine cranberries, sugar and water; bring to a boil. Reduce heat to medium; cook, uncovered, until berries pop, about 10 minutes, stirring occasionally. Remove from heat; cool slightly. Stir in pear, onion, jalapeno, celery, lemon zest and juice, and cumin.
2. Preheat griddle over medium heat. Top one half of each tortilla with ½ cup of the turkey; sprinkle with ¼ cup of the cheese. Fold tortilla to close. Cook on griddle until tortilla is golden brown and the cheese is melted, 1-2 minutes per side. Serve with salsa.
NOTE: Wear disposable gloves when you're cutting hot peppers; the oils can burn skin. Avoid touching your face.
1 QUESADILLA WITH ⅓ CUP SALSA: 321 cal., 10g fat (4g sat. fat), 80mg chol., 449mg sod., 27g carb. (12g sugars, 2g fiber), 32g pro. **DIABETIC EXCHANGES:** 3 lean meat, 1½ starch, 1 fat, ½ fruit.

TEST KITCHEN TIP

As long as you're making this recipe, go ahead and make extra salsa; it goes well with chicken or pork, too!

SALADS & BOWLS

The ideal combination of healthy, fast and delicious, a salad or a colorful bowl makes a great light option on a busy night—especially in the summer, when fresh veggies are plentiful!

POACHED EGG BUDDHA BOWLS

My husband and I like to celebrate the arrival of spring with this dish, enjoying it in the backyard. I often include fresh peas and other spring delights—whatever is in season.
—Amy McDonough, Carlton, OR

- -

Prep: 5 min. • **Cook:** 65 min.
Makes: 2 servings

- ¾   cup wheat berries
- 3½ cups water, divided
- 2   Tbsp. olive oil
- 2   Tbsp. lemon juice
- 1   Tbsp. thinly sliced fresh mint leaves
- ¼   tsp. salt
- ⅛   tsp. freshly ground pepper
- ½   cup quartered cherry tomatoes
- ½   cup reduced-fat ricotta cheese
- 2   Tbsp. sliced Greek olives
- 2   large eggs
     Additional olive oil and pepper, optional

1. Place wheat berries and 2½ cups of water in a large saucepan; bring to a boil. Reduce heat; simmer, covered, until tender, about 1 hour. Drain; transfer to a bowl. Cool slightly.
2. Stir in oil, lemon juice, mint, salt and pepper; divide between 2 bowls. Top with tomatoes, ricotta cheese and olives.
3. To poach egg, place ½ cup water in a small microwave-safe bowl or glass measuring cup. Break an egg into the water. Microwave, covered, on high 1 minute. Microwave in 10-second intervals until egg white is set and the yolk begins to thicken; let stand 1 minute.
4. Using a slotted spoon, transfer the egg to 1 of the bowls. Repeat. If desired, drizzle with additional oil and sprinkle with more pepper.
1 SERVING: 526 cal., 24g fat (5g sat. fat), 201mg chol., 563mg sod., 58g carb. (5g sugars, 10g fiber), 21g pro.

DID YOU KNOW?
Buddha bowls, or grain bowls, are highly adaptable dishes that are all about balance. The only rules for building your own Buddha bowl are that it should combine a grain, a protein and a variety of vegetables (raw or cooked); and that it should be served in a bowl!

MEDITERRANEAN TORTELLINI SALAD

One of my childhood friends moved to Italy 20 years ago. While visiting her, I enjoyed a scrumptious salad made with tortellini and fresh vegetables—this is my re-creation.
—*Kelly Mapes, Fort Collins, CO*

Takes: 30 min. • **Makes:** 6 servings

- 1 pkg. (19 oz.) frozen cheese tortellini
- 1 pkg. (14 oz.) smoked turkey sausage, sliced
- ¾ cup prepared pesto
- 2 cups fresh baby spinach, chopped
- 2 cups sliced baby portobello mushrooms
- 1 can (15 oz.) cannellini beans, rinsed and drained
- 1 cup roasted sweet red peppers, chopped
- 1 cup crumbled feta cheese
- ¼ cup pitted Greek olives, sliced

1. Cook cheese tortellini according to the package directions.
2. Meanwhile, in a large skillet coated with cooking spray, cook and stir sausage over medium heat for 6-7 minutes or until lightly browned. Transfer to a large bowl.
3. Drain the tortellini; add to the sausage. Stir in pesto. Add the remaining ingredients; toss to combine. Serve warm or refrigerate until chilled.
1½ CUPS: 334 cal., 17g fat (6g sat. fat), 45mg chol., 981mg sod., 25g carb. (2g sugars, 4g fiber), 19g pro.

PEPPERONI-ARTICHOKE PASTA SALAD

Everyone loves a good pasta salad, and this one will make them feel like special guests. Store-bought salad dressing makes it super convenient; artichoke hearts, olives, pepperoni and mozzarella cubes give it extra flair.
—*Clara Coulson Minney,
Washington Court House, OH*

Takes: 30 min. • **Makes:** 6 servings

- 1 cup uncooked bow tie pasta
- 1 cup cubed part-skim mozzarella cheese
- ¾ cup water-packed artichoke hearts, rinsed, drained and chopped
- 1 can (2¼ oz.) sliced ripe olives, drained
- 2 oz. sliced pepperoni
- 1 small red onion, halved and sliced
- ¼ cup shredded Parmesan cheese
- ¼ cup chopped green pepper
- ½ cup Italian salad dressing

1. Cook pasta according to the package directions. Meanwhile, in a large bowl, combine the mozzarella cheese, artichokes, olives, pepperoni, onion, Parmesan cheese and green pepper.
2. Drain pasta and rinse in cold water. Add to salad. Drizzle with salad dressing and toss to coat. Chill until serving.
¾ CUP: 270 cal., 18g fat (6g sat. fat), 22mg chol., 840mg sod., 15g carb. (2g sugars, 1g fiber), 11g pro.

KELLY MAPES
Fort Collins, CO

BLT CHICKEN SALAD

Featuring all the fun fixings for a BLT chicken sandwich, this salad is so easy to love. I can prep the ingredients ahead of time and just throw it together at the last minute. Barbecue sauce in the dressing gives it unexpected flavor. Even picky eaters enjoy it.
—*Cindy Moore, Mooresville, NC*

- -

Takes: 20 min. • **Makes:** 8 servings

- ½ cup mayonnaise
- 3 to 4 Tbsp. barbecue sauce
- 2 Tbsp. finely chopped onion
- 1 Tbsp. lemon juice
- ¼ tsp. pepper
- 8 cups torn salad greens
- 2 large tomatoes, chopped
- 1½ lbs. boneless skinless chicken breasts, cooked and cubed
- 10 bacon strips, cooked and crumbled
- 2 hard-boiled large eggs, sliced

In a small bowl, combine first 5 ingredients; mix well. Cover and refrigerate until serving. Place salad greens in a large serving bowl. Sprinkle with tomatoes, chicken and bacon; garnish with eggs. Drizzle with dressing.
1 SERVING: 281 cal., 19g fat (4g sat. fat), 112mg chol., 324mg sod., 5g carb. (3g sugars, 2g fiber), 23g pro.

KOREAN SAUSAGE BOWL

When we hosted a student from South Korea, she shared some of her favorite Korean dishes. We especially liked bibimbap. I created a variation on the dish with Italian sausage.
—*Michal Riege, Cedarburg, WI*

- -

Prep: 15 min. + marinating • **Cook:** 25 min.
Makes: 4 servings

- 1 pkg. (19 oz.) Italian sausage links, cut into 1-in. pieces
- ¾ cup Korean barbecue sauce, divided
- 1 tsp. plus 1 Tbsp. canola oil, divided
- 1 large egg
- 2 medium carrots, julienned
- 1 medium sweet red pepper, julienned
- 3 green onions, thinly sliced
- 2 garlic cloves, minced
- ½ tsp. salt
- ¼ tsp. crushed red pepper flakes
- ¼ tsp. pepper
- 8 oz. uncooked angel hair pasta
  Additional sliced green onions, optional

1. In a large bowl, toss sausage pieces with ½ cup of the barbecue sauce; refrigerate, covered, 4 hours.
2. In a large skillet, heat 1 tsp. oil over medium heat. Break egg into pan; cook until the yolk is set, turning once. Remove from pan; cut into thin strips.
3. In same pan, heat the remaining oil over medium-high heat. Add carrots and red pepper; cook and stir until crisp-tender. Stir in green onions, garlic and seasonings; cook 1 minute longer. Remove from pan.
4. Drain the sausage, discarding the marinade. In same pan, cook and stir sausage until no longer pink, 12-15 minutes.
5. Cook the pasta according to the package directions; drain, reserving ¼ cup pasta water. Add pasta, pasta water, carrot mixture and the remaining barbecue sauce to the sausage. Toss to combine. Divide among 4 bowls; top with egg strips and, if desired, additional sliced green onions.
1¾ CUPS: 672 cal., 39g fat (10g sat. fat), 119mg chol., 1620mg sod., 56g carb. (9g sugars, 4g fiber), 25g pro.

CONGA LIME PORK

Dinner guests won't be too shy to get in line when this yummy pork in chipotle and molasses sauce moves to the buffet table.
—*Janice Elder, Charlotte, NC*

- -

Prep: 20 min. • **Cook:** 4 hours
Makes: 6 servings

1	tsp. salt, divided
½	tsp. pepper, divided
1	boneless pork shoulder butt roast (2 to 3 lbs.)
1	Tbsp. canola oil
1	large onion, chopped
3	garlic cloves, peeled and thinly sliced
½	cup water
2	chipotle peppers in adobo sauce, seeded and chopped
2	Tbsp. molasses
2	cups broccoli coleslaw mix
1	medium mango, peeled and chopped
2	Tbsp. lime juice
1½	tsp. grated lime zest
6	prepared corn muffins
	Lime wedges, optional

1. Sprinkle ¾ tsp. salt and ¼ tsp. pepper over the roast. In a large skillet, brown pork in oil on all sides. Transfer meat to a 3- or 4-qt. slow cooker.

2. In the same skillet, saute onion until tender. Add garlic; cook 1 minute longer. Add water, chipotle peppers and molasses, stirring to loosen any browned bits from pan. Pour over pork. Cover and cook on high for 4-5 hours or until the meat is tender.

3. Remove roast; cool slightly. Skim fat from the cooking juices. Shred pork with 2 forks and return to slow cooker; heat through.

4. In a large bowl, combine the coleslaw mix, mango, lime juice, lime zest and remaining salt and pepper. Serve pork with muffins and, if desired, lime wedges; top with slaw.

NOTE: Wear disposable gloves when cutting hot peppers; the oils can burn skin. Avoid touching your face.

⅔ CUP PORK MIXTURE WITH 1 MUFFIN AND ½ CUP SLAW: 514 cal., 23g fat (7g sat. fat), 135mg chol., 877mg sod., 46g carb. (21g sugars, 3g fiber), 31g pro.

WHOLE WHEAT ORZO SALAD

In less than 30 minutes, I can put together this hearty salad of pasta, cannellini beans and veggies—and it's good for a crowd.
—*Seth Canada, Washington, DC*

Takes : 30 min. • **Makes:** 8 servings

2½ cups uncooked whole wheat orzo pasta (about 1 lb.)
1 can (15 oz.) cannellini beans, rinsed and drained
3 medium tomatoes, finely chopped
1 English cucumber, finely chopped
2 cups crumbled feta cheese
1¼ cups pitted Greek olives (about 6 oz.), chopped
1 medium sweet yellow pepper, finely chopped
1 medium green pepper, finely chopped
1 cup fresh mint leaves, chopped
½ medium red onion, finely chopped
¼ cup lemon juice
2 Tbsp. olive oil
1 Tbsp. grated lemon zest
3 garlic cloves, minced
½ tsp. pepper

1. Cook the orzo according to the package directions. Drain orzo; rinse with cold water.
2. Meanwhile, in a large bowl, the combine remaining ingredients. Stir in orzo. Refrigerate until serving.

1¾ CUPS: 411 cal., 17g fat (4g sat. fat), 15mg chol., 740mg sod., 51g carb. (3g sugars, 13g fiber), 14g pro.

SWISS COBB SALAD

Topped with ham, roast beef, bacon and other fixings, this hearty salad has an excellent blend of flavors. A from-scratch vinaigrette adds the refreshing final touch.
—Taste of Home *Test Kitchen*

Takes: 25 min. • **Makes:** 4 servings

8 cups torn leaf lettuce
½ lb. sliced deli roast beef, cut into strips
¼ lb. cubed fully cooked ham
1 medium tomato, chopped
2 hard-boiled large eggs, chopped
4 bacon strips, cooked and crumbled
½ cup shredded Swiss cheese
DRESSING
½ cup olive oil
3 Tbsp. red wine vinegar
2 Tbsp. honey mustard
2 tsp. sugar
¾ tsp. dried oregano
⅛ tsp. pepper

On a serving platter, layer first 7 ingredients. Place the dressing ingredients in a jar with a tight-fitting lid; shake well. Serve with salad.
2 CUPS: 531 cal., 42g fat (9g sat. fat), 171mg chol., 922mg sod., 14g carb. (8g sugars, 3g fiber), 28g pro.s

SOUTHWEST SHREDDED PORK SALAD

This knockout shredded pork makes a healthy, delicious and hearty salad with black beans, corn, cotija cheese and plenty of fresh greens.
—*Mary Shivers, Ada, OK*

- -

Prep: 20 min. • **Cook:** 6 hours
Makes: 12 servings

- 1   boneless pork loin roast (3 to 4 lbs.)
- 1½ cups apple cider or juice
- 1   can (4 oz.) chopped green chiles, drained
- 3   garlic cloves, minced
- 1½ tsp. salt
- 1½ tsp. hot pepper sauce
- 1   tsp. chili powder
- 1   tsp. pepper
- ½   tsp. ground cumin
- ½   tsp. dried oregano
- 12 cups torn mixed salad greens
- 1   can (15 oz.) black beans, rinsed and drained
- 2   medium tomatoes, chopped
- 1   small red onion, chopped
- 1   cup fresh or frozen corn
- 1   cup crumbled cotija or shredded part-skim mozzarella cheese
  Salad dressing of your choice

1. Place pork in a 5- or 6-qt. slow cooker. In a small bowl, mix cider, green chiles, garlic, salt, pepper sauce, chili powder, pepper, cumin and oregano; pour over pork. Cook, covered, on low for 6-8 hours or until the meat is tender.
2. Remove roast from slow cooker; discard the cooking juices. Shred pork with 2 forks. Arrange the salad greens on a large serving platter. Top with the pork, black beans, tomatoes, onion, corn and cheese. Serve with salad dressing.
FREEZE OPTION: Place shredded pork in a freezer container; top with cooking juices. Cool and freeze. To use, partially thaw in refrigerator overnight. Heat through in a saucepan, stirring occasionally.
1 SERVING: 233 cal., 8g fat (4g sat. fat), 67mg chol., 321mg sod., 12g carb. (2g sugars, 3g fiber), 28g pro. **DIABETIC EXCHANGES:** 4 lean meat, 1 vegetable, ½ starch.

FIESTA BEEF BOWLS

This easy entree will knock your socks off. Zesty ingredients turn round steak, beans and rice into a phenomenal meal.
—*Deborah Linn, Valdez, AK*

- -

Prep: 25 min. • **Cook:** 8½ hours
Makes: 6 servings

- 1½ lbs. boneless beef top round steak
- 1   can (10 oz.) diced tomatoes and green chiles
- 1   medium onion, chopped
- 2   garlic cloves, minced
- 1   tsp. dried oregano
- 1   tsp. chili powder
- 1   tsp. ground cumin
- ¼   tsp. salt
- ¼   tsp. pepper
- 2   cans (15 oz. each) pinto beans, rinsed and drained
- 3   cups hot cooked rice
- ½   cup shredded cheddar cheese
- 6   Tbsp. sliced ripe olives
- 6   Tbsp. thinly sliced green onions
- 6   Tbsp. guacamole

1. Place round steak in a 3-qt. slow cooker. In a small bowl, combine the tomatoes, onion, garlic and seasonings; pour over steak. Cover and cook on low for 8-9 hours or until the meat is tender.
2. Remove meat from slow cooker. Add beans to the tomato mixture. Cover and cook on high for 30 minutes or until the beans are heated through.
3. When cool enough to handle, slice the meat. In individual bowls, layer the rice, meat and bean mixture. Top with cheese, olives, onions and guacamole.
1 SERVING: 460 cal., 11g fat (4g sat. fat), 74mg chol., 720mg sod., 52g carb. (4g sugars, 9g fiber), 38g pro.

READER REVIEW
"So easy and delicious! I've tweaked it by adding black beans and replacing pepper with fajita seasoning. The rice is also good with cilantro and lime."
TROSIE74, TASTEOFHOME.COM

GINGERED SPAGHETTI SALAD

We love this chilled chicken salad brimming with colorful veggies. You can easily make it meatless by omitting the chicken and tossing in more edamame.

—*Cindy Heinbaugh, Aurora, CO*

Takes: 30 min. • **Makes:** 8 servings

- 1 pkg. (16 oz.) whole wheat spaghetti
- 1 cup frozen shelled edamame
- 1 tsp. minced fresh gingerroot
- 1 cup reduced-fat sesame ginger salad dressing
- 3 cups cubed cooked chicken breast
- 1 English cucumber, chopped
- 1 medium sweet red pepper, chopped
- 1 small sweet yellow pepper, chopped
- 1 small red onion, finely chopped
- 3 green onions, sliced

1. Cook the spaghetti according to package directions, adding edamame during the last 5 minutes of cooking. Rinse in cold water and drain well. Meanwhile, stir the ginger into the salad dressing.

2. In a large bowl, combine the spaghetti, chicken, cucumber, peppers and red onion. Add dressing; toss to coat. Sprinkle with green onions.

1¾ CUPS: 353 cal., 5g fat (1g sat. fat), 40mg chol., 432mg sod., 53g carb. (6g sugars, 8g fiber), 26g pro.

VEGGIE RICE BOWL

This yummy recipe makes a lot, so it's great for a gathering. Packed with vegetables and two kinds of rice, it's a quick and easy dish.

—*Sherry Hulsman, Louisville, KY*

Takes: 20 min. • **Makes:** 12 servings

- 1 pkg. (6.2 oz.) fast-cooking long grain and wild rice mix
- 2 cups uncooked instant rice
- ½ cup chopped green onions
- ½ cup chopped celery
- ½ cup chopped fresh mushrooms
- ½ cup chopped carrot
- 3 Tbsp. butter
- 1 cup frozen peas

Prepare rice mix and instant rice separately according to their package directions. Meanwhile, in a large skillet, saute the onions, celery, mushrooms and carrot in butter for 4-6 minutes or until tender. Stir in peas and the prepared rice; cook for 2-4 minutes or until heated through.

¾ CUP: 105 cal., 5g fat (3g sat. fat), 13mg chol., 265mg sod., 13g carb. (1g sugars, 1g fiber), 2g pro.

GREEK BROWN & WILD RICE BOWLS

This fresh rice and vegetable dish tastes like the Mediterranean in a bowl! It's short on ingredients but packs in so much flavor. For a hand-held version, leave out the rice and tuck the rest of the ingredients in a pita pocket.
—*Darla Andrews, Schertz, TX*

Takes: 15 min. • **Makes:** 2 Servings

- 1 pkg. (8½ oz.) ready-to-serve whole grain brown and wild rice medley
- ¼ cup Greek vinaigrette, divided
- ½ medium ripe avocado, peeled and sliced
- ¾ cup cherry tomatoes, halved
- ¼ cup crumbled feta cheese
- ¼ cup pitted Greek olives, sliced
  Minced fresh parsley, optional

In a microwave-safe bowl, combine the rice mix and 2 Tbsp. of vinaigrette. Cover and cook on high until heated through, about 2 minutes. Divide between 2 bowls. Top with avocado, tomatoes, cheese, olives, remaining dressing and, if desired, parsley.

1 SERVING: 433 cal., 25g fat (4g sat. fat), 8mg chol., 1355mg sod., 44g carb. (3g sugars, 6g fiber), 8g pro.

CAMILLE BECKSTRAND
Layton, UT

BARBECUE CHICKEN COBB SALAD

I turned barbecue chicken into a major salad with romaine and carrots, sweet peppers and avocados. That's how I got my family to eat more veggies.
—*Camille Beckstrand, Layton, UT*

Prep: 30 min. • **Cook:** 3 hours
Makes: 6 servings

- 1 bottle (18 oz.) barbecue sauce
- 2 Tbsp. brown sugar
- ½ tsp. garlic powder
- ¼ tsp. paprika
- 1½ lbs. boneless skinless chicken breasts
- 12 cups chopped romaine
- 2 avocados, peeled and chopped
- 3 plum tomatoes, chopped
- 2 small carrots, thinly sliced
- 1 medium sweet red or green pepper, chopped
- 3 hard-boiled large eggs, chopped
- 6 bacon strips, cooked and crumbled
- 1½ cups shredded cheddar cheese
  Salad dressing of your choice

1. In a greased 3-qt. slow cooker, mix the barbecue sauce, brown sugar, garlic powder and paprika. Add chicken; turn to coat. Cook, covered, on low for 3-4 hours or until the chicken is tender (a thermometer should read at least 165°).

2. Remove chicken from slow cooker; cut into bite-sized pieces. In a bowl, toss chicken with 1 cup barbecue sauce mixture. Place romaine on a large serving platter; arrange chicken, avocado, vegetables, eggs, bacon and cheese over romaine. Drizzle with dressing.

1 SERVING: 571 cal., 26g fat (9g sat. fat), 192mg chol., 1314mg sod., 47g carb. (32g sugars, 7g fiber), 39g pro.

PIZZA IN A BOWL

On busy days, it's a comfort to know that my family can sit down to dinner minutes after we walk in the door. Double the recipe to impress at a potluck.

—*Virginia Krites, Cridersville, OH*

Takes: 25 min. • **Makes:** 6 servings

- 8 oz. uncooked rigatoni (about 3 cups)
- ¾ lb. ground beef
- ½ cup chopped onion
- 1 can (15 oz.) pizza sauce
- ⅔ cup condensed cream of mushroom soup, undiluted
- 2 cups shredded part-skim mozzarella cheese
- 1 pkg. (3½ oz.) sliced pepperoni
   Chopped fresh basil or arugula, optional

1. Cook the rigatoni according to the package directions; drain. Meanwhile, in a large skillet, cook the beef and onion over medium heat for 6-8 minutes or until the beef is no longer pink, breaking up beef into crumbles; drain. Add pizza sauce, soup and cheese; cook and stir over low heat until the cheese is melted.
2. Add the rigatoni and pepperoni to the beef mixture. Heat through, stirring to combine. If desired, top with basil before serving.

1 CUP: 495 cal., 25g fat (9g sat. fat), 74mg chol., 1056mg sod., 37g carb. (6g sugars, 3g fiber), 30g pro.

BALSAMIC-SALMON SPINACH SALAD

This healthy and tasty dish is a cinch to make after a hard day of work. It comes together fast, but the fresh salmon makes it taste like a meal for a special occasion.

—*Karen Schlyter, Calgary, AB*

Takes: 20 min. • **Makes:** 2 servings

- 1 salmon fillet (6 oz.)
- 2 Tbsp. reduced-fat balsamic vinaigrette, divided
- 3 cups fresh baby spinach
- ¼ cup cubed avocado
- 1 Tbsp. chopped walnuts, toasted
- 1 Tbsp. sunflower kernels, toasted
- 1 Tbsp. dried cranberries

1. Drizzle salmon with 1 Tbsp. vinaigrette. Place on a broiler pan coated with cooking spray. Broil 3-4 in. from the heat until the fish flakes easily with a fork, 10-15 minutes. Cut the salmon into 2 pieces.
2. Meanwhile, in a large bowl, toss spinach with the remaining vinaigrette. Divide between 2 plates. Top with the salmon, avocado, walnuts, sunflower kernels and cranberries.

1 SALAD: 265 cal., 18g fat (3g sat. fat), 43mg chol., 261mg sod., 10g carb. (4g sugars, 3g fiber), 18g pro. **DIABETIC EXCHANGES:** 2 medium-fat meat, 2 fat, 1 vegetable.

GRILLED CHICKEN SALAD WITH BLUEBERRY VINAIGRETTE

We love adding grilled chicken to our salads in the summer, but the real star here is the vinaigrette made with blueberry preserves and maple syrup. It goes great with a fresh baguette and a frosty glass of minted lemonade.
—*Susan Gauthier, Falmouth, ME*

Prep: 20 min. + marinating • **Grill:** 10 min.
Makes: 4 servings

- 2 boneless skinless chicken breast halves (6 oz. each)
- 1 Tbsp. olive oil
- 1 garlic clove, minced
- ¼ tsp. salt
- ¼ tsp. pepper

VINAIGRETTE
- ¼ cup olive oil
- ¼ cup blueberry preserves
- 2 Tbsp. balsamic vinegar
- 2 Tbsp. maple syrup
- ¼ tsp. ground mustard
- ⅛ tsp. salt
  Dash pepper

SALADS
- 1 pkg. (10 oz.) ready-to-serve salad greens
- 1 cup fresh blueberries
- ½ cup canned mandarin oranges
- 1 cup crumbled goat cheese

1. Toss the chicken with oil, garlic, salt and pepper; refrigerate, covered, 30 minutes. In a small bowl, whisk together the vinaigrette ingredients; refrigerate, covered, until serving.
2. Grill chicken, covered, over medium heat until a thermometer reads 165°, 5-7 minutes per side. Let stand 5 minutes before slicing.
3. Place greens on a serving plate; top with chicken, blueberries and mandarin oranges. Whisk the vinaigrette again; drizzle over the salad. Top with cheese.

1 SERVING: 455 cal., 26g fat (7g sat. fat), 82mg chol., 460mg sod., 36g carb. (27g sugars, 4g fiber), 24g pro.

TEST KITCHEN TIP
Look for plump blueberries with a silver frosted appearance. Place the berries on a paper towel-lined plate, cover loosely and refrigerate. Don't wash the berries until ready to use them; use within five days.

STIR-FRY RICE BOWL

My meatless version of Korean bibimbap is tasty, pretty and so easy to tweak for different spice levels.
—*Devon Delaney, Westport, CT*

Takes: 30 min. • **Makes:** 4 servings

- 1 Tbsp. canola oil
- 2 medium carrots, julienned
- 1 medium zucchini, julienned
- ½ cup sliced baby portobello mushrooms
- 1 cup bean sprouts
- 1 cup fresh baby spinach
- 1 Tbsp. water
- 1 Tbsp. reduced-sodium soy sauce
- 1 Tbsp. chili garlic sauce
- 4 large eggs
- 3 cups hot cooked brown rice
- 1 tsp. sesame oil

1. In a large skillet, heat the canola oil over medium-high heat. Add carrots, zucchini and mushrooms; cook and stir 3-5 minutes or until carrots are crisp-tender. Add bean sprouts, spinach, water, soy sauce and chili sauce; cook and stir just until the spinach is wilted. Remove from heat; keep warm.
2. Place 2-3 in. of water in a large skillet with high sides. Bring to a boil; adjust heat to maintain a gentle simmer. Break cold eggs, 1 at a time, into a small bowl; holding bowl close to surface of water, slip egg into water.
3. Cook, uncovered, 3-5 minutes or until whites are completely set and yolks begin to thicken but are not hard. Using a slotted spoon, lift eggs out of water.
4. Serve rice in bowls; top with vegetables. Drizzle with sesame oil. Top each serving with a poached egg.

1 SERVING: 305 cal., 11g fat (2g sat. fat), 186mg chol., 364mg sod., 40g carb. (4g sugars, 4g fiber), 12g pro. **DIABETIC EXCHANGES:** 2 starch, 1 medium-fat meat, 1 vegetable, 1 fat.

SPICY TILAPIA RICE BOWL

I love eating well, and tilapia is a staple in my kitchen. Fresh vegetables are always good but take more prep time, so I like the frozen veggie blend here.
—*Rosalin Johnson, Tupelo, MS*

Takes: 30 min. • **Makes:** 4 servings

- 4 tilapia fillets (4 oz. each)
- 1¼ tsp. Cajun seasoning
- 3 Tbsp. olive oil, divided
- 1 medium yellow summer squash, halved lengthwise and sliced
- 1 pkg. (16 oz.) frozen pepper and onion stir-fry blend
- 1 can (14½ oz.) diced tomatoes, drained
- 1 envelope fajita seasoning mix
- 1 can (15 oz.) black beans, rinsed and drained
- ⅛ tsp. salt
- ⅛ tsp. pepper
- 3 cups hot cooked brown rice
  Optional toppings: Cubed avocado, sour cream and salsa

1. Sprinkle fillets with Cajun seasoning. In a large skillet, heat 2 Tbsp. oil over medium heat. Add fillets; cook until fish just begins to flake easily with a fork, 4-6 minutes on each side. Remove and keep warm. Wipe pan clean.
2. In same skillet, heat the remaining oil. Add squash; cook and stir 3 minutes. Add stir-fry blend and tomatoes; cook until the vegetables are tender, 6-8 minutes longer. Stir in fajita seasoning mix; cook and stir until slightly thickened, 1-2 minutes longer.
3. In a small bowl, mix beans, salt and pepper. Divide rice among 4 serving bowls; layer with beans, vegetables and fillets. If desired, serve with toppings.
1 SERVING: 538 cal., 13g fat (2g sat. fat), 55mg chol., 1365mg sod., 71g carb. (11g sugars, 10g fiber), 33g pro.

SLOW-COOKER CHICKEN TACO SALAD

We use this super duper chicken for several meals including tacos, sandwiches, omelets and enchiladas. My little guys love to help measure the seasonings.
—*Karie Houghton, Lynnwood, WA*

Prep: 10 min. • **Cook:** 3 hours
Makes: 6 servings

- 3 tsp. chili powder
- 1 tsp. each ground cumin, seasoned salt and pepper
- ½ tsp. each white pepper, ground chipotle pepper and paprika
- ¼ tsp. dried oregano
- ¼ tsp. crushed red pepper flakes
- 1½ lbs. boneless skinless chicken breasts
- 1 cup chicken broth
- 9 cups torn romaine
  Optional toppings: Sliced avocado, shredded cheddar cheese, chopped tomato, sliced green onions and ranch salad dressing

1. Mix seasonings; rub over chicken. Place in a 3-qt. slow cooker. Add broth. Cook, covered, on low 3-4 hours or until the chicken is tender.
2. Remove chicken; cool slightly. Shred with 2 forks. Serve over romaine; top as desired.
1¾ CUPS: 143 cal., 3g fat (1g sat. fat), 63mg chol., 516mg sod., 4g carb. (1g sugars, 2g fiber), 24g pro. **DIABETIC EXCHANGES:** 3 lean meat, 1 vegetable.

HEALTH TIP
Switch to a baby kale salad blend for more fiber, vitamin C, calcium and iron.

KARIE HOUGHTON
Lynnwood, WA

GRILLED JERK SHRIMP ORZO SALAD

Celebrate summer with this colorful main-dish salad that delivers a tasty little Caribbean kick.
—*Eileen Budnyk, Palm Beach Gardens, FL*

Prep: 25 min. • **Grill:** 10 min.
Makes: 2 servings

- ⅓ cup uncooked whole wheat orzo pasta
- ½ lb. uncooked shrimp (31-40 per lb.), peeled and deveined
- 1 Tbsp. Caribbean jerk seasoning
- 1 medium ear sweet corn
- 1 tsp. olive oil
- 6 fresh asparagus spears, trimmed
- 1 small sweet red pepper, chopped

DRESSING

- 3 Tbsp. lime juice
- 1 Tbsp. water
- 1 Tbsp. olive oil
- ⅛ tsp. salt
- ⅛ tsp. pepper

1. Cook orzo according to package directions. Drain and rinse with cold water; drain well.
2. Meanwhile, toss shrimp with jerk seasoning; thread onto metal or soaked wooden skewers. Brush corn with oil.
3. On a covered grill over medium heat, cook the corn 10-12 minutes or until tender and lightly browned, turning occasionally; cook the asparagus until crisp-tender, 5-7 minutes, turning occasionally. Grill the shrimp until they turn pink, 1-2 minutes per side.
4. Cut corn from the cob; cut the asparagus into 1-in. pieces. Remove the shrimp from skewers. In a large bowl, combine the orzo, grilled vegetables, shrimp and red pepper. Whisk together the dressing ingredients; toss with salad.

2 CUPS: 340 cal., 12g fat (2g sat. fat), 138mg chol., 716mg sod., 35g carb. (6g sugars, 7g fiber), 25g pro. **DIABETIC EXCHANGES:** 2 starch, 3 lean meat, 1 vegetable, 1 fat.

PESTO TORTELLINI SALAD

I came up with this recipe when I tried re-creating a pasta salad I had at a wedding rehearsal. It's easy to make and now I'm always asked to bring it to potlucks and parties.
—*Danielle Weets, Grandview, WA*

Takes: 20 min. • **Makes:** 5 servings

- 1 pkg. (19 oz.) frozen cheese tortellini
- ¾ cup shredded Parmesan cheese
- 1 can (2¼ oz.) sliced ripe olives, drained
- 5 bacon strips, cooked and crumbled
- ¼ cup prepared pesto

Cook tortellini according to the package directions; drain and rinse in cold water. Place in a small bowl. Add the remaining ingredients; toss to coat.

¾ CUP: 376 cal., 20g fat (8g sat. fat), 36mg chol., 832mg sod., 31g carb. (1g sugars, 2g fiber), 19g pro.

SHRIMP & NOODLE BOWLS

It'll look as if you picked up takeout, but this dish comes from your kitchen. Convenience items reduce the prep time.
—Mary Bergfeld, Eugene, OR

Takes: 25 min. • **Makes:** 6 servings

- 8 oz. uncooked angel hair pasta
- 1 lb. cooked small shrimp
- 2 cups broccoli coleslaw mix
- 6 green onions, thinly sliced
- ½ cup minced fresh cilantro
- ⅔ cup reduced-fat sesame ginger salad dressing

Cook pasta according to package directions; drain and rinse in cold water. Transfer to a large bowl. Add shrimp, coleslaw mix, onions and cilantro. Drizzle with the dressing; toss to coat. Cover and refrigerate until serving.

1⅓ CUPS: 260 cal., 3g fat (0 sat. fat), 147mg chol., 523mg sod., 36g carb. (6g sugars, 2g fiber), 22g pro. **DIABETIC EXCHANGES:** 2 starch, 2 lean meat, 1 vegetable.

HEALTH TIP
Use whole wheat pasta and you'll boost the fiber to 5 grams per serving.

CHICKEN QUINOA BOWLS WITH BALSAMIC DRESSING

The simplicity of this recipe allows me to spend time with my family while not sacrificing taste or nutrition. Plus, the fresh spring flavors really shine through!
—Allyson Meyler, Greensboro, NC

Prep: 30 min. + cooling • **Broil:** 10 min.
Makes: 2 servings

- ¼ cup balsamic vinegar
- ⅔ cup water
- ⅓ cup quinoa, rinsed
- 2 boneless skinless chicken breast halves (6 oz. each)
- 3 tsp. olive or coconut oil, divided
- ¼ tsp. garlic powder
- ½ tsp. salt, divided
- ¼ tsp. pepper, divided
- ½ lb. fresh asparagus, trimmed
- ¼ cup plain Greek yogurt
- ½ tsp. spicy brown mustard
- ½ medium ripe avocado, peeled and sliced
- 6 cherry tomatoes, halved

1. Place vinegar in a small saucepan; bring to a boil. Cook until slightly thickened, 2-3 minutes. Transfer to a bowl; cool completely.

2. In a small saucepan, bring water to a boil. Add quinoa. Reduce heat; simmer, covered, until the liquid is absorbed, 10-12 minutes. Keep warm.

3. Preheat the broiler. Toss chicken with 2 tsp. oil, the garlic powder, ¼ tsp. salt and ⅛ tsp. pepper. Place on 1 half of a 15x10x1-in. pan coated with cooking spray. Broil 4 in. from heat for 5 minutes. Meanwhile, toss asparagus with the remaining oil, salt and pepper.

4. Remove the pan from the broiler; turn chicken over. Add asparagus. Return to oven and broil until a thermometer inserted in chicken reads 165° and asparagus is tender, 3-5 minutes. Let the chicken stand 5 minutes before slicing.

5. For dressing, stir yogurt and mustard into the balsamic reduction. To serve, spoon quinoa into bowls; top with the chicken, asparagus, avocado and tomatoes. Serve with dressing.

1 SERVING: 491 cal., 21g fat (5g sat. fat), 101mg chol., 715mg sod., 35g carb. (12g sugars, 6g fiber), 42g pro.

ASIAN BARBECUE CHICKEN SLAW

When it's springtime in the South, cabbage is plentiful and we use it. One of our favorite recipes is this combination of Asian slaw and barbecued chicken. It's easy to halve or double the servings as needed.
—*Paula Todora, Maple Valley, WA*

- -

Takes: 25 min. • **Makes:** 4 servings

- ¼ cup reduced-sodium soy sauce
- ¼ cup honey
- 4 Tbsp. canola oil, divided
- 2 Tbsp. rice vinegar
- ½ cup barbecue sauce
- 1 lb. boneless skinless chicken breasts, cut into strips
- ¼ tsp. pepper
- ¼ cup honey mustard salad dressing
- 1 pkg. (14 oz.) coleslaw mix
- 3 green onions, chopped
- 4 Tbsp. sliced almonds, toasted, divided
- 3 tsp. sesame seeds, toasted, divided

1. In a large bowl, whisk soy sauce, honey, 3 Tbsp. oil and the vinegar until blended. Pour half of the honey mixture into a small bowl; stir in barbecue sauce. Sprinkle the chicken with pepper.

2. In a large nonstick skillet heat the remaining oil over medium-high heat. Add chicken; cook and stir until no longer pink, 4-6 minutes. Add the barbecue sauce mixture; heat through.

3. Meanwhile, whisk salad dressing into the remaining honey mixture until blended. Add coleslaw mix, green onions, 3 Tbsp. almonds and 2 tsp. sesame seeds; toss to coat. Serve with the chicken. Sprinkle each individual serving with the remaining almonds and sesame seeds.

NOTE: To toast nuts, bake in a shallow pan in a 350° oven for 5-10 minutes or cook in a skillet over low heat until the nuts are lightly browned, stirring occasionally.

½ CUP CHICKEN MIXTURE WITH 1¼ CUPS SLAW: 531 cal., 27g fat (3g sat. fat), 67mg chol., 1202mg sod., 47g carb. (37g sugars, 4g fiber), 27g pro.

EASY GROUND BEEF TACO SALAD

Every time I have to bring a dish to a party, friends ask for my taco salad. Even players on my son's football team ask for it!
—*Lori Buntrock, Wisconsin Rapids, WI*

- -

Takes: 30 min. • **Makes:** 6 servings

- 1 lb. ground beef
- 1 envelope reduced-sodium taco seasoning
- ¾ cup water
- 1 medium head iceberg lettuce, torn (about 8 cups)
- 2 cups shredded cheddar cheese
- 2 cups broken nacho-flavored tortilla chips
- ¼ cup Catalina salad dressing

1. In a large skillet, cook beef over medium heat 6-8 minutes or until meat is no longer pink, breaking into crumbles; drain. Stir in taco seasoning and water; bring to a boil. Reduce heat; simmer, uncovered, 4-6 minutes or until thickened, stirring occasionally. Cool slightly.

2. In a large bowl, toss lettuce with cheese. Top with the beef mixture and chips; drizzle with the Catalina dressing and toss salad to combine. Serve immediately.

1⅔ CUPS: 416 cal., 27g fat (12g sat. fat), 86mg chol., 830mg sod., 19g carb. (7g sugars, 2g fiber), 25g pro.

CURRIED CHICKEN & PEACH SALAD

This is a healthy and simple salad to make; even my non-cooking husband can whip it together in minutes. We've served this to friends over the years, and they always ask for the recipe.
—Radelle Knappenberger, Oviedo, FL

- -

Takes: 10 min. • **Makes:** 4 servings

- ½ cup fat-free mayonnaise
- 1 tsp. curry powder
- 2 cups cubed cooked chicken breasts
- ½ cup chopped walnuts
- ¼ cup raisins
- 2 medium peaches, sliced
- 1 pkg. (5 oz.) spring mix salad greens

Mix mayonnaise and curry powder; toss gently with chicken, walnuts and raisins. Serve the chicken mixture and peaches over greens.
1 SERVING: 286 cal., 12g fat (2g sat. fat), 54mg chol., 315mg sod., 23g carb. (14g sugars, 4g fiber), 24g pro. **DIABETIC EXCHANGES:** 3 lean meat, 1½ fat, 1 vegetable, 1 fruit.

READER REVIEW

"Refreshing, satisfying and quite delicious. My family has given it a thumbs-up for a repeat performance... Thanks for a great recipe that helped expand our tastes a bit!"

DOVECANYON, TASTEOFHOME.COM

MEDITERRANEAN BULGUR BOWL

You can transform this tasty bowl into an Italian version with mozzarella, pesto, tomatoes, spinach and basil.
—Renata Smith, Brookline, MA

- -

Takes: 30 min. • **Makes:** 4 servings

- 1 cup bulgur
- ½ tsp. ground cumin
- ¼ tsp. salt
- 2 cups water
- 1 can (15 oz.) garbanzo beans or chickpeas, rinsed and drained
- 6 oz. fresh baby spinach (about 8 cups)
- 2 cups cherry tomatoes, halved
- 1 small red onion, halved and thinly sliced
- ½ cup crumbled feta cheese
- ¼ cup hummus
- 2 Tbsp. chopped fresh mint
- 2 Tbsp. lemon juice

1. In a 6-qt. stockpot, combine the first 4 ingredients; bring to a boil. Reduce heat; simmer, covered, 10-12 minutes or until bulgur is tender. Stir in garbanzo beans; heat through.
2. Remove from heat; stir in the spinach. Let stand, covered, until the spinach is wilted, about 5 minutes. Stir in remaining ingredients. Serve warm or refrigerate and serve cold.
2 CUPS: 311 cal., 7g fat (2g sat. fat), 8mg chol., 521mg sod., 52g carb. (6g sugars, 12g fiber), 14g pro.

HEALTH TIP
With the spinach, tomatoes and feta cheese, this dish supplies all the vitamin A you need in a day.

EAST COAST SHRIMP & LENTIL BOWLS

If you have frozen shrimp, a few seasoning ingredients, bagged spinach and lentils in your pantry, you can make this dish in no time. It's healthy, but it's so delicious, nobody needs to know!

—Mary Kay LaBrie, Clermont, FL

- -

Prep: 10 min. • **Cook:** 25 min.
Makes: 4 servings

- ½ cup dried brown lentils, rinsed
- 1 Tbsp. olive oil
- ⅛ tsp. salt
- 1¾ cups water
- 2 Tbsp. garlic powder, divided
- 1 lb. uncooked shrimp (26-30 per lb.), peeled and deveined
- 2 tsp. seafood seasoning
- 2 Tbsp. butter
- ½ tsp. crushed red pepper flakes
- 2 tsp. lemon juice
- 3 cups fresh baby spinach
- ¼ tsp. ground nutmeg
- ¼ cup finely chopped sweet onion
  Lemon wedges

1. Place the first 4 ingredients and 1 Tbsp. garlic powder in a small saucepan; bring to a boil. Reduce heat; simmer, covered, until the lentils are tender, 17-20 minutes.

2. Toss shrimp with seafood seasoning. In a large skillet, melt butter over medium-high heat. Add pepper flakes and the remaining garlic powder; cook and stir 30 seconds. Add shrimp; cook and stir until shrimp turn pink, 3-4 minutes. Stir in lemon juice; remove from pan and keep warm.

3. Add spinach and nutmeg to pan; cook and stir over medium-high heat until the spinach is wilted. Remove from heat.

4. To serve, divide lentils among 4 bowls. Top with shrimp, spinach and onion. Serve with lemon wedges.

1 SERVING: 289 cal., 11g fat (5g sat. fat), 153mg chol., 645mg sod., 22g carb. (1g sugars, 4g fiber), 26g pro. **DIABETIC EXCHANGES:** 3 lean meat, 1½ starch, 1 fat.

STEAK SALAD WITH TOMATOES & AVOCADO

My family loves a good steak dinner, but with our busy schedules, I'm often thinking about ways to put simple twists on things. This salad is flavored with the freshness of lemon and cilantro, and is one of my husband's favorite weeknight dishes.

—*Lyndsay Wells, Ladysmith, BC*

Takes: 30 min. • **Makes:** 6 servings

- 1 beef top sirloin steak (1¼ in. thick and 1½ lbs.)
- 1 Tbsp. olive oil
- 3 tsp. Creole seasoning
- 2 large tomatoes, chopped
- 1 can (15 oz.) cannellini beans, rinsed and drained
- 1 can (15 oz.) black beans, rinsed and drained
- 3 green onions, chopped
- ¼ cup minced fresh cilantro
- 2 tsp. grated lemon zest
- 2 Tbsp. lemon juice
- ¼ tsp. salt
- 1 medium ripe avocado, peeled and cubed (½ in.)

1. Rub both sides of steak with oil; sprinkle with Creole seasoning. Grill, covered, over medium heat or broil 4 in. from heat for 5-8 minutes on each side or until the meat reaches desired doneness (for medium-rare, a thermometer should read 135°; medium, 140°; medium-well, 145°). Let stand for 5 minutes.

2. In a large bowl, combine tomatoes, beans, green onions, cilantro, lemon zest, lemon juice and salt; gently stir in avocado. Cut steak into slices; serve with bean mixture.

NOTE: The following may be substituted for 3 tsp. Creole seasoning: ¾ tsp. each salt, garlic powder and paprika; and ⅛ tsp. each dried thyme, ground cumin and cayenne pepper.

1 SERVING: 328 cal., 11g fat (3g sat. fat), 46mg chol., 710mg sod., 25g carb. (3g sugars, 8g fiber), 31g pro. **DIABETIC EXCHANGES:** 3 lean meat, 1½ starch, 1½ fat.

EDAMAME & SOBA NOODLE BOWL

Made from buckwheat flour, soba noodles are toothsome and hearty.

—*Matthew Hass, Ellison Bay, WI*

Takes: 30 min. • **Makes:** 6 servings

- 1 pkg. (12 oz.) uncooked Japanese soba noodles or whole wheat spaghetti
- 2 Tbsp. sesame oil
- 2 cups fresh small broccoli florets
- 1 medium onion, halved and thinly sliced
- 3 cups frozen shelled edamame, thawed
- 2 large carrots, cut into ribbons with a vegetable peeler
- 4 garlic cloves, minced
- 1 cup reduced-fat Asian toasted sesame salad dressing
- ¼ tsp. pepper
  Sesame seeds, toasted, optional

1. In a 6 qt. stockpot, cook noodles according to package directions; drain and return to pan.
2. Meanwhile, in a large skillet, heat oil over medium heat. Add broccoli and onion; cook and stir until crisp-tender, 4-6 minutes. Add edamame and carrots; cook and stir until tender, 6-8 minutes. Add garlic; cook 1 minute longer. Add the vegetable mixture, dressing and pepper to noodles; toss to combine. Sprinkle with sesame seeds if desired.
1⅓ CUPS: 414 cal., 12g fat (1g sat. fat), 0 chol., 867mg sod., 64g carb. (12g sugars, 4g fiber), 18g pro.

THAI SALMON BROWN RICE BOWLS

Turn to this salmon recipe for a quick and nourishing meal. The store-bought dressing saves time and adds extra flavor to this healthy dish.
—*Naylet LaRochelle, Miami, FL*

Takes: 15 min. • **Makes:** 4 servings

- 4 **salmon fillets (4 oz. each)**
- ½ **cup sesame ginger salad dressing, divided**
- 3 **cups hot cooked brown rice**
- ½ **cup chopped fresh cilantro**
- ¼ **tsp. salt**
- 1 **cup julienned carrot**
  Thinly sliced red cabbage, optional

1. Preheat oven to 400°. Place salmon in a foil-lined 15x10x1-in. pan; brush with ¼ cup of the dressing. Bake until the fish just begins to flake easily with a fork, 8-10 minutes. Meanwhile, toss rice with cilantro and salt.
2. To serve, divide rice mixture among 4 bowls. Top with the salmon fillets, carrots and, if desired, cabbage. Drizzle with the remaining dressing.
1 SERVING: 486 cal., 21g fat (4g sat. fat), 57mg chol., 532mg sod., 49g carb. (8g sugars, 3g fiber), 24g pro.

CHICKEN FAJITA SALAD

This recipe came from Texas, which is famous for its Tex-Mex food. I love to cook, even though it's just for my husband and me now. I invite our grown kids over a lot, and they just love this recipe. I'm happy to share it!
—*Lois Proudfit, Eugene, OR*

Takes: 30 min. + marinating
Makes: 6 servings

- 4 **Tbsp. canola oil, divided**
- ½ **cup lime juice**
- 2 **garlic cloves, minced**
- 1 **tsp. ground cumin**
- 1 **tsp. dried oregano**
- 1 **lb. boneless skinless chicken breasts, cut into thin strips**
- 1 **medium onion, cut into thin wedges**
- 1 **medium sweet red pepper, cut into thin strips**
- 2 **cans (4 oz. each) chopped green chiles**
- 1 **cup unblanched almonds, toasted**
- 3 **cups shredded lettuce**
- 3 **medium tomatoes, cut into wedges**
- 1 **medium ripe avocado, peeled and sliced**

1. In a small bowl, combine 2 Tbsp. of oil, the lime juice, garlic, cumin and oregano. Pour half of the mixture into a large bowl or dish; add chicken and turn to coat. Marinate for at least 30 minutes. Cover and refrigerate the remaining marinade.
2. In a large skillet, heat the remaining oil on medium-high. Saute onion for 2-3 minutes or until crisp-tender.
3. Drain chicken, discarding marinade. Add to skillet; stir-fry until meat is no longer pink. Add the red pepper, chiles and reserved marinade; cook 2 minutes or until heated through. Stir in almonds. Serve immediately over shredded lettuce; top with tomatoes and avocado.
1½ CUPS: 372 cal., 26g fat (3g sat. fat), 42mg chol., 203mg sod., 16g carb. (5g sugars, 6g fiber), 22g pro.

FETA CHICKEN SALAD

I grew up eating lots of chicken because my father was the manager at a poultry facility. This is one dish that never gets boring!
—*Cheryl Snavely, Hagerstown, MD*

Prep: 20 min. + chilling • **Makes:** 4 servings

- 2 **cups shredded cooked chicken breasts**
- ½ **cup cherry tomatoes, halved**
- ½ **cup finely chopped red onion**
- ½ **cup chopped seedless cucumber**
- ½ **cup chopped sweet yellow pepper**
- 4 **tsp. lemon juice**
- 4 **tsp. olive oil**
- ½ **tsp. Greek seasoning**
- ½ **tsp. salt**
- ⅛ **tsp. pepper**
- ¼ **cup crumbled feta cheese**

In a large bowl, combine first 5 ingredients. In a small bowl, whisk the lemon juice, oil, Greek seasoning, salt and pepper. Pour over the chicken mixture; toss to coat. Refrigerate for at least 1 hour. Just before serving, sprinkle with cheese.

1 CUP: 198 cal., 9g fat (2g sat. fat), 63mg chol., 540mg sod., 5g carb. (2g sugars, 1g fiber), 24g pro. **DIABETIC EXCHANGES:** 3 lean meat, 1 vegetable, 1 fat.

GINGER-CASHEW CHICKEN SALAD

I revamped an Asian-style chicken salad recipe to create this gingery, crunchy salad. It's a huge success when I serve it at ladies' luncheons.
—*Shelly Gramer, Long Beach, CA*

Prep: 20 min. + marinating • **Broil:** 10 min.
Makes: 8 servings

- ½ **cup cider vinegar**
- ½ **cup molasses**
- ⅓ **cup canola oil**
- 2 **Tbsp. minced fresh gingerroot**
- 2 **tsp. reduced-sodium soy sauce**
- 1 **tsp. salt**
- ⅛ **tsp. cayenne pepper**
- 4 **boneless skinless chicken breast halves (6 oz. each)**

SALAD
- 8 **oz. fresh baby spinach (about 10 cups)**
- 1 **can (11 oz.) mandarin oranges, drained**
- 1 **cup shredded red cabbage**
- 2 **medium carrots, shredded**
- 3 **green onions, thinly sliced**
- 2 **cups chow mein noodles**

- ¾ **cup salted cashews, toasted**
- 2 **Tbsp. sesame seeds, toasted**

1. In a small bowl, whisk the first 7 ingredients until blended. Pour ¾ cup of the marinade into a large shallow dish. Add the chicken; turn to coat. Cover and refrigerate at least 3 hours. Cover and refrigerate the remaining marinade.
2. Preheat the broiler. Drain the chicken, discarding the marinade in the bag. Place chicken in a 15x10x1-in. baking pan. Broil 4-6 in. from the heat for 4-6 minutes on each side or until a thermometer reads 165°. Cut chicken into strips.
3. Place spinach on a serving platter. Arrange chicken, oranges, cabbage, carrots and green onions on top. Sprinkle with the chow mein noodles, cashews and sesame seeds. Stir reserved molasses mixture; drizzle over salad and toss to coat. Serve immediately.

NOTE: To toast nuts, bake in a shallow pan in a 350° oven for 5-10 minutes or cook in a skillet over low heat until the nuts are lightly browned, stirring occasionally.

1½ CUPS: 379 cal., 18g fat (3g sat. fat), 47mg chol., 533mg sod., 33g carb. (16g sugars, 3g fiber), 23g pro. **DIABETIC EXCHANGES:** 2½ fat, 2 lean meat, 1½ starch, 1 vegetable.

SHRIMP & AVOCADO SALADS

This gorgeous salad has such authentic flavor, you can close your eyes and imagine you're sitting at a beachside cantina in Acapulco!
—*Heidi Hall, North Saint Paul, MN*

Takes: 25 min. • **Makes:** 4 servings

- 1 lb. uncooked large shrimp, peeled and deveined
- 1 small garlic clove, minced
- ½ tsp. chili powder
- ¼ tsp. salt
- ¼ tsp. ground cumin
- 2 tsp. olive oil
- 5 cups hearts of romaine salad mix
- 1 cup fresh or frozen corn, thawed
- 1 cup frozen peas, thawed
- ½ cup chopped sweet red pepper
- 1 medium ripe avocado, peeled and thinly sliced

CILANTRO VINAIGRETTE

- 7 Tbsp. olive oil
- ¼ cup minced fresh cilantro
- ¼ cup lime juice
- 1½ tsp. sugar
- 1 small garlic clove, minced
- ½ tsp. salt
- ¼ tsp. pepper

1. In a large skillet, cook shrimp, garlic, chili powder, salt and cumin in oil over medium heat for 3-4 minutes or until the shrimp turn pink; set aside.

2. In a large bowl, combine the romaine, corn, peas and chopped red pepper; divide among 4 serving plates. Top each serving with shrimp and avocado. In a small bowl, whisk the vinaigrette ingredients; drizzle over each individual salad.

1 SERVING: 489 cal., 35g fat (5g sat. fat), 138mg chol., 638mg sod., 24g carb. (7g sugars, 8g fiber), 24g pro.

ASIAN CHICKEN RICE BOWL

This super flavorful, nutrient-packed dish makes use of supermarket conveniences like coleslaw mix and rotisserie chicken. The recipe is easily doubled or tripled for large families.
—*Christianna Gozzi, Astoria, NY*

Takes: 20 min. • **Makes:** 4 servings

- ¼ cup rice vinegar
- 1 green onion, minced
- 2 Tbsp. reduced-sodium soy sauce
- 1 Tbsp. toasted sesame seeds
- 1 Tbsp. sesame oil
- 1 Tbsp. honey
- 1 tsp. minced fresh gingerroot
- 1 pkg. (8.8 oz.) ready-to-serve brown rice
- 4 cups coleslaw mix (about 9 oz.)
- 2 cups shredded rotisserie chicken, chilled
- 2 cups frozen shelled edamame, thawed

1. For the dressing, whisk together the first 7 ingredients. Cook rice according to package directions. Divide among 4 bowls.

2. In a large bowl, toss coleslaw mix and chicken with half of the dressing. Serve edamame and slaw mixture over rice; drizzle with the remaining dressing.

1 SERVING: 429 cal., 15g fat (2g sat. fat), 62mg chol., 616mg sod., 38g carb. (13g sugars, 5g fiber), 32g pro. **DIABETIC EXCHANGES:** 3 lean meat, 2 starch, 1 vegetable, 1 fat.

> **TEST KITCHEN TIP**
> Pulled pork also works well in this bowl. If you want a little extra crunch, add some chopped peanuts to the mix.

SOUPS, STEWS & CHILI

Is there anything better than a bowl of homemade happiness? Whether you're in the mood for something spicy, meaty or loaded with veggies, these dishes will have your family asking for more.

5i 🍲

POTATO CHOWDER

One of the ladies in our church quilting group brought this savory potato soup to a meeting, and everyone loved how the cream cheese and bacon made it so rich. It's easy to assemble in the morning so it can simmer on its own all day.
—*Anna Mayer, Fort Branch, IN*

- -

Prep: 15 min. • **Cook:** 8 hours
Makes: 12 servings (3 qt.)

8	cups diced potatoes
3	cans (14½ oz. each) chicken broth
1	can (10¾ oz.) condensed cream of chicken soup, undiluted
⅓	cup chopped onion
¼	tsp. pepper
1	pkg. (8 oz.) cream cheese, cubed, at room temperature
½	lb. sliced bacon, cooked and crumbled, optional
	Minced chives, optional

1. In a 5-qt. slow cooker, combine the first 5 ingredients. Cover and cook on low for 8-10 hours or until the potatoes are tender.

2. Add cream cheese; stir until blended. Garnish with bacon and chives if desired.

1 CUP: 179 cal., 9g fat (5g sat. fat), 25mg chol., 690mg sod., 21g carb. (2g sugars, 2g fiber), 4g pro.

READER REVIEW

"This is one of our family favorites and it's easy to add corn or ham— whatever your family fancies. We absolutely love it."

DANETTEMROY, TASTEOFHOME.COM

WHITE TURKEY CHILI

Cut the fat and calories while savoring all the comfort, heartiness and flavor you love. This recipe makes it easy!
—*Tina Barrett, Houston, TX*

- -

Prep: 10 min. • **Cook:** 35 min.
Makes: 6 servings (1½ qt.)

- 2 cans (15 oz. each) cannellini beans, rinsed and drained
- 1 can (10¾ oz.) reduced-fat reduced-sodium condensed cream of chicken soup, undiluted
- 2 cups cubed cooked turkey breast
- 1⅓ cups fat-free milk
- 1 can (4 oz.) chopped green chiles, drained
- 1 Tbsp. minced fresh cilantro
- 1 Tbsp. dried minced onion
- 1 tsp. garlic powder
- 1 tsp. ground cumin
- 1 tsp. dried oregano
- 6 Tbsp. fat-free sour cream

In a large saucepan, combine the first 10 ingredients; bring to a boil, stirring occasionally. Reduce heat; simmer, covered, 25-30 minutes or until heated through. Top individual servings with sour cream.

1 CUP WITH 1 TBSP. SOUR CREAM: 250 cal., 2g fat (1g sat. fat), 47mg chol., 510mg sod., 31g carb. (0 sugars, 6g fiber), 23g pro. **DIABETIC EXCHANGES:** 3 lean meat, 2 starch.

PRISCILLA'S VEGETABLE CHOWDER

This is the perfect soup to warm up with on a cold fall or winter day. Serve it in a bread bowl to make it extra special.
—*Jenna Jackson, Salt Lake City, UT*

- -

Prep: 25 min. • **Cook:** 30 min.
Makes: 12 servings (3 qt.)

- 3 cups diced peeled potatoes
- 2½ cups broccoli florets
- 1 cup chopped onion
- 1 cup grated carrots
- 2 celery ribs, diced
- 4 tsp. chicken bouillon granules
- 3 cups water
- ¾ cup butter, cubed
- ¾ cup all-purpose flour
- 4 cups whole milk
- 1 tsp. salt
- ¼ tsp. pepper
- 1 cup cubed fully cooked ham
- 1 cup shredded cheddar cheese

1. In a Dutch oven, combine the potatoes, broccoli, onion, carrots, celery, bouillon and water; simmer for 20 minutes or until vegetables are tender.

2. In a large saucepan, melt butter; stir in flour. Cook and stir over medium heat for 2 minutes. Whisk in milk, salt and pepper. Bring to a boil; cook and stir for 2 minutes or until thickened. Add to the vegetable mixture with the ham; simmer for 10 minutes or until heated through. Stir in cheese just until melted.

1 CUP: 281 cal., 18g fat (11g sat. fat), 58mg chol., 853mg sod., 22g carb. (6g sugars, 2g fiber), 9g pro.

BLACK BEAN, CHORIZO & SWEET POTATO CHILI

Chili is one of my all-time favorite dishes. This recipe takes it to the next level by changing up the flavors and adding a surprise ingredient— sweet potatoes.
—*Julie Merriman, Seattle, WA*

Prep: 20 min. • **Cook:** 6 hours
Makes: 16 servings (4 qt.)

- 1 lb. uncooked chorizo, casings removed, or spicy bulk pork sausage
- 1 large onion, chopped
- 2 poblano peppers, finely chopped
- 2 jalapeno peppers, seeded and finely chopped
- 3 Tbsp. tomato paste
- 3 large sweet potatoes, peeled and cut into ½-in. cubes
- 4 cans (14½ oz. each) fire-roasted diced tomatoes, undrained
- 2 cans (15 oz. each) black beans, rinsed and drained
- 2 cups beef stock
- 2 Tbsp. chili powder
- 1 Tbsp. dried oregano
- 1 Tbsp. ground coriander
- 1 Tbsp. ground cumin
- 1 Tbsp. smoked paprika
- ¼ cup lime juice
  Optional: Chopped jalapenos, chopped red onion and crumbled queso fresco

1. In a large skillet, cook and stir the chorizo, onion, poblanos and jalapenos over medium heat for 8-10 minutes or until the chorizo is cooked. Using a slotted spoon, transfer to a 6-qt. slow cooker.

2. Stir in tomato paste. Add the potatoes, tomatoes, beans, stock and spices; stir to combine. Cover and cook on low for 6-7 hours or until the potatoes are tender. Stir in lime juice. If desired, top individual servings with chopped jalapenos, chopped red onion and crumbled queso fresco.

NOTE: Wear disposable gloves when cutting hot peppers; the oils can burn skin exposed skin. Avoid touching your face.

1 CUP: 263 cal., 9g fat (3g sat. fat), 25mg chol., 823mg sod., 33g carb. (11g sugars, 6g fiber), 12g pro.

JULIE MERRIMAN
Seattle, WA

COMFORTING CHICKEN NOODLE SOUP

A good friend made us this rich, comforting soup after the birth of our son. It was such a help to have dinner taken care of until I was back on my feet. I now give a pot of it (along with the recipe) to other new mothers.
—Joanna Sargent, Sandy, UT

- -

Takes: 25 min.
Makes: 12 servings (3 qt.)

 2 qt. water
 8 tsp. chicken bouillon granules
 6½ cups uncooked wide egg noodles
 2 cans (10¾ oz. each) condensed
    cream of chicken soup, undiluted
 3 cups cubed cooked chicken
 1 cup sour cream
    Minced fresh parsley

1. In a large saucepan, bring water and bouillon to a boil. Add the noodles; cook, uncovered, until tender, about 10 minutes. Do not drain. Add the soup and chicken; heat through.
2. Remove from the heat; stir in the sour cream. Sprinkle with minced parsley.

1 CUP: 218 cal., 9g fat (4g sat. fat), 67mg chol., 980mg sod., 18g carb. (2g sugars, 1g fiber), 15g pro.

❄ WEEKNIGHT TACO SOUP

This soup turned out delicious on the first try when I was working without a recipe. For a heartier meal, you could add cooked ground beef or stew meat dredged in seasoned flour and browned.
—Amanda Swartz, Goderich, ON

- -

Takes: 30 min. • **Makes:** 6 servings (2½ qt.)

 1 Tbsp. canola oil
 1 large onion, chopped
 1 medium sweet red pepper, chopped
 1 medium green pepper, chopped
 1 can (28 oz.) diced tomatoes,
    undrained
 3 cups vegetable broth
 1 can (15 oz.) pinto beans,
    rinsed and drained
 1½ cups frozen corn
 1 envelope taco seasoning
 ¼ tsp. salt
 ¼ tsp. pepper
 1 pkg. (8.8 oz.) ready-to-serve
    long grain rice
 1 cup sour cream
    Optional toppings: Shredded cheddar
    cheese, crushed tortilla chips and
    additional sour cream

1. In a Dutch oven, heat oil over medium heat. Add onion and peppers; cook and stir until crisp-tender, 3-5 minutes.
2. Add tomatoes, broth, beans, corn, taco seasoning, salt and pepper; bring to a boil. Reduce heat; simmer, uncovered, until the vegetables are tender, 10-15 minutes. Reduce heat. Stir in rice and sour cream; heat through. Serve with toppings as desired.
FREEZE OPTION: Freeze cooled soup in freezer containers. To use, partially thaw in refrigerator overnight. Heat through in a saucepan, stirring occasionally; add a little broth if necessary.

1¾ CUPS: 333 cal., 12g fat (5g sat. fat), 9mg chol., 1288mg sod., 49g carb. (10g sugars, 7g fiber), 9g pro.

READER REVIEW

"A quick, delicious meal. I thought it was a fantastic meatless dish—the beans give it a good 'fill your tummy' texture. Dinner will be early at our home this evening!"

KANSASFOODIE, TASTEOFHOME.COM

30-MINUTE CHICKEN NOODLE SOUP

This great soup is perfect for a cold, wintry day. It is my favorite thing to eat when I'm under the weather; it makes me feel so much better.

—*Lacey Waadt, Payson, UT*

Takes: 30 min. • **Makes:** 6 servings (2¼ qt.)

- 4 cups water
- 1 can (14½ oz.) chicken broth
- 1½ cups cubed cooked chicken breast
- 1 can (10¾ oz.) condensed cream of chicken soup, undiluted
- ¾ cup sliced celery
- ¾ cup sliced carrots
- 1 small onion, chopped
- 1½ tsp. dried parsley flakes
- 1 tsp. reduced-sodium chicken bouillon granules
- ¼ tsp. pepper
- 3 cups uncooked egg noodles

In a Dutch oven, combine first 10 ingredients. Bring to a boil. Reduce heat; cover and simmer for 10 minutes or until the vegetables are crisp-tender. Stir in noodles; cook 5-7 minutes longer or until the noodles and vegetables are tender.

1½ CUPS: 196 cal., 5g fat (1g sat. fat), 49mg chol., 759mg sod., 22g carb. (3g sugars, 2g fiber), 15g pro. **DIABETIC EXCHANGES:** 2 lean meat, 1 starch, ½ fat.

🍎 SHRIMP PAD THAI SOUP

Pad thai is one of my favorite foods, but it is often loaded with extra calories. This soup is a healthier option that has all the flavor of traditional pad thai.

—*Julie Merriman, Seattle, WA*

Prep: 15 min. • **Cook:** 30 min.
Makes: 8 servings (2¾ qt.)

- 1 Tbsp. sesame oil
- 2 shallots, thinly sliced
- 1 Thai chili pepper or serrano pepper, seeded and finely chopped
- 1 can (28 oz.) no-salt-added crushed tomatoes
- ¼ cup creamy peanut butter
- 2 Tbsp. reduced-sodium soy sauce or fish sauce
- 6 cups reduced-sodium chicken broth
- 1 lb. uncooked shrimp (31-40 per lb.), peeled and deveined
- 6 oz. uncooked thick rice noodles
- 1 cup bean sprouts
- 4 green onions, sliced
  Chopped peanuts, optional
  Lime wedges

1. In a 6-qt. stockpot, heat oil over medium heat. Add shallots and chili pepper; cook and stir 4-6 minutes or until tender. Stir in crushed tomatoes, peanut butter and soy sauce until blended; add the broth. Bring to a boil; cook, uncovered, 15 minutes to allow the flavors to blend.

2. Add shrimp and noodles; cook 4-6 minutes longer or until the shrimp turn pink and the noodles are tender. Top individual servings with bean sprouts, green onions and, if desired, chopped peanuts and additional chopped chili pepper. Serve with lime wedges.

NOTE: Wear disposable gloves when cutting hot peppers; the oils can burn skin exposed skin. Avoid touching your face.

1⅓ CUPS: 252 cal., 7g fat (1g sat. fat), 69mg chol., 755mg sod., 31g carb. (5g sugars, 4g fiber), 17g pro. **DIABETIC EXCHANGES:** 2 lean meat, 1½ starch, 1 vegetable, 1 fat.

COUNTRY FISH CHOWDER

You'll think you're on Cape Cod when you taste this thick, wholesome chowder. I've treasured this recipe for many years—it's one of my husband's favorites. He likes it more and more because over the years I've customized the basic recipe by including ingredients he enjoys.
—Linda Lazaroff, Hebron, CT

Prep: 15 min. • **Cook:** 25 min.
Makes: 10 servings (2½ qt.)

- 1 cup chopped onion
- 4 bacon strips, chopped
- 3 cans (12 oz. each) evaporated milk
- 1 can (15¼ oz.) whole kernel corn, undrained
- 1 can (6½ oz.) chopped clams, undrained
- 3 medium potatoes, peeled and cubed
- 3 Tbsp. butter
- 1 tsp. salt
- ¾ tsp. pepper
- 1 lb. fish fillets (haddock, cod or flounder), cooked and broken into pieces
  Crumbled cooked bacon, optional
  Minced chives, optional

In a large saucepan, cook onion and bacon over medium heat until the onion is tender; drain. Add milk, corn, clams, potatoes, butter, salt and pepper. Cover and cook over medium heat, stirring occasionally, until the potatoes are tender, about 20 minutes. Stir in fish and heat through. Ladle into bowls. If desired, top with bacon and chives.

1 CUP: 250 cal., 12g fat (6g sat. fat), 57mg chol., 598mg sod., 19g carb. (7g sugars, 2g fiber), 15g pro.

DID YOU KNOW?
A chowder is a chunky, thick, rich soup frequently made with seafood or vegetables (such as corn), but it also can be made with other meat. What makes a chowder a chowder is that it has a milk or cream base and may be thickened with flour.

BONNIE'S CHILI

This chili is incredibly easy to make, and has a surprising depth of flavor—it tastes like a chili that takes all day to create! I can make this for people who like it hot or mild just by changing the salsa. You can make it *really* spicy if you add hot peppers and hot salsa.
—Bonnie Altig, North Pole, AK

Prep: 25 min. • **Cook:** 5 hours
Makes: 8 servings (2½ qt.)

- 2 lbs. lean ground beef (90% lean)
- 2 cans (16 oz. each) kidney beans, rinsed and drained
- 2 cans (15 oz. each) tomato sauce
- 1½ cups salsa
- ½ cup water or reduced-sodium beef broth
- 4½ tsp. chili powder
- ½ tsp. garlic powder
- ½ tsp. pepper
- ¼ tsp. salt
  Optional toppings: Corn chips, sliced jalapeno peppers and shredded cheddar cheese

In a Dutch oven, cook beef over medium heat until no longer pink, 8-10 minutes, breaking into crumbles; drain. Transfer to a 4- or 5-qt. slow cooker. Stir in the remaining ingredients. Cook, covered, on low until heated through, 5-6 hours. Serve with optional toppings as desired.

1¼ CUPS: 323 cal., 10g fat (4g sat. fat), 71mg chol., 1027mg sod., 27g carb. (5g sugars, 8g fiber), 31g pro.

GONE-ALL-DAY STEW

This healthy, hearty stew is one of my husband's favorite meals. I always use fresh mushrooms and low-sodium bouillon granules.
—*Patricia Kile, Elizabethtown, PA*

- -

Prep: 25 min. • **Cook:** 4 hours
Makes: 8 servings

- ¼ cup all-purpose flour
- 2 lbs. boneless beef chuck roast, trimmed and cut into 1-in. cubes
- 2 Tbsp. canola oil
- 1 can (10¾ oz.) condensed tomato soup, undiluted
- 1 cup water or red wine
- 2 tsp. beef bouillon granules
- 3 tsp. Italian seasoning
- 1 bay leaf
- ½ tsp. coarsely ground pepper
- 6 white onions or yellow onions, quartered
- 4 medium potatoes, cut into 1½-in. slices
- 3 medium carrots, cut into 1-in. slices
- 12 large fresh mushrooms
- ½ cup sliced celery

1. Place flour in a large shallow dish. Add beef, a few pieces at a time, and turn to coat.
2. In a large skillet, brown the meat in oil in batches; drain. Transfer to a 5-qt. slow cooker. Combine the tomato soup, water or wine, bouillon and seasonings; pour over the beef. Add onions, potatoes, carrots, mushrooms and celery.
3. Cover and cook on low for 4-5 hours or until the meat is tender. Discard the bay leaf. Serve with noodles or French bread.
1 SERVING: 385 cal., 15g fat (5g sat. fat), 74mg chol., 416mg sod., 36g carb. (7g sugars, 5g fiber), 27g pro.

SPICY CHEESEBURGER SOUP

This creamy soup always brings my family to the table in a hurry. I love the warming zip of cayenne, but it also tastes terrific without it if you like milder flavor. With a few simple side dishes, this soup is a full meal.
—*Lisa Mast, White Cloud, MI*

- -

Prep: 15 min. • **Cook:** 30 min.
Makes: 8 servings (2 qt.)

- 1½ cups water
- 2 cups cubed peeled potatoes
- 2 small carrots, grated
- 1 small onion, chopped
- ¼ cup chopped green pepper
- 1 jalapeno pepper, seeded and chopped
- 1 garlic clove, minced
- 1 Tbsp. beef bouillon granules
- ½ tsp. salt
- 1 lb. ground beef, cooked and drained
- 2½ cups whole milk, divided
- 3 Tbsp. all-purpose flour
- 8 oz. cubed Velveeta
- ¼ to 1 tsp. cayenne pepper, optional
- ½ lb. sliced bacon, cooked and crumbled

1. In a large saucepan, combine the first 9 ingredients; bring to a boil. Reduce heat; cover and simmer for 15-20 minutes or until the potatoes are tender.
2. Stir in beef and 2 cups of milk; heat through. Combine flour and the remaining milk until smooth; gradually stir into soup. Bring to a boil; cook and stir for 2 minutes or until thickened and bubbly. Reduce heat; stir in cheese until melted. Add cayenne pepper if desired. Top with bacon just before serving.
NOTE: Wear disposable gloves when cutting hot peppers; the oils can burn skin exposed skin. Avoid touching your face.
1 CUP: 351 cal., 20g fat (10g sat. fat), 81mg chol., 1063mg sod., 19g carb. (7g sugars, 1g fiber), 22g pro.

BEEF & BLACK BEAN SOUP

I lead a busy life, so I'm always trying to come up with timesaving recipes. This zippy and colorful soup is one of my husband's favorites. It has been a hit at family gatherings, too.
—*Vickie Gibson, Gardendale, AL*

Prep: 10 min. • **Cook:** 6 hours
Makes: 10 servings (2½ qt.)

- 1 lb. lean ground beef (90% lean)
- 2 cans (14½ oz. each) chicken broth
- 1 can (14½ oz.) diced tomatoes, undrained
- 8 green onions, thinly sliced
- 3 medium carrots, thinly sliced
- 2 celery ribs, thinly sliced
- 2 garlic cloves, minced
- 1 Tbsp. sugar
- 1½ tsp. dried basil
- ½ tsp. salt
- ½ tsp. dried oregano
- ½ tsp. ground cumin
- ½ tsp. chili powder
- 2 cans (15 oz. each) black beans, rinsed and drained
- 1½ cups cooked rice

In a skillet over medium heat, cook beef until no longer pink; drain. Transfer to a 5-qt. slow cooker. Add the next 12 ingredients. Cover and cook on high for 1 hour. Reduce heat to low; cook until the vegetables are tender, 4-5 hours. Add beans and rice; cook until heated through, about 1 hour longer.

1 CUP: 203 cal., 4g fat (2g sat. fat), 28mg chol., 630mg sod., 26g carb. (5g sugars, 5g fiber), 16g pro. **DIABETIC EXCHANGES:** 2 lean meat, 1 starch, 1 vegetable.

HUNGARIAN STEW

As the owner of a busy fitness center, I rely on a slow cooker many days to create nutritious meals for my family. This hearty stew feels reminiscent of the old days.
—*Susan Kain, Woodbine, MD*

Prep: 30 min. • **Cook:** 7 hours
Makes: 6 servings (2¼ qt.)

- 4 medium potatoes, cut into 1-in. cubes
- 2 medium onions, chopped
- 1 lb. beef stew meat, cut into 1-in. cubes
- 2 Tbsp. canola oil
- 1½ cups water
- 3 tsp. paprika
- 1 tsp. salt
- 1 tsp. caraway seeds
- 1 tsp. tomato paste
- 1 garlic clove, minced
- 2 medium green peppers, cut into 1-in. pieces
- 2 medium tomatoes, peeled, seeded and chopped
- 3 Tbsp. all-purpose flour
- 3 Tbsp. cold water
- ½ cup sour cream

1. Place potatoes and onions in a 3-qt. slow cooker. In a large skillet, brown meat in oil on all sides. Place over the potato mixture.
2. Pour off excess fat from skillet. Add water to the drippings, stirring to loosen browned bits from pan; heat through. Stir in paprika, salt, caraway seeds, tomato paste and garlic. Pour into the slow cooker. Cover and cook on low for 6-8 hours.
3. Add green peppers and tomatoes; cover and cook 1 hour longer or until the meat and vegetables are tender. With a slotted spoon, transfer meat and vegetables to a large serving bowl; cover and keep warm.
4. Pour the cooking juices into a small saucepan. Combine flour and cold water until smooth; gradually whisk into the pan. Bring to a boil; cook and stir for 2 minutes or until thickened. Remove from the heat; whisk in sour cream. Stir into meat mixture.

1½ CUPS: 358 cal., 14g fat (5g sat. fat), 60mg chol., 446mg sod., 39g carb. (8g sugars, 5g fiber), 20g pro.

QUICK GOLDEN SQUASH SOUP

This delectable soup feels like fall! Its golden color and rich, satisfying flavor have made it a favorite of mine—which is really amazing because I was convinced I didn't like squash until I tried this recipe.
—*Becky Ruff, McGregor, IA*

Takes: 30 min. • **Makes:** 6 servings (1½ qt.)

5	medium leeks (white portion only), sliced
2	Tbsp. butter
4	cups cubed peeled butternut squash
4	cups chicken broth
¼	tsp. dried thyme
¼	tsp. pepper
1¾	cups shredded cheddar cheese
¼	cup sour cream
1	green onion, thinly sliced

1. In a large saucepan, saute leeks in butter until tender. Stir in squash, broth, thyme and pepper. Bring to a boil. Reduce heat; cover and simmer 10-15 minutes or until the squash is tender. Cool slightly.

2. In a blender, cover and process the squash mixture in small batches until smooth; return all to the pan. Bring to a boil. Reduce heat to low. Add cheese; stir until soup is heated through and the cheese is melted. Garnish with sour cream and onion.

1 CUP: 294 cal., 18g fat (10g sat. fat), 48mg chol., 922mg sod., 26g carb. (7g sugars, 4g fiber), 11g pro.

READER REVIEW

"I lighten this up by using light butter, reduced-fat cheddar and fat-free sour cream, and it is still delicious! Plus, it makes my house smell like Thanksgiving when it's cooking."

KIMICLARK777, TASTEOFHOME.COM

BECKY RUFF
McGregor, LA

PUMPKIN TURKEY CHILI

I love pumpkin and my husband loves chili. So I combined them into a dish we would both be happy about. It has also become a big hit with the rest of my family—they are always happy to see it at suppertime!

—*Catherine Walmsley, Phoenix, AZ*

Prep: 20 min. • **Cook:** 1¾ hours
Makes: 6 servings (2¼ qt.)

- 1 lb. ground turkey
- 1 medium sweet yellow pepper, chopped
- 1 medium onion, chopped
- 3 garlic cloves, minced
- 2 tsp. olive oil
- 2 cups chicken broth
- 1 can (15 oz.) kidney beans, rinsed and drained
- 1 can (15 oz.) black beans, rinsed and drained
- 1 can (15 oz.) solid-pack pumpkin
- 1 can (15 oz.) tomato sauce
- 4 medium tomatoes, chopped
- ⅔ cup chili sauce
- 3 Tbsp. brown sugar
- 1 Tbsp. dried oregano
- 1 Tbsp. dried parsley flakes
- 1 tsp. dried tarragon
- ¾ tsp. salt
- ¾ tsp. pepper
  Dash crushed red pepper flakes
  Dash cayenne pepper

In a Dutch oven, cook the turkey, pepper, onion and garlic in oil over medium heat until the meat is no longer pink; drain. Stir in the remaining ingredients. Bring to a boil. Reduce heat; simmer, uncovered, for 1½ hours or until the chili reaches desired thickness.

1½ CUPS: 422 cal., 13g fat (4g sat. fat), 53mg chol., 1695mg sod., 54g carb. (22g sugars, 12g fiber), 24g pro.

> **HEALTH TIP**
> Not all ground turkey is the same. If you want to save calories, look for labels that say ground turkey breast (instead of just ground turkey, which may contain light and dark meat) or lean ground turkey.

SANTA FE CHIPOTLE CHILI

Sausage and ground beef make this spiced-up chili a meat lover's delight. I also can freeze and reheat it later without sacrificing any flavor.

—*Angela Spengler, Niceville, FL*

Prep: 15 min. • **Cook:** 35 min.
Makes: 8 servings (3 qt.)

- 1 lb. ground beef
- 1 lb. bulk pork sausage
- 1 medium onion, chopped
- 2 cans (14½ oz. each) diced tomatoes, undrained
- 2 cans (15 oz. each) tomato sauce
- 2 cans (16 oz. each) kidney beans, rinsed and drained
- 1 cup frozen corn
- ¼ cup canned diced jalapeno peppers
- ¼ cup chili powder
- 1 chipotle pepper in adobo sauce, finely chopped
- 1 tsp. salt
  Optional toppings: Sour cream, shredded Monterey Jack cheese and crushed tortilla chips

1. In a 6-qt. stockpot, cook beef, sausage and onion over medium heat 8-10 minutes or until the beef and sausage are no longer pink and the onion is tender, breaking up the beef and sausage into crumbles; drain.

2. Add the tomatoes, tomato sauce, beans, corn, jalapeno peppers, chili powder, chipotle pepper and salt. Bring to a boil. Reduce heat; simmer, covered, 20-25 minutes or until heated through. Serve with optional toppings as desired.

NOTE: Wear disposable gloves when cutting hot peppers; the oils can burn exposed skin. Avoid touching your face.

1½ CUPS: 419 cal., 21g fat (6g sat. fat), 66mg chol., 1646mg sod., 36g carb. (8g sugars, 11g fiber), 27g pro.

ORZO SHRIMP STEW

My husband and I really enjoy seafood, so I don't skimp on shrimp in this mildly seasoned stew. We also adore the broccoli, tomatoes and pasta.

—*Lisa Stinger, Hamilton, NJ*

- -

Takes: 20 min. • **Makes:** 4 servings (1¾ qt.)

- 2½ cups reduced-sodium chicken broth
- 5 cups fresh broccoli florets
- 1 can (14½ oz.) diced tomatoes, undrained
- 1 cup uncooked orzo
- 1 lb. uncooked medium shrimp, peeled and deveined
- ¾ tsp. salt
- ¼ tsp. pepper
- 2 tsp. dried basil
- 2 Tbsp. butter

1. Bring broth to a boil in a Dutch oven. Add broccoli florets, tomatoes and orzo. Reduce the heat; simmer, uncovered, for 5 minutes, stirring occasionally.

2. Add the shrimp, salt and pepper. Cover and cook for 4-5 minutes or until the shrimp turn pink and orzo is tender. Stir in basil and butter.

1¾ CUPS: 401 cal., 10g fat (5g sat. fat), 190mg chol., 919mg sod., 45g carb. (0 sugars, 4g fiber), 35g pro. **DIABETIC EXCHANGES:** 3 lean meat, 2½ starch, 1 vegetable.

TEST KITCHEN TIP
To remove the black vein down the back of shrimp, make a shallow slit with a paring knife along the back from head to tail. Rinse under cold running water to remove the vein.

ZESTY BEEF STEW

Preparation couldn't be simpler for this hearty stew. I created the dish when I didn't have some of my usual ingredients for vegetable beef soup. My husband says it's the best I have ever made!

—*Margaret Turza, South Bend, IN*

- -

Prep: 10 min. • **Cook:** 3½ hours
Makes: 6 servings (1½ qt.)

- 1 lb. beef stew meat, cut into 1-in. cubes
- 1 pkg. (16 oz.) frozen mixed vegetables, thawed
- 1 can (15 oz.) pinto beans, rinsed and drained
- 1½ cups water
- 1 can (8 oz.) pizza sauce
- 2 Tbsp. medium pearl barley
- 1 Tbsp. dried minced onion
- 2 tsp. beef bouillon granules
- ¼ tsp. crushed red pepper flakes

In a 3-qt. slow cooker, combine all the ingredients. Cover and cook on low until the meat is tender, 3½-4½ hours.

1 CUP: 251 cal., 6g fat (2g sat. fat), 47mg chol., 526mg sod., 28g carb. (5g sugars, 8g fiber), 21g pro. **DIABETIC EXCHANGES:** 3 lean meat, 2 starch.

TOMATO HAMBURGER SOUP

As a full-time teacher, I only have time to cook from scratch a few nights each week. This recipe makes a big enough batch to feed my family for two nights. You can vary the flavor of this soup each time you make it by using different blends of frozen mixed vegetables.

—*Julie Kruger, St. Cloud, MN*

- -

Prep: 10 min. • **Cook:** 4 hours
Makes: 12 servings (3 qt.)

- 1 can (46 oz.) V8 juice
- 2 pkg. (16 oz. each) frozen mixed vegetables
- 1 lb. ground beef, cooked and drained
- 1 can (10¾ oz.) condensed cream of mushroom soup, undiluted
- 2 tsp. dried minced onion
  Salt and pepper to taste

In a 5-qt. slow cooker, combine the first 5 ingredients. Cover and cook on high for 4-5 hours or until heated through. Season with salt and pepper.

1 CUP: 125 cal., 5g fat (2g sat. fat), 20mg chol., 494mg sod., 12g carb. (5g sugars, 2g fiber), 9g pro.

SOUTHWESTERN PORK & SQUASH SOUP

I adapted a pork and squash stew recipe, using tomatoes and southwestern-style seasonings. My husband and sons loved it, and the leftovers were even better the next day! Try it with fresh corn muffins.

—*Molly Andersen, Portland, OR*

- -

Prep: 20 min. • **Cook:** 4 hours
Makes: 6 servings (2¼ qt.)

- 1 lb. pork tenderloin, cut into
    1-in. cubes
- 1 medium onion, chopped
- 1 Tbsp. canola oil
- 3 cups reduced-sodium chicken broth
- 1 medium butternut squash,
    peeled and cubed
- 2 medium carrots, sliced
- 1 can (14½ oz.) diced tomatoes with
    mild green chiles, undrained
- 1 Tbsp. chili powder
- 1 tsp. ground cumin
- 1 tsp. dried oregano
- ½ tsp. pepper
- ¼ tsp. salt

In a large skillet, brown pork and onion in oil; drain. Transfer to a 4- or 5-qt. slow cooker. Stir in the remaining ingredients. Cover and cook on low for 4-5 hours or until the meat is tender.

1½ CUPS: 220 cal., 5g fat (1g sat. fat), 42mg chol., 708mg sod., 26g carb. (10g sugars, 7g fiber), 19g pro. **DIABETIC EXCHANGES:** 4 vegetable, 2 lean meat, ½ fat.

ITALIAN SAUSAGE & BEAN STEW

The combo of sausage, beans and coleslaw may sound unusual, but it is comforting and delicious. The recipe doubles easily to serve a crowd.

—*Stacey Bennett, Locust Grove, VA*

- -

Takes: 30 min. • **Makes:** 6 servings (2 qt.)

- 1 lb. bulk hot Italian sausage
- 2 cans (15½ oz. each) great northern
    beans, rinsed and drained
- 1 pkg. (16 oz.) coleslaw mix
- 1 jar (24 oz.) garlic and herb
    spaghetti sauce
- 3 cups water

In a Dutch oven, cook sausage over medium heat until no longer pink; drain. Stir in the remaining ingredients. Bring to a boil. Reduce heat; simmer, uncovered, until flavors are blended, 16-20 minutes. Serve immediately or may be frozen for up to 3 months.

1⅓ CUPS: 416 cal., 21g fat (8g sat. fat), 53mg chol., 1411mg sod., 35g carb. (9g sugars, 12g fiber), 23g pro.

FREEZE OPTION: Freeze cooled soup in freezer containers. To use, partially thaw in refrigerator overnight. Transfer to a saucepan. Cover and cook stew over medium heat until heated through.

1¼ CUPS: 172 cal., 5g fat (1g sat. fat), 24mg chol., 1251mg sod., 20g carb. (7g sugars, 4g fiber), 12g pro.

MARGEE BERRY
White Salmon, WA

SEAFOOD GUMBO

Gumbo is one of the dishes that makes Louisiana cuisine famous. We live across the state line in Texas and can't get enough of this traditional Cajun dish that features sliced okra, shrimp, spicy seasonings and the "holy trinity"—onions, green peppers and celery. This recipe calls for seafood, but you could also use chicken, duck or sausage.
—*Ruth Aubey, San Antonio, TX*

- -

Prep: 20 min. • **Cook:** 30 min.
Makes: 24 servings (6 qt.)

- 1   cup all-purpose flour
- 1   cup canola oil
- 4   cups chopped onion
- 2   cups chopped celery
- 2   cups chopped green pepper
- 1   cup sliced green onion and tops
- 4   cups chicken broth
- 8   cups water
- 4   cups sliced okra
- 2   Tbsp. paprika
- 2   Tbsp. salt
- 2   tsp. oregano
- 1   tsp. ground black pepper
- 6   cups small shrimp, rinsed and drained, or seafood of your choice
- 1   cup minced fresh parsley
- 2   Tbsp. Cajun seasoning

1. In a heavy Dutch oven, combine flour and oil until smooth. Cook over medium-high heat for 5 minutes, stirring constantly. Reduce heat to medium. Cook and stir about 10 minutes more, or until the mixture is reddish brown.
2. Add onion, celery, green pepper and green onions; cook and stir for 5 minutes. Add chicken broth, water, okra, paprika, salt, oregano and pepper. Bring to boil; reduce heat and simmer, covered, for 10 minutes.
3. Add the shrimp and parsley. Simmer, uncovered, about 5 minutes more or until the seafood is done. Remove from heat; stir in Cajun seasoning.
1 CUP: 175 cal., 9g fat (1g sat. fat), 115mg chol., 1574mg sod., 10g carb. (3g sugars, 2g fiber), 12g pro.

TURKEY POSOLE

I love making this soup because it makes good use of leftover roasted turkey. It is quick, easy and tasty. No one feels as if they're eating leftovers because it tastes so different from traditional turkey with gravy.
—*Margee Berry, White Salmon, WA*

- -

Takes: 30 min. • **Makes:** 6 servings (1½ qt.)

- 2   cans (14½ oz. each) reduced-sodium chicken broth
- 1   jar (16 oz.) chunky salsa
- 1   can (15 oz.) hominy, rinsed and drained
- 2   tsp. chipotle hot pepper sauce
- ½   tsp. ground cumin
- 2   cups cubed cooked turkey breast
- ¼   cup sour cream
- ⅓   cup shredded cheddar or Monterey Jack cheese
- ⅓   cup minced fresh cilantro
- ⅓   cup crushed blue tortilla chips
- ¼   cup shredded red or green cabbage

In a large saucepan, combine the first 5 ingredients. Bring to a boil; reduce heat. Simmer, uncovered, 10 minutes. Stir in turkey; heat through. Top servings with sour cream, cheese, cilantro, tortilla chips and cabbage.
1 CUP: 193 cal., 5g fat (3g sat. fat), 53mg chol., 1080mg sod., 16g carb. (4g sugars, 2g fiber), 19g pro.

DID YOU KNOW?
Cilantro—also known as Chinese parsley—has a slightly sharp flavor that gives a distinctive taste to Mexican, Latin American and Asian dishes. The spice coriander comes from the seed of the cilantro plant.

SHRIMP GAZPACHO

Here's a refreshing take on the classic chilled tomato soup. Our twist features shrimp, lime and plenty of avocado. This recipe is best served the same day it's made.
—Taste of Home *Test Kitchen*

- -

Prep: 15 min. + chilling
Makes: 12 servings (3 qt.)

6	cups spicy hot V8 juice
2	cups cold water
½	cup lime juice
½	cup minced fresh cilantro
½	tsp. salt
¼	to ½ tsp. hot pepper sauce
1	lb. peeled and deveined cooked shrimp (31-40 per lb.), tails removed
1	medium cucumber, seeded and diced
2	medium tomatoes, seeded and chopped
2	medium ripe avocados, peeled and chopped

In a large nonreactive bowl, mix the first 6 ingredients. Gently stir in the remaining ingredients. Refrigerate, covered, 1 hour before serving.

1 CUP: 112 cal., 4g fat (1g sat. fat), 57mg chol., 399mg sod., 9g carb. (5g sugars, 3g fiber), 10g pro. **DIABETIC EXCHANGES:** 1 lean meat, 2 vegetable, 1 fat.

TEST KITCHEN TIP

Use nonreactive bowls when you're working with acidic ingredients such as tomatoes, citrus and chiles. Reactive metals—aluminum, iron and unlined copper—can give food a metallic flavor. Go for glass, ceramic, enamel or stainless steel.

SPINACH & TORTELLINI SOUP

My tomato-y broth is perfect for cheese tortellini and fresh spinach. Add extra garlic and Italian seasoning to suit your taste.
—*Debbie Wilson, Burlington, NC*

- -

Takes: 20 min. • **Makes:** 6 servings (2 qt.)

- 1 tsp. olive oil
- 2 garlic cloves, minced
- 1 can (14½ oz.) no-salt-added diced tomatoes, undrained
- 3 cans (14½ oz. each) vegetable broth
- 2 tsp. Italian seasoning
- 1 pkg. (9 oz.) refrigerated cheese tortellini
- 4 cups fresh baby spinach
  Shredded Parmesan cheese and freshly ground pepper

1. In a large saucepan, heat oil over medium heat. Add garlic; cook and stir 1 minute. Stir in tomatoes, broth and Italian seasoning; bring to a boil. Add tortellini; bring to a gentle boil. Cook, uncovered, just until the tortellini are tender, 7-9 minutes.

2. Stir in spinach. Sprinkle servings with cheese and pepper.

1⅓ CUPS: 164 cal., 5g fat (2g sat. fat), 18mg chol., 799mg sod., 25g carb. (4g sugars, 2g fiber), 7g pro.

SLOW-COOKER PEA SOUP

This slow-cooker soup is one of my favorite meals to make during a busy workweek. When I get home all I have to do add the milk, and supper is served!
—*Deanna Waggy, South Bend, IN*

- -

Prep: 10 min. • **Cook:** 4 hours
Makes: 9 servings (2¼ qt.)

- 1 pkg. (16 oz.) dried split peas
- 2 cups cubed fully cooked ham
- 1 cup diced carrots
- 1 medium onion, chopped
- 2 garlic cloves, minced
- 2 bay leaves
- ½ tsp. salt
- ½ tsp. pepper
- 5 cups boiling water
- 1 cup hot whole milk

In a 5-qt. slow cooker, layer first 9 ingredients in the order listed (do not stir). Cover and cook on high for 4-5 hours or until vegetables are tender. Stir in milk. Discard the bay leaves before serving.

1 CUP: 244 cal., 3g fat (1g sat. fat), 21mg chol., 537mg sod., 36g carb. (7g sugars, 14g fiber), 20g pro. **DIABETIC EXCHANGES:** 2½ starch, 2 lean meat.

SKILLET SOUTHWESTERN CHICKEN SOUP

This hearty soup is loaded with chicken, corn, black beans and diced tomatoes seasoned with zippy southwestern flavor. Mexican cornbread makes a delicious accompaniment.
—*Terri Stevens, Ardmore, OK*

Prep: 10 min. • **Cook:** 25 min.
Makes: 4 servings (1 qt.)

2   Tbsp. olive oil
½   lb. boneless skinless chicken breast, cut into ½-in. cubes
¼   cup finely chopped onion
2   garlic cloves, minced
1   can (15¼ oz.) whole-kernel corn, drained
1   can (15 oz.) black beans, rinsed and drained
1   can (14½ oz.) chicken broth
1   can (10 oz.) diced tomatoes and green chiles, undrained
1   tsp. ground cumin
½   tsp. salt
½   tsp. chili powder
⅛   tsp. cayenne pepper
    Optional: Plain yogurt and minced fresh cilantro

1. In a large skillet, heat oil over medium heat. Add chicken and onion; cook and stir for 5-6 minutes or until the chicken is no longer pink. Add garlic; cook 1 minute longer.
2. Stir in corn, beans, broth, tomatoes and seasonings. Bring to a boil. Reduce heat; simmer, covered, for 10-15 minutes to allow flavors to blend. Top individual servings with yogurt and cilantro if desired.
1 CUP: 302 cal., 9g fat (1g sat. fat), 31mg chol., 1106mg sod., 32g carb. (6g sugars, 7g fiber), 19g pro.

❄ MINESTRONE WITH TURKEY

I remember my mom making this soup; now I make it as often as I can. It's a good way to use up leftover vegetables. Sometimes I add a can of rinsed and drained kidney beans or garbanzo beans.
—*Angela Goodman, Kaneohe, HI*

Takes: 30 min. • **Makes:** 6 servings (2 qt.)

1   Tbsp. olive oil
1   medium onion, chopped
1   medium carrot, sliced
1   celery rib, sliced
1   garlic clove, minced
4   cups chicken broth or homemade turkey stock
1   can (14½ oz.) diced tomatoes, undrained
⅔   cup each frozen peas, corn and cut green beans, thawed
½   cup uncooked elbow macaroni
1   tsp. salt
¼   tsp. dried basil
¼   tsp. dried oregano
¼   tsp. pepper
1   bay leaf
1   cup cubed cooked turkey
1   small zucchini, halved lengthwise and cut into ¼-in. slices
¼   cup grated Parmesan cheese, optional

1. In a Dutch oven, heat oil over medium-high heat. Add onion, carrot and celery; cook and stir until tender. Add garlic; cook 1 minute longer. Add broth, vegetables, macaroni and seasonings. Bring to a boil.
2. Reduce heat; simmer, uncovered, 5 minutes or until the macaroni is al dente. Stir in cubed turkey and zucchini; cook until the zucchini is crisp-tender. Discard the bay leaf. If desired, sprinkle individual servings with cheese.
FREEZE OPTION: Transfer cooled soup to freezer container and freeze up to 3 months. To use, thaw in the refrigerator overnight. Transfer to a saucepan. Cover and cook over medium heat until heated through. Serve with cheese if desired.
1¼ CUPS: 172 cal., 5g fat (1g sat. fat), 24mg chol., 1251mg sod., 20g carb. (7g sugars, 4g fiber), 12g pro.

JAMAICAN-STYLE BEEF STEW

This delicious stew makes a hearty supper with a lighter touch. It's so flavorful, you won't want to stop at just one bowlful!
—*James Hayes, Ridgecrest, CA*

Prep: 25 min. • **Cook:** 1¼ hours
Makes: 5 servings (1¼ qt.)

- 1 Tbsp. canola oil
- 1 Tbsp. sugar
- 1½ lbs. beef top sirloin steak, cut into ¾-in. cubes
- 5 plum tomatoes, finely chopped
- 3 large carrots, cut into ½-in. slices
- 3 celery ribs, cut into ½-in. slices
- 4 green onions, chopped
- ¾ cup reduced-sodium beef broth
- ¼ cup barbecue sauce
- ¼ cup reduced-sodium soy sauce
- 2 Tbsp. steak sauce
- 1 Tbsp. garlic powder
- 1 tsp. dried thyme
- ¼ tsp. ground allspice
- ¼ tsp. pepper
- ⅛ tsp. hot pepper sauce
- 1 Tbsp. cornstarch
- 2 Tbsp. cold water
  Hot cooked rice or mashed potatoes, optional

1. In a Dutch oven, heat oil over medium-high heat. Add sugar; cook and stir until lightly browned, 1 minute. Add beef and brown on all sides.
2. Stir in the vegetables, broth, barbecue sauce, soy sauce, steak sauce and seasonings. Bring to a boil. Reduce heat; cover and simmer until the meat and vegetables are tender, 1-1¼ hours.
3. Combine cornstarch and water until smooth; stir into stew. Bring to a boil; cook and stir until thickened, about 2 minutes. If desired, serve with rice or mashed potatoes.
FREEZE OPTION: Freeze cooled stew in freezer containers. To use, partially thaw in refrigerator overnight. Heat through in a saucepan, stirring occasionally; adding water if necessary.
1 CUP: 285 cal., 9g fat (2g sat. fat), 56mg chol., 892mg sod., 18g carb. (10g sugars, 3g fiber), 32g pro.

TURKEY CHILI

I've taken my mother's milder recipe for chili and made it thicker and more robust. It's a favorite, especially in fall and winter.
—*Celesta Zanger, Bloomfield Hills, MI*

Prep: 20 min. • **Cook:** 6½ hours
Makes: 12 servings (3 qt.)

- 1 lb. lean ground turkey
- ¾ cup chopped celery
- ¾ cup chopped onion
- ¾ cup chopped green pepper
- 2 Tbsp. chili powder
- 1 tsp. ground cumin
- ¼ tsp. pepper
- ⅛ to ¼ tsp. cayenne pepper
- 2 cans (14½ oz. each) no-salt-added diced tomatoes, undrained
- 1 jar (24 oz.) meatless pasta sauce
- 1 can (16 oz.) hot chili beans, undrained
- 1½ cups water
- ½ cup frozen corn
- 1 can (16 oz.) kidney beans, rinsed and drained
- 1 can (15 oz.) pinto beans, rinsed and drained
  Optional toppings: Sour cream, cubed avocado, diced jalapeno peppers

1. In a large skillet, cook and crumble turkey with celery, onion and pepper over medium-high heat until the turkey is no longer pink, 6-8 minutes. Transfer to a 5-qt. slow cooker. Stir in seasonings, tomatoes, pasta sauce, chili beans, water and corn.
2. Cook, covered, on high for 1 hour. Reduce setting to low; cook, covered, until flavors are blended, 5-6 hours.
3. Stir in the kidney and pinto beans; cook, covered, on low 30 minutes longer. If desired, serve with sour cream, avocado and jalapeno.
1 CUP: 200 cal., 4g fat (1g sat. fat), 26mg chol., 535mg sod., 29g carb. (8g sugars, 8g fiber), 15g pro. **DIABETIC EXCHANGES:** 2 lean meat, 2 vegetable, 1 starch.

ZIPPY VEGETARIAN CHILI

Hominy, green chiles and garbanzo beans are deliciously different additions to my chili. No one will miss the meat in this satisfying recipe!
—*Karen Hunt, Bellvue, CO*

Prep: 10 min. • **Cook:** 30 min.
Makes: 12 servings (3 qt.)

- 2 cans (15 oz. each) pinto beans, rinsed and drained
- 1 can (28 oz.) crushed tomatoes
- 1 can (16 oz.) kidney beans, rinsed and drained
- 1 can (15½ oz.) hominy, rinsed and drained
- 1 can (15 oz.) garbanzo beans or chickpeas, rinsed and drained
- 1 can (6 oz.) tomato paste
- 1 can (4 oz.) chopped green chiles, undrained
- 2 small zucchini, halved and thinly sliced
- 1 medium onion, chopped
- 1½ to 2 cups water
- 1 to 2 Tbsp. chili powder
- 1 tsp. ground cumin
- 1 tsp. salt, optional
- ½ tsp. garlic powder
- ½ tsp. sugar
- ½ cup shredded Monterey Jack cheese Chopped green onions, optional

In a Dutch oven, combine first 15 ingredients. Bring to a boil. Reduce heat; cover and simmer for 30-35 minutes or until the vegetables are tender. Sprinkle with shredded cheese and, if desired, green onions.
1 CUP: 210 cal., 3g fat (1g sat. fat), 4mg chol., 524mg sod., 37g carb. (5g sugars, 9g fiber), 11g pro. **DIABETIC EXCHANGES:** 2 vegetable, 1½ starch, 1 lean meat.

DID YOU KNOW?

Hominy is dried corn that's been soaked in an alkaline solution. This improves the nutritional content of the corn and gives it a complex flavor and aroma. Look for it in the canned bean aisle.

MEXICAN CHICKEN CORN CHOWDER

I like to make this creamy soup when company comes to visit. Its zippy flavor is full of southwestern flair. Sometimes I top it with toasted strips of leftover tortillas.
—*Susan Garoutte, Georgetown, TX*

Takes: 30 min. • **Makes:** 8 servings (2 qt.)

- 1½ lbs. boneless skinless chicken breasts, cut into 1-in. pieces
- ½ cup chopped onion
- 3 Tbsp. butter
- 1 to 2 garlic cloves, minced
- 1 cup hot water
- 2 tsp. chicken bouillon granules
- ½ to 1 tsp. ground cumin
- 2 cups half-and-half cream
- 2 cups shredded Monterey Jack cheese
- 1 can (14¾ oz.) cream-style corn
- 1 can (4 oz.) chopped green chiles, undrained
- ¼ to 1 tsp. hot pepper sauce
- 1 medium tomato, chopped Optional toppings: Minced fresh cilantro and fried tortilla strips

1. In a Dutch oven, brown chicken and onion in butter until the chicken is no longer pink. Add garlic; cook for 1 minute longer. Add water, bouillon and cumin; bring to a boil. Reduce heat; cover and simmer for 5 minutes.
2. Stir in cream, cheese, corn, chiles and hot pepper sauce. Cook and stir over low heat until the cheese is melted; add tomato. If desired, top with cilantro and tortilla strips.
1 CUP: 368 cal., 21g fat (13g sat. fat), 114mg chol., 753mg sod., 14g carb. (5g sugars, 1g fiber), 28g pro.

HEARTY VEGETABLE LENTIL SOUP

My mother has diabetes, so I often prepare this healthy dish for her. I wanted a hearty soup that would hit the spot on cold autumn nights, so I paired the lentils with turkey bacon and a handful of spices.
—*Nicole Hopping, Pinole, CA*

- -

Prep: 15 min. • **Cook:** 45 min.
Makes: 6 servings (1½ qt.)

- 6 bacon strips, chopped
- 1 lb. red potatoes (about 3 medium), chopped
- 2 medium carrots, chopped
- 1 medium onion, chopped
- 6 garlic cloves, minced
- ¾ tsp. ground cumin
- ½ tsp. salt
- ½ tsp. rubbed sage
- ½ tsp. dried thyme
- ¼ tsp. pepper
- 1½ cups dried lentils, rinsed
- 4 cups chicken stock

1. In a large saucepan, cook the bacon over medium heat until crisp, stirring occasionally. Remove with a slotted spoon; drain on paper towels. Discard drippings, reserving 1 Tbsp. in pan. Add the potatoes, carrots and onion; cook and stir for 6-8 minutes or until the carrots and onion are tender. Add the garlic and seasonings; cook 1 minute longer.
2. Add lentils and stock; bring to a boil. Reduce heat; simmer, covered, 30-35 minutes or until the lentils and potatoes are tender. Top each individual serving with bacon.
1 CUP: 314 cal., 6g fat (2g sat. fat), 10mg chol., 708mg sod., 47g carb. (4g sugars, 17g fiber), 20g pro. **DIABETIC EXCHANGES:** 3 starch, 2 lean meat.

CHICKEN GNOCCHI PESTO SOUP

After tasting a delicious gnocchi soup at a restaurant, I created this tasty version at home.
—*Deanna Smith, Des Moines, IA*

- -

Takes: 25 min. • **Makes:** 4 servings (1½ qt.)

- 1 jar (15 oz.) roasted garlic Alfredo sauce
- 2 cups water
- 2 cups rotisserie chicken, roughly chopped
- 1 tsp. Italian seasoning
- ¼ tsp. salt
- ¼ tsp. pepper
- 1 pkg. (16 oz.) potato gnocchi
- 3 cups coarsley chopped fresh spinach
- 4 tsp. prepared pesto

In a saucepan, combine first 6 ingredients; bring to a gentle boil, stirring occasionally. Stir in the gnocchi and spinach; cook until gnocchi float, 3-8 minutes. Top servings with pesto.
1½ CUPS: 586 cal., 26g fat (11g sat. fat), 158mg chol., 1650mg sod., 56g carb. (3g sugars, 4g fiber), 31g pro

HAM & BEAN STEW

You need only five ingredients for this thick and flavorful stew. It's so easy to make and it's always a favorite with my family. I top bowls of it with a sprinkling of shredded cheese.
—*Teresa D'Amato, East Granby, CT*

- -

Prep: 5 min. • **Cook:** 7 hours
Makes: 6 servings (1½ qt.)

- 2 cans (16 oz. each) baked beans
- 2 medium potatoes, peeled and cubed
- 2 cups cubed fully cooked ham
- 1 celery rib, chopped
- ½ cup water

In a 3-qt. slow cooker, combine all ingredients; mix well. Cover and cook on low for 7 hours or until the potatoes are tender.
1 CUP: 213 cal., 5g fat (2g sat. fat), 30mg chol., 919mg sod., 29g carb. (6g sugars, 5g fiber), 14g pro.

CHICKPEA & POTATO CURRY

I make chana masala, the classic Indian dish, in my slow cooker. Browning the onion, ginger and garlic first really makes the sauce amazing.
—*Anjana Devasahayam, San Antonio, TX*

Prep: 25 min. • **Cook:** 6 hours
Makes: 6 servings

- 1 Tbsp. canola oil
- 1 medium onion, chopped
- 2 garlic cloves, minced
- 2 tsp. minced fresh gingerroot
- 2 tsp. ground coriander
- 1 tsp. garam masala
- 1 tsp. chili powder
- ½ tsp. salt
- ½ tsp. ground cumin
- ¼ tsp. ground turmeric
- 1 can (15 oz.) crushed tomatoes
- 2 cans (15 oz. each) chickpeas or garbanzo beans, rinsed and drained
- 1 large baking potato, peeled and cut into ¾-in. cubes
- 2½ cups vegetable stock
- 1 Tbsp. lime juice
  Chopped fresh cilantro
  Hot cooked rice
  Sliced red onion, optional
  Lime wedges, optional

1. In a large skillet, heat oil over medium-high heat; saute onion until tender, 2-4 minutes. Add garlic, ginger and dry seasonings; cook and stir 1 minute. Stir in tomatoes; transfer to a 3- or 4-qt. slow cooker.

2. Stir in chickpeas, potato and stock. Cook, covered, on low until potato is tender and flavors are blended, 6-8 hours.

3. Stir in the lime juice; sprinkle with cilantro. Serve with rice and, if desired, red onion and lime wedges.

1¼ CUPS CHICKPEA MIXTURE: 240 cal., 6g fat (0 sat. fat), 0 chol., 767mg sod., 42g carb. (8g sugars, 9g fiber), 8g pro.

PICO DE GALLO BLACK BEAN SOUP

Everyone at my table goes for this feel-good soup. It's a quick and tasty option when you're pressed for time and it beats fast food, hands down.
—*Darlis Wilfer, West Bend, WI*

Takes: 20 min.
Makes: 6 servings (about 2 qt.)

- 4 cans (15 oz. each) black beans, rinsed and drained
- 2 cups vegetable broth
- 2 cups pico de gallo
- ½ cup water
- 2 tsp. ground cumin
  Optional toppings: Chopped fresh cilantro and additional pico de gallo

1. In a Dutch oven, combine first 5 ingredients; bring to a boil over medium heat, stirring occasionally. Reduce heat; simmer, uncovered, until the vegetables in the pico de gallo are softened, about 5-7 minutes; stir occasionally.

2. Puree the soup using an immersion blender, or cool soup slightly and puree in batches in a blender. Return to pan and heat through. Serve with fresh cilantro and more pico de gallo, if desired.

FREEZE OPTION: Freeze cooled soup in freezer containers. To use, partially thaw in refrigerator overnight. Heat through in a saucepan, stirring occasionally; add broth or water if necessary. Top as desired.

1¼ CUPS: 241 cal., 0 fat (0 sat. fat), 0 chol., 856mg sod., 44g carb. (4g sugars, 12g fiber), 14g pro.

SLOW-COOKED CHUNKY CHILI

Pork sausage, ground beef and plenty of beans make this chili a marvelous meal. I keep serving-size containers of it in my freezer at all times so I can quickly warm up bowls on busy days.
—*Margie Shaw, Greenbrier, AR*

Prep: 15 min. • **Cook:** 4 hours
Makes: 12 servings (3 qt.)

- 1 **lb. ground beef**
- 1 **lb. bulk pork sausage**
- 4 **cans (16 oz. each) kidney beans, rinsed and drained**
- 2 **cans (14½ oz. each) diced tomatoes, undrained**
- 2 **cans (10 oz. each) diced tomatoes and green chiles, undrained**
- 1 **large onion, chopped**
- 1 **medium green pepper, chopped**
- 1 **envelope taco seasoning**
- ½ **tsp. salt**
- ¼ **tsp. pepper**
   Optional: Shredded cheddar cheese, chopped red onion and sour cream

1. In a large skillet, cook beef and sausage over medium heat until the meat is no longer pink; drain. Transfer to a 5-qt. slow cooker. Stir in the remaining ingredients.
2. Cover and cook on high for 4-5 hours or until vegetables are tender. If desired, serve with cheese, onions and sour cream.
FREEZE OPTION: Before adding toppings, cool chili. Freeze chili and toppings separately in freezer containers. To use, partially thaw in refrigerator overnight. Heat through in a saucepan, stirring occasionally and adding a little water if necessary. Sprinkle with toppings.
1 CUP: 329 cal., 13g fat (4g sat. fat), 44mg chol., 1158mg sod., 33g carb. (5g sugars, 9g fiber), 21g pro.

CREAMY RED PEPPER SOUP

Everyone loves this soup, but no one ever guesses that pears are the secret ingredient!
—*Connie Summers, Augusta, MI*

Prep: 15 min. • **Cook:** 30 min. + cooling
Makes: 12 servings (3 qt.)

- 2 **large onions, chopped**
- ¼ **cup butter, cubed**
- 4 **garlic cloves, minced**
- 2 **large potatoes, peeled and diced**
- 2 **jars (7 oz. each) roasted red peppers, drained, patted dry and chopped**
- 5 **cups chicken broth**
- 2 **cans (15 oz. each) pears in juice**
- ⅛ **tsp. cayenne pepper**
- ⅛ **tsp. black pepper**
   Optional: Chopped chives, heavy cream and croutons

1. In a Dutch oven, saute onions in butter until tender. Add garlic; cook 1 minute longer. Add potatoes, red peppers and broth. Bring to a boil. Reduce heat; cover and simmer for 15-20 minutes or until the vegetables are tender. Remove from the heat. Add pears; let cool.
2. In a blender, cover and puree the soup in batches. Return to the pan. Stir in cayenne and black pepper. Cook until heated through. If desired, serve with chopped chives, heavy cream and croutons.
1 CUP: 127 cal., 4g fat (2g sat. fat), 10mg chol., 494mg sod., 20g carb. (9g sugars, 2g fiber), 3g pro.

VEGGIE SALMON CHOWDER

I wanted to use up odds and ends in my fridge (waste not, want not!) and came up with this chowder. I thought others might enjoy a recipe that began as an experiment but became a mainstay for me.
—*Liv Vors, Peterborough, ON*

Takes: 30 min. • **Makes:** 2 servings

- 1   medium sweet potato, peeled and cut into ½-in. cubes
- 1   cup reduced-sodium chicken broth
- ½   cup fresh or frozen corn
- ½   small onion, chopped
- 2   garlic cloves, minced
- 1½ cups fresh spinach, torn
- ½   cup flaked smoked salmon fillet
- 1   tsp. pickled jalapeno slices, chopped
- 1   Tbsp. cornstarch
- ½   cup 2% milk
- 1   Tbsp. minced fresh cilantro
       Dash pepper

1. In a large saucepan, combine the first 5 ingredients; bring to a boil. Reduce heat; simmer, covered, 8-10 minutes or until the potato is tender.

2. Stir in spinach, salmon and jalapeno; cook 1-2 minutes or until the spinach is wilted. In a small bowl, mix cornstarch and milk until smooth; stir into the soup. Bring to a boil; cook and stir 2 minutes or until thickened. Stir in cilantro and pepper.

1¼ CUPS: 202 cal., 3g fat (1g sat. fat), 12mg chol., 645mg sod., 32g carb. (11g sugars, 4g fiber), 13g pro. **DIABETIC EXCHANGES:** 2 starch, 1 lean meat, 1 vegetable.

Weeknight Favorite

OVEN ENTREES

Fire up the oven! From casseroles to potpies, and mac & cheese to Mexican-inspired meals, adding these recipes to your lineup will make your weeknight dinners sure to impress.

ERIN CHILCOAT
Central Islip, NY

BALSAMIC ROASTED CHICKEN THIGHS WITH ROOT VEGETABLES

I will never forget the way my grandmother's house smelled when she made this chicken every Sunday. She gave me the recipe, and the heartwarming flavors always take me back to my childhood.
—*Erin Chilcoat, Central Islip, NY*

Prep: 15 min. + marinating • **Bake:** 35 min.
Makes: 6 servings

4	Tbsp. olive oil, divided
3	Tbsp. stone-ground mustard
2	Tbsp. balsamic vinaigrette
¾	tsp. kosher salt, divided
¾	tsp. freshly ground pepper, divided
6	bone-in chicken thighs (about 2¼ lbs.)
4	medium parsnips, peeled and cut into ½-in. pieces
1	medium sweet potato, peeled and cut into ½-in. pieces
4	shallots, chopped
¼	tsp. caraway seeds
4	Tbsp. minced fresh parsley, divided
3	bacon strips, cooked and crumbled, divided

1. In a bowl, whisk 3 Tbsp. olive oil, mustard, vinaigrette and ½ tsp. each salt and pepper until blended. Add chicken, turning to coat. Refrigerate, covered, 6 hours or overnight.
2. Preheat oven to 425°. Place chicken, skin side up, on half of a greased 15x101-in. baking pan. Place parsnips and sweet potato in a large bowl; add the shallots, caraway seeds and the remaining oil, salt and pepper and toss to combine. Arrange in a single layer on the remaining half of pan.
3. Roast chicken and vegetables 20 minutes. Stir the vegetables; roast 15-20 minutes longer or until a thermometer inserted in chicken reads 170°-175° and vegetables are tender.
4. Transfer the vegetables to a bowl; toss with 2 Tbsp. parsley and half the bacon. Serve the chicken with vegetables; sprinkle with the remaining parsley and bacon.
1 SERVING: 480 cal., 27g fat (6g sat. fat), 85mg chol., 604mg sod., 33g carb. (10g sugars, 5g fiber), 27g pro.

🍎
DIJON-CRUSTED FISH

Dijon, Parmesan and a hint of horseradish give this toasty fish lots of flavor. The preparation is so easy, it takes just 5 to 7 minutes to get all four servings ready for the oven.
—*Scott Schmidtke, Chicago, IL*

- -

Takes: 25 min. • **Makes:** 4 servings

- 3 Tbsp. reduced-fat mayonnaise
- 1 Tbsp. lemon juice
- 2 tsp. Dijon mustard
- 1 tsp. prepared horseradish
- 2 Tbsp. grated Parmesan cheese, divided
- 4 tilapia fillets (5 oz. each)
- ¼ cup dry bread crumbs
- 2 tsp. butter, melted

1. Preheat oven to 425°. Mix first 4 ingredients and 1 Tbsp. cheese. Place tilapia on a baking sheet coated with cooking spray; spread evenly with mayonnaise mixture.
2. Toss bread crumbs with melted butter and the remaining cheese; sprinkle over fillets.

Bake until the fish just begins to flake easily with a fork, 12-15 minutes.

1 FILLET: 214 cal., 8g fat (3g sat. fat), 80mg chol., 292mg sod., 7g carb. (1g sugars, 1g fiber), 28g pro. **DIABETIC EXCHANGES:** 4 lean meat, 1½ fat, ½ starch.

> **HEALTH TIP**
> Tilapia is low in calories, rich in high-quality protein and a good source of many B vitamins.

CHICKEN ENCHILADAS FOR FOUR

These enchiladas put zip into any menu. The tortillas are filled with cheese, chicken and green chiles and then topped with a creamy sauce—and more cheese! I sometimes use leftover turkey instead of chicken.
—*Karen Bourne, Magrath, AB*

- -

Takes: 30 min. • **Makes:** 4 servings

- 2 Tbsp. butter
- ¼ cup all-purpose flour
- 2½ cups chicken broth
- 1 tsp. dried coriander
- 1 can (4 oz.) chopped green chiles, divided
- 2 cups cubed cooked chicken
- 1 cup shredded Monterey Jack cheese
- 8 flour tortillas (8 in.), warmed
- 1 cup shredded cheddar cheese

1. Preheat oven to 375°. Melt butter in a large saucepan. Stir in flour until smooth. Gradually add broth. Bring to a boil; cook and stir for 2 minutes or until thickened. Stir in coriander and half of the chiles. In a large bowl, combine the chicken, Monterey Jack cheese and the remaining chilies.
2. Spoon ⅓ cup of the chicken mixture onto each tortilla; roll up. Place seam side down in an ungreased 13x9-in. baking dish. Pour sauce over the enchiladas. Sprinkle with shredded cheddar cheese.
3. Bake, uncovered, until heated through and the cheese is melted, 15-18 minutes.

2 ENCHILADAS: 767 cal., 36g fat (18g sat. fat), 134mg chol., 1654mg sod., 64g carb. (1g sugars, 4g fiber), 44g pro.

CHEESY BEEF CASSEROLE

My noodle bake has the flavor of a lasagna without all the effort. The meaty casserole makes a satisfying meal when served with a green salad and garlic bread.
—*Ardyce Piehl, Poynette, WI*

Prep: 20 min. • **Bake:** 30 min.
Makes: 6 servings

- 4 cups uncooked medium egg noodles
- 1 lb. ground beef
- ¾ cup chopped onion
- 2 cans (8 oz. each) tomato sauce
- ½ tsp. garlic powder
- ½ tsp. salt
- ¼ tsp. pepper
- 1 pkg. (8 oz.) cream cheese, softened
- 1 cup 4% cottage cheese
- ½ cup grated Parmesan cheese
- ⅓ cup sliced green onions
- ¼ cup chopped green pepper
  Additional Parmesan cheese, optional

1. Preheat oven to 350°. Cook the noodles according to package directions. Meanwhile, in a large skillet, cook the beef and onion over medium heat until the meat is no longer pink; drain. Add tomato sauce, garlic powder, salt and pepper.
2. In a large bowl, combine the cream cheese, cottage cheese, Parmesan cheese, onions and green pepper. Drain the noodles; place half in a greased 13x9-in. baking dish. Top with half each of the meat and cheese mixtures. Repeat layers. Sprinkle with additional Parmesan cheese if desired.
3. Cover and bake for 30-35 minutes or until heated through.
1 CUP: 468 cal., 27g fat (14g sat. fat), 129mg chol., 783mg sod., 26g carb. (5g sugars, 2g fiber), 30g pro.

BUSY-DAY PORK CHOPS

I created this recipe one day when I had pork chops and needed to find a simple way to make them. It was so easy and the response was a rave review! They're crispy on the outside, even though the preparation technique uses less fat.
—*Dee Maltby, Wayne, OH*

Takes: 25 min. • **Makes:** 4 servings

- ¼ cup fat-free milk
- ¼ cup seasoned bread crumbs
- ¼ cup grated Parmesan cheese
- ¼ tsp. salt
- ¼ tsp. garlic powder
- ⅛ tsp. pepper
- 4 boneless pork loin chops (4 oz. each)
  Cooking spray

1. Preheat oven to 375°. Place milk in a shallow bowl. In another shallow bowl, toss the bread crumbs with cheese and seasonings.
2. Dip the pork chops in milk, then coat with crumb mixture. Place on a baking sheet coated with cooking spray; lightly spritz chops with cooking spray.
3. Bake for 8-10 minutes on each side or until a thermometer reads 145°. Let stand 5 minutes before serving.
1 PORK CHOP: 178 cal., 7g fat (3g sat. fat), 57mg chol., 207mg sod., 3g carb. (0 sugars, 0 fiber), 23g pro. **DIABETIC EXCHANGES:** 3 lean meat.

CAPRESE CHICKEN

I love a Caprese salad of tomatoes, basil and cheese, so why not use them with chicken? You can grill this dish, but my family agrees that it's juicier straight from the oven.
—*Dana Johnson, Scottsdale, AZ*

- -

Prep: 10 min. + marinating • **Bake:** 20 min.
Makes: 4 servings

- ⅔ cup Italian salad dressing
- 2 tsp. chicken seasoning
- 2 tsp. Italian seasoning
- 4 boneless skinless chicken breast halves (6 oz. each)
- 2 Tbsp. canola oil
- ½ lb. fresh mozzarella cheese, cut into 4 slices
- 2 medium tomatoes, sliced
- 1 Tbsp. balsamic vinegar or balsamic glaze
  Torn fresh basil leaves

1. In a large shallow dish, combine salad dressing, chicken seasoning and Italian seasoning. Add the chicken; turn to coat. Cover and refrigerate 4-6 hours. Drain chicken, discarding marinade.

2. Preheat oven to 450°. In an ovenproof skillet, heat oil over medium-high heat. Brown chicken on both sides. Transfer skillet to oven; bake 15-18 minutes or until a thermometer reads 165°.

3. Top each chicken breast half with cheese and tomato. Bake 3-5 minutes longer or until the cheese is melted. Drizzle with the vinegar; top with basil.

1 SERVING: 525 cal., 34g fat (11g sat. fat), 139mg chol., 761mg sod., 5g carb. (4g sugars, 1g fiber), 45g pro.

DANA JOHNSON
Scottsdale, AZ

🗊
AFRICAN CHICKEN & SWEET POTATOES

I came up with this when I combined some of my favorite ingredients: sweet potatoes, chicken and peanut butter. It's a fantastic busy-week recipe.
—*Devon Delaney, Westport, CT*

- -

Prep: 10 min. • **Bake:** 40 min.
Makes: 6 servings

- 6 bone-in chicken thighs (about 2¼ lbs.)
- ½ tsp. salt
- ¼ tsp. pepper
- 2 Tbsp. canola oil
- 2 medium sweet potatoes, peeled and finely chopped (about 4 cups)
- ½ cup mango chutney
- ¼ cup creamy peanut butter
- 1 can (10 oz.) diced tomatoes and green chiles, undrained

1. Preheat oven to 375°. Place the chicken in a greased 13x9-in. baking dish; sprinkle with salt and pepper. Bake, uncovered, 30 minutes.

2. Meanwhile, in a large skillet, heat oil over medium-high heat. Add sweet potatoes; cook and stir for 10-12 minutes or until tender. In a small bowl, mix chutney and peanut butter; stir into sweet potatoes. Add the tomatoes; heat through.

3. Spoon the potato-chutney mixture over the chicken. Bake 10-15 minutes longer or until a thermometer inserted in chicken reads 170°-175°.

1 CHICKEN THIGH WITH ½ CUP POTATO MIXTURE: 480 cal., 24g fat (5g sat. fat), 81mg chol., 733mg sod., 38g carb. (19g sugars, 3g fiber), 26g pro.

TILAPIA WITH CORN SALSA

My family loves fish, and this super fast and delicious dish is popular at my house. Though it tastes like it takes a long time to make, it actually cooks in just minutes under the broiler. We like it garnished with lemon wedges with couscous on the side.
—*Brenda Coffey, Singer Island, FL*

Takes: 10 min. • **Makes:** 4 servings

- 4 tilapia fillets (6 oz. each)
- 1 Tbsp. olive oil
- ¼ tsp. salt
- ¼ tsp. pepper
- 1 can (15 oz.) black beans, rinsed and drained
- 1 can (11 oz.) whole kernel corn, drained
- ½ cup Italian salad dressing
- 2 Tbsp. chopped green onion
- 2 Tbsp. chopped sweet red pepper

1. Drizzle both sides of fillets with oil; sprinkle with salt and pepper.
2. Broil 4-6 in. from the heat until fish flakes easily with a fork, 5-7 minutes.
3. Meanwhile, in a small bowl, combine the remaining ingredients. Serve with the fish.
1 FILLET WITH ¾ CUP SALSA: 354 cal., 10g fat (2g sat. fat), 83mg chol., 934mg sod., 25g carb. (7g sugars, 6g fiber), 38g pro.

PINWHEEL STEAK POTPIE

On cool nights, nothing hits the spot like a steaming homemade potpie—I especially love this one for its relatively easy preparation.
—*Kristin Shaw, Castleton, NY*

Prep: 25 min. • **Bake:** 20 min.
Makes: 6 servings

- 2 Tbsp. butter
- 1¼ lbs. beef top sirloin steak, cut into ½-in. cubes
- ¼ tsp. pepper
- 1 pkg. (16 oz.) frozen vegetables for stew
- 2 Tbsp. water
- ½ tsp. dried thyme
- 1 jar (12 oz.) mushroom or beef gravy
- 1 tube (8 oz.) refrigerated crescent rolls

1. Preheat oven to 375°. In a 10-in. cast-iron or other ovenproof skillet, heat butter over medium-high heat. Brown beef in batches; remove from pan. Sprinkle with pepper; keep warm.
2. In the same skillet, combine vegetables, water and thyme; stir in gravy. Bring to a boil. Reduce heat; simmer, uncovered, until the vegetables are thawed. Stir in the beef; remove from heat.
3. Unroll crescent dough and separate into 8 triangles. Starting from the wide end of each triangle, roll up a third of the length and place over the beef mixture with the pointed ends toward the center.
4. Bake, uncovered, until golden brown, 16-18 minutes.
1 SERVING: 365 cal., 18g fat (6g sat. fat), 67mg chol., 716mg sod., 29g carb. (4g sugars, 1g fiber), 22g pro.

BROWN SUGAR-GLAZED SALMON

Pop these protein-packed salmon fillets in the oven before whipping up the basting sauce. This tangy entree cooks in minutes, so it's ideal for busy families and unexpected guests.
—*Debra Martin, Belleville, MI*

- -

Takes: 25 min. • **Makes:** 4 servings

- 1   **salmon fillet (1 lb.)**
- ¼   **tsp. salt**
- ¼   **tsp. pepper**
- 3   **Tbsp. brown sugar**
- 4   **tsp. Dijon mustard**
- 1   **Tbsp. reduced-sodium soy sauce**
- 1   **tsp. rice vinegar**

1. Preheat oven to 425°. Cut salmon into 4 portions; place in a foil-lined 15x10x1-in. pan. Sprinkle with salt and pepper. Roast for 10 minutes. Remove from oven; preheat the broiler.

2. In a small saucepan, mix the remaining ingredients; bring just to a boil. Brush over salmon. Broil 6 in. from heat until fish just begins to flake easily with a fork, 1-2 minutes.

3 OZ. COOKED SALMON: 225 cal., 10g fat (2g sat. fat), 57mg chol., 491mg sod., 11g carb. (10g sugars, 0 fiber), 19g pro. **DIABETIC EXCHANGES:** 3 lean meat, 1 starch.

DEVILED CHICKEN

My family has always loved this flavorful golden-brown chicken. I watch for frequent sales on leg quarters to keep the cost per serving low.
—*Linda Trammell, Kingston, MO*

- -

Prep: 10 min. • **Bake:** 50 min.
Makes: 6 servings

- 6   **chicken leg quarters**
- ¼   **cup butter, melted**
- 1   **Tbsp. lemon juice**
- 1   **Tbsp. prepared mustard**
- 1   **tsp. salt**
- 1   **tsp. paprika**
- ¼   **tsp. pepper**

1. Preheat oven to 375°. Place chicken in a 15x10x1-in. baking pan. In a small bowl, combine the remaining ingredients. Pour over chicken.

2. Bake, uncovered, 50-60 minutes or until a thermometer reads 170°-175°, basting occasionally with pan juices.

1 LEG QUARTER: 345 cal., 24g fat (9g sat. fat), 125mg chol., 567mg sod., 1g carb. (0 sugars, 0 fiber), 30g pro.

CHILI-STUFFED POBLANO PEPPERS

While exploring Mexican restaurants, I tasted chiles rellenos and wanted to make them at home. My husband and I teamed up to create this new favorite recipe.
—*Lorrie Grabczynski,*
Commerce Township, MI

Takes: 30 min. • **Makes:** 4 servings

- 1 **lb. lean ground turkey**
- 1 **can (15 oz.) chili without beans**
- ¼ **tsp. salt**
- 1½ **cups shredded Mexican cheese blend, divided**
- 1 **medium tomato, finely chopped**
- 4 **green onions, chopped**
- 4 **large poblano peppers**
- 1 **Tbsp. olive oil**

1. Preheat the broiler. In a large skillet over medium heat, cook turkey, crumbling meat, until no longer pink, 5-7 minutes; drain. Add chili and salt; heat through. Stir in ½ cup cheese, the tomato and green onions.

2. Cut peppers lengthwise in half; remove seeds. Place on a foil-lined 15x10x1-in. baking pan, cut side down; brush with oil. Broil 4 in. from heat until skins blister, about 5 minutes.

3. With tongs, turn peppers. Fill with turkey mixture; sprinkle with remaining cheese. Broil until cheese is melted, 1-2 minutes longer.

NOTE: Wear disposable gloves when cutting hot peppers; the oils can burn skin. Avoid touching your face.

2 STUFFED PEPPER HALVES: 496 cal., 30g fat (11g sat. fat), 134mg chol., 913mg sod., 17g carb. (5g sugars, 4g fiber), 40g pro.

READER REVIEW

"My family loved this recipe. We added a half pound of chorizo for a little extra heat. This dish is fast, easy and delicious!"

SHARI, TASTEOFHOME.COM

TOMATO-BASIL BAKED FISH

This recipe can be made with different kinds of fish as desired, and I usually have the rest of the ingredients on hand. Baked fish is wonderful, and I fix this healthy dish often.
—Annie Hicks, Zephyrhills, FL

Takes: 15 min. • **Makes:** 2 servings

- 1 Tbsp. lemon juice
- 1 tsp. olive oil
- 8 oz. red snapper, cod or haddock fillets
- ¼ tsp. dried basil
- ⅛ tsp. salt
- ⅛ tsp. pepper
- 2 plum tomatoes, thinly sliced
- 2 tsp. grated Parmesan cheese

1. Preheat oven to 400°. In a shallow bowl, combine lemon juice and oil. Add fish fillets; turn to coat. Place in a greased 9-in. pie plate. Sprinkle with half the basil, salt and pepper. Arrange tomatoes over top; sprinkle with cheese and the remaining seasonings.
2. Cover and bake for 10-12 minutes or until the fish flakes easily with a fork.

1 SERVING: 121 cal., 4g fat (1g sat. fat), 24mg chol., 256mg sod., 4g carb. (2g sugars, 1g fiber), 18g pro. **DIABETIC EXCHANGES:** 3 lean meat, 1 vegetable, ½ fat.

GARLIC BEEF ENCHILADAS

We prefer flour tortillas in this saucy enchilada casserole with a subtle kick.
—Jennifer Standridge, Dallas, GA

Prep: 30 min. • **Bake:** 40 min.
Makes: 5 servings

- 1 lb. ground beef
- 1 medium onion, chopped
- 2 Tbsp. all-purpose flour
- 1 Tbsp. chili powder
- 1 tsp. salt
- 1 tsp. garlic powder
- ½ tsp. ground cumin
- ¼ tsp. rubbed sage
- 1 can (14½ oz.) stewed tomatoes, cut up

SAUCE
- ⅓ cup butter
- 4-6 garlic cloves, minced
- ½ cup all-purpose flour
- 1 can (14½ oz.) beef broth
- 1 can (15 oz.) tomato sauce
- 1-2 Tbsp. chili powder
- 1-2 tsp. ground cumin
- 1-2 tsp. rubbed sage
- ½ tsp. salt
- 10 flour tortillas (6 inches), warmed
- 2 cups shredded Colby-Monterey Jack cheese, divided

Optional toppings: Halved grape tomatoes, minced fresh cilantro, sliced jalapeno peppers and chopped or sliced medium red onion

1. Preheat oven to 350°. In a large skillet, cook beef and onion over medium heat, crumbling meat, until beef is no longer pink, 6-8 minutes; drain. Stir in the flour and seasonings. Add the stewed tomatoes; bring to a boil. Reduce heat; simmer, covered, 15 minutes.
2. In a saucepan, heat butter over medium-high heat. Add garlic; cook and stir 1 minute or until tender. Stir in the flour until blended; gradually whisk in broth. Bring to a boil; cook and stir until thickened, about 2 minutes. Stir in tomato sauce and seasonings; heat through.
3. Pour 1½ cups sauce into an ungreased 13x9-in. baking dish. Place about ¼ cup of the beef mixture off center on each tortilla; top with 1-2 tablespoons cheese. Roll up and place over sauce, seam side down. Top with the remaining sauce.
4. Bake, covered, until heated through, 30-35 minutes. Sprinkle with the remaining cheese. Bake, uncovered, until the cheese is melted, 10-15 minutes longer. Serve with toppings as desired.

2 ENCHILADAS: 751 cal., 43g fat (21g sat. fat), 128mg chol., 2536mg sod., 56g carb. (8g sugars, 4g fiber), 38g pro.

CASHEW CHICKEN CASSEROLE

I like this dish because I can get it ready the day before I need it. It's easy to whip up with common pantry items, including macaroni, canned soup and saltine crackers.
—*Julie Ridlon, Solway, MN*

Prep: 15 min. + chilling • **Bake:** 35 min.
Makes: 8 servings

- 2 cups uncooked elbow macaroni
- 3 cups cubed cooked chicken
- ½ cup Velveeta
- 1 small onion, chopped
- ½ cup chopped celery
- ½ cup chopped green pepper
- 1 can (8 oz.) sliced water chestnuts, drained
- 1 can (10¾ oz.) condensed cream of mushroom soup, undiluted
- 1 can (10¾ oz.) condensed cream of chicken soup, undiluted
- 1⅓ cups whole milk
- 1 can (14½ oz.) chicken broth
- ¼ cup butter, melted
- ⅔ cup crushed saltines (about 20 crackers)
- ¾ cup cashew halves

1. In a greased 13x9-in. baking dish, layer the first 7 ingredients in the order listed. In a large bowl, combine the soups, milk and broth. Pour over the water chestnuts. Cover and refrigerate overnight.
2. Preheat oven to 350°. Toss butter and cracker crumbs; sprinkle over casserole. Top with cashews. Bake, uncovered, for 35-40 minutes or until macaroni is tender.
1¼ CUPS: 464 cal., 25g fat (9g sat. fat), 79mg chol., 1095mg sod., 36g carb. (6g sugars, 4g fiber), 24g pro.

TURKEY BUNDLES

For this must-try recipe, just bundle up creamy turkey filling in crescent dough. Double the recipe to have enough for lunch the next day!
—*Lydia Garrod, Tacoma, WA*

Takes: 30 min. • **Makes:** 6 servings

- 4 oz. cream cheese, softened
- 2 Tbsp. whole milk
- ½ tsp. dill weed
- ¼ tsp. celery salt
- ¼ tsp. pepper
- 2 cups cubed cooked turkey
- ¼ cup chopped water chestnuts
- 1 green onion, chopped
- 2 tubes (one 8 oz., one 4 oz.) refrigerated crescent rolls
- 2 Tbsp. butter, melted
- 2 Tbsp. seasoned bread crumbs

1. Preheat oven to 375°. In a large bowl, beat the first 5 ingredients until smooth. Stir in the turkey, water chestnuts and green onion.
2. Unroll both tubes of crescent dough and separate the dough into 6 rectangles; press perforations to seal. Place ⅓ cup of the turkey mixture in the center of each rectangle. Bring the 4 corners of the dough together above the filling; twist and pinch seams to seal.
3. Place on an ungreased baking sheet. Brush tops with butter; sprinkle with bread crumbs. Bake until golden brown, 15-20 minutes.
1 BUNDLE: 418 cal., 25g fat (10g sat. fat), 67mg chol., 674mg sod., 26g carb. (5g sugars, 0 fiber), 20g pro.

CREAMY SEAFOOD ENCHILADAS

Shrimp and crab plus a flavorful sauce make these enchiladas outstanding. I made them for an annual fundraiser, and now they're always in demand. Spice up the recipe to your taste by adding more green chiles and salsa.
—*Evelyn Gebhardt, Kasilof, AK*

Prep: 20 min. • **Bake:** 30 min.
Makes: 6 servings

- ¼ cup butter
- ¼ cup all-purpose flour
- 1 cup chicken broth
- 1 can (10¾ oz.) condensed cream of chicken soup, undiluted
- 1 cup sour cream
- ½ cup salsa
- ⅛ tsp. salt
- 1 cup 4% cottage cheese
- 1 lb. small shrimp, cooked, peeled and deveined
- 1 cup cooked or canned crabmeat, drained, flaked and cartilage removed
- 1½ cups shredded Monterey Jack cheese
- 1 can (4 oz.) chopped green chiles
- 1 Tbsp. dried cilantro flakes
- 12 flour tortillas (6 in.)
  Optional: Sliced jalapeno pepper, thinly sliced green onions and chopped cilantro leaves
  Additional salsa

1. Preheat oven to 350°. In a saucepan over low heat, melt butter; stir in the flour until smooth. Gradually stir in the broth and soup until blended. Bring to a boil; cook and stir for 2 minutes or until slightly thickened. Remove from heat. Stir in sour cream, salsa and salt; set aside.
2. Place cottage cheese in a blender; cover and process until smooth. Transfer to a bowl; add shrimp, crab, Monterey Jack cheese, chiles and cilantro.
3. Spread 1½ cups of sauce in a greased 13x9-in. baking dish. Place about ⅓ cup of the seafood mixture down the center of each tortilla. Roll up tortillas and place seam side down over the sauce. Top with the remaining sauce. Bake, uncovered, until heated through, 30-35 minutes. If desired, top with sliced jalapeno pepper, green onions and chopped cilantro. Serve with additional salsa.
2 ENCHILADAS: 645 cal., 35g fat (17g sat. fat), 252mg chol., 1812mg sod., 40g carb. (4g sugars, 2g fiber), 42g pro.

BAKED MAC & CHEESE

Even people who have had their own macaroni and cheese recipe for years ask for mine when they taste this crumb-topped version. When baking mac and cheese, make it with extra-sharp white cheddar for more flavor.
—*Shelby Thompson, Dover, DE*

Prep: 15 min. • **Bake:** 30 min.
Makes: 8 servings

- 1 pkg. (16 oz.) uncooked elbow macaroni
- ⅓ cup plus ¼ cup butter, divided
- ¾ cup finely chopped onion
- 6 Tbsp. all-purpose flour
- 1 tsp. ground mustard
- ¾ tsp. salt
- ¼ tsp. pepper
- 4½ cups 2% milk
- 4 cups shredded sharp cheddar cheese
- ¾ cup dry bread crumbs

1. Preheat oven to 350°. Cook the macaroni according to the package directions for al dente; drain.
2. In a Dutch oven, heat ⅓ cup butter over medium heat; saute onion until tender. Stir in flour and seasonings until blended; gradually stir in milk. Bring to a boil, stirring constantly; cook and stir until thickened. Stir in cheese until melted. Stir in macaroni. Transfer to a greased 13x9-in. baking dish.
3. In a microwave, melt remaining butter; toss with bread crumbs. Sprinkle over casserole. Bake, uncovered, until heated through, 30-35 minutes.
1 CUP: 689 cal., 37g fat (22g sat. fat), 104mg chol., 834mg sod., 62g carb. (10g sugars, 3g fiber), 28g pro.

BAKED COD PICCATA WITH ASPARAGUS

It takes longer for the oven to preheat than it does to prepare this delicious dish. While it's baking, I throw together a quick salad.
—Barbara Lento, Houston, PA

Takes: 30 min. • **Makes:** 4 servings

- 1 lb. fresh asparagus, trimmed
- ¼ cup water
- 1 lb. cod fillet, cut into 4 pieces
- 2 Tbsp. lemon juice
- 1 tsp. salt-free lemon-pepper seasoning
- ½ tsp. garlic powder
- 2 Tbsp. butter, cubed
- 2 tsp. capers
  Minced fresh parsley, optional

1. Preheat oven to 400°. Place asparagus in an ungreased 11x7-in. baking dish; add water. Arrange cod over asparagus. Sprinkle with lemon juice, lemon pepper and garlic powder. Dot with butter; sprinkle with capers.
2. Bake, uncovered, for 12-15 minutes or until the fish flakes easily with a fork and the asparagus is tender. If desired, sprinkle with parsley.
1 SERVING: 150 cal., 7g fat (4g sat. fat), 58mg chol., 265mg sod., 3g carb. (1g sugars, 1g fiber), 20g pro. **DIABETIC EXCHANGES:** 3 lean meat, 1 fat.

CRANBERRY CHICKEN & WILD RICE

This tender chicken in a sweet-tart cranberry sauce is delicious, and it's so easy to prepare. I love that I can do other things while it bakes.
—Evelyn Lewis, Independence, MO

Prep: 10 min. • **Bake:** 35 min.
Makes: 6 servings

- 6 boneless skinless chicken breast halves (4 oz. each)
- 1½ cups hot water
- 1 pkg. (6.2 oz.) fast-cooking long grain and wild rice mix
- 1 can (14 oz.) whole-berry cranberry sauce
- 1 Tbsp. lemon juice
- 1 Tbsp. reduced-sodium soy sauce
- 1 Tbsp. Worcestershire sauce

1. Preheat oven to 350°. Place chicken in a 13x9-in. baking dish coated with cooking spray. In a bowl, mix hot water, rice mix and contents of seasoning packet; pour around the chicken.
2. In a small bowl, mix remaining ingredients; pour over the chicken. Bake, covered, until a thermometer inserted in chicken reads 165°, 35-45 minutes.
1 CHICKEN BREAST HALF WITH ½ CUP RICE MIXTURE: 332 cal., 3g fat (1g sat. fat), 63mg chol., 592mg sod., 50g carb. (19g sugars, 2g fiber), 26g pro.

ROASTED CHICKEN & RED POTATOES

Pop this homey, flavorful dinner in the oven for about an hour, then enjoy!
—*Sherri Melotik, Oak Creek, WI*

- -

Prep: 15 min. • **Bake:** 55 min.
Makes: 6 servings

- 2 lbs. red potatoes, cut into 1-in. pieces
- 1 pkg. (9 oz.) fresh spinach
- 1 large onion, cut into 1-in. pieces
- 2 Tbsp. olive oil
- 4 garlic cloves, minced
- 1 tsp. salt, divided
- 1 tsp. dried thyme
- ¾ tsp. pepper, divided
- 6 chicken leg quarters
- ¾ tsp. paprika

1. Preheat oven to 375°. Place potatoes, spinach and onion in a greased shallow roasting pan. Add oil, garlic, ¾ tsp. salt, thyme and ½ tsp. pepper; toss to combine.
2. Arrange chicken over vegetables; sprinkle with paprika and the remaining salt and pepper. Roast on an upper oven rack until a thermometer inserted in the chicken reads 170°-175° and potatoes are tender, 55-60 minutes.
1 CHICKEN LEG QUARTER WITH 1 CUP VEGETABLE MIXTURE: 449 cal., 21g fat (5g sat. fat), 105mg chol., 529mg sod., 29g carb. (3g sugars, 4g fiber), 35g pro.

BROCCOLI BEEF BRAIDS

Each slice of this fast-to-fix, golden bread is like a hot sandwich packed with beef, broccoli and mozzarella.
—*Penny Lapp, North Royalton, OH*

- -

Takes: 30 min.
Makes: 2 loaves (4 servings each)

- 1 lb. ground beef
- ½ cup chopped onion
- 3 cups frozen chopped broccoli
- 1 cup shredded part-skim mozzarella cheese
- ½ cup sour cream
- ¼ tsp. salt
- ¼ tsp. pepper
- 2 tubes (8 oz. each) refrigerated crescent rolls

1. Preheat oven to 350°. In a large skillet, cook beef and onion over medium heat 6-8 minutes or until the beef is no longer pink, breaking up the beef into crumbles; drain. Stir in chopped broccoli, cheese, sour cream, salt and pepper; heat through.
2. Unroll 1 tube of crescent dough onto a greased baking sheet; form into a 12x8-in. rectangle, pressing the perforations to seal. Spoon half the beef mixture lengthwise down the center of the rectangle.
3. On each long side, cut 1-in.-wide strips at an angle, about 3 in. into the center. Fold 1 strip from each side over the filling and pinch the ends together; repeat.
4. Repeat with the remaining ingredients to make a second braid. Bake 15-20 minutes or until golden brown.
1 PIECE: 396 cal., 23g fat (6g sat. fat), 48mg chol., 644mg sod., 29g carb. (8g sugars, 2g fiber), 20g pro.

ROASTED PORK TENDERLOIN & VEGETABLES

There are no complicated steps to follow when preparing this medley of tender pork and veggies. Just season with herbs, then pop in the oven—that's all it takes.

—*Diane Martin, Brown Deer, WI*

Prep: 20 min. • **Bake:** 25 min.
Makes: 6 servings

- 2 pork tenderloins (¾ lb. each)
- 2 lbs. red potatoes, quartered
- 1 lb. carrots, halved and cut into 2-in. pieces
- 1 medium onion, cut into wedges
- 1 Tbsp. olive oil
- 2 tsp. dried rosemary, crushed
- 1 tsp. rubbed sage
- ½ tsp. salt
- ¼ tsp. pepper

1. Preheat oven to 450°. Place the pork in a shallow roasting pan coated with cooking spray; arrange the potatoes, carrots and onion around pork. Drizzle with oil. Combine the seasonings; sprinkle over the meat and vegetables.

2. Bake, uncovered, for 25-35 minutes or until a thermometer reads 145° and the vegetables are tender, stirring vegetables occasionally. Remove from oven; tent pork with foil. Let stand 5 minutes before slicing. If pork is done before the vegetables are tender, remove pork from oven and keep warm; continue cooking vegetables until tender.

1 SERVING: 301 cal., 7g fat (2g sat. fat), 64mg chol., 304mg sod., 33g carb. (6g sugars, 5g fiber), 26g pro. **DIABETIC EXCHANGES:** 3 lean meat, 2 starch, 1 vegetable.

LEMON & ROSEMARY CHICKEN

This baked chicken with a tangy lemon and rosemary sauce is my husband's favorite, and my sister always wants it for her special birthday dinner.

—*Laurel Dalzell, Manteca, CA*

Takes: 30 min. • **Makes:** 4 servings

- 4 boneless skinless chicken breast halves (4 oz. each)
- ¼ tsp. salt
- ¼ tsp. pepper
- 2 tsp. canola oil
- 1 shallot, finely chopped
- 1 Tbsp. minced fresh rosemary or 1 tsp. dried rosemary, crushed
- ½ cup reduced-sodium chicken broth
- 2 tsp. grated lemon zest
- 4½ tsp. lemon juice
- ¼ cup cold butter

1. Preheat oven to 400°. Sprinkle chicken with salt and pepper. In a large cast-iron or other heavy skillet, heat oil over medium heat; brown chicken on both sides. Transfer the chicken to a 15x10x1-in. baking pan; reserve the drippings in the skillet. Bake the chicken, uncovered, until a thermometer reads 165°, 8-10 minutes.

2. Meanwhile, in the same skillet, cook and stir the shallot and rosemary in the drippings until tender. Stir in broth. Bring to a boil; cook until the liquid is reduced by half. Reduce heat to low; stir in lemon zest and juice. Whisk in the butter, 1 Tbsp. at a time, until creamy. Serve with chicken.

1 CHICKEN BREAST HALF WITH 1 TBSP. SAUCE: 252 cal., 16g fat (8g sat. fat), 93mg chol., 355mg sod., 2g carb. (0 sugars, 0 fiber), 24g pro.

TUNA NOODLE CASSEROLE

Families are sure to love the creamy texture and comforting taste of this traditional tuna casserole. It goes together in a jiffy, and I serve it with a green salad and warm rolls for a fast and nutritious supper.

—*Ruby Wells, Cynthiana, KY*

Prep: 10 min. • **Bake:** 30 min.
Makes: 4 servings

- 1 can (10¾ oz.) reduced-fat reduced-sodium condensed cream of celery soup, undiluted
- ½ cup fat-free milk
- 2 cups cooked yolk-free wide noodles
- 1 cup frozen peas, thawed
- 1 can (6 oz.) light water-packed tuna, drained and flaked
- 1 jar (2 oz.) diced pimientos, drained
- 2 Tbsp. dry bread crumbs
- 1 Tbsp. butter, melted

1. Preheat the oven to 400°. In a large bowl, combine soup and milk until smooth. Add the noodles, peas, tuna and pimientos; mix well.
2. Pour into a 1½-qt. baking dish coated with cooking spray. Bake, uncovered, 25 minutes. Toss the bread crumbs and butter; sprinkle over the top. Bake 5 minutes longer or until golden brown.
1 CUP: 238 cal., 5g fat (2g sat. fat), 27mg chol., 475mg sod., 32g carb. (6g sugars, 4g fiber), 15g pro. **DIABETIC EXCHANGES:** 2 starch, 2 lean meat, ½ fat.

CRUNCHY BAKED CHICKEN

I've fixed this dish many times for company, and everyone always asks for the recipe. The leftovers—if there are any—are very good heated up in the microwave.

—*Elva Jean Criswell, Charleston, MS*

Prep: 10 min. • **Bake:** 50 min.
Makes: 6 servings

- 1 large egg
- 1 Tbsp. whole milk
- 1 can (2.8 oz.) french-fried onions, crushed
- ¾ cup grated Parmesan cheese
- ¼ cup dry bread crumbs
- 1 tsp. paprika
- ½ tsp. salt
  Dash pepper
- 1 broiler/fryer chicken (3 to 4 lbs.), cut up
- ¼ cup butter, melted

1. Preheat oven to 350°. In a shallow bowl, whisk egg and milk. In another shallow bowl, combine the onions, cheese, bread crumbs, paprika, salt and pepper. Dip chicken in egg the mixture, then roll in the onion mixture.
2. Place in a greased 13x9-in. baking dish. Drizzle with butter. Bake, uncovered, 50-60 minutes or until juices run clear.
1 SERVING: 418 cal., 28g fat (11g sat. fat), 148mg chol., 423mg sod., 8g carb. (1g sugars, 0 fiber), 32g pro.

ZESTY BAKED CATFISH

This catfish combines common pantry seasonings for a taste that's anything but basic. Catfish is a southern classic, but you can also use the seasoning rub on other kinds of fish if you like.

—*Karen Conklin, Supply, NC*

Takes: 20 min. • **Makes:** 2 servings

- 1 tsp. canola oil
- 1 tsp. lemon juice
- 2 catfish fillets (6 oz. each)
- 1½ tsp. paprika
- ½ tsp. dried tarragon
- ½ tsp. dried basil
- ½ tsp. pepper
- ¼ tsp. salt
- ⅛ tsp. cayenne pepper

1. Combine oil and lemon juice; brush over both sides of fillets. Combine the remaining ingredients; rub over both sides of the fillets. Place in an ungreased 15x10x1-in. baking pan.
2. Bake, uncovered, at 350° for 10-15 minutes or until fish flakes easily with a fork.
1 SERVING: 259 cal., 16g fat (3g sat. fat), 80mg chol., 386mg sod., 2g carb. (0 sugars, 1g fiber), 27g pro.

HOMEMADE CHICKEN POTPIE

We don't get our potpies in the frozen food aisle—we make our own. Savory filling tucked inside golden brown crust is the ultimate comfort food.

—*Amy Briggs, Gove, KS*

Takes: 30 min. • **Makes:** 6 servings

- 2 Tbsp. canola oil
- 1 medium onion, chopped
- ½ cup all-purpose flour
- 1 tsp. poultry seasoning
- 1 can (14½ oz.) chicken broth
- ¾ cup 2% milk
- 3 cups cubed cooked chicken
- 2 cups frozen mixed vegetables (about 10 oz.), thawed
- 1 sheet refrigerated pie crust

1. Preheat oven to 450°. In a large saucepan, heat oil over medium-high heat. Add onion; cook and stir until tender. Stir in flour and poultry seasoning until blended; gradually whisk in broth and milk. Bring to a boil, stirring constantly; cook and stir 2-3 minutes or until thickened. Stir in chicken and vegetables.
2. Transfer to a greased 9-in. deep-dish pie plate; place crust over the filling. Trim, seal and flute edges. Cut slits in crust. Bake until the crust is golden brown and the filling is bubbly, 15-20 minutes.
1 SERVING: 439 cal., 20g fat (6g sat. fat), 73mg chol., 526mg sod., 37g carb. (6g sugars, 3g fiber), 26g pro.

MAPLE-ROASTED CHICKEN & ACORN SQUASH

When I became a new mother, my mom helped me find comforting and simple recipes to have on hand. This terrific roast chicken was a very happy discovery.
—*Sara Eilers, Surprise, AZ*

- -

Prep: 15 min. • **Bake:** 35 min.
Makes: 6 servings

1   **medium acorn squash**
4   **medium carrots, chopped (about 2 cups)**
1   **medium onion, cut into 1-in. pieces**
6   **bone-in chicken thighs (about 2¼ lbs.)**
½   **cup maple syrup**
1   **tsp. salt**
½   **tsp. coarsely ground pepper**

1. Preheat oven to 450°. Cut acorn squash lengthwise in half; remove and discard seeds. Cut each half crosswise into ½-in. slices; discard ends. Place squash, carrots and onion in a greased 13x9-in. baking pan; top with chicken, skin side down. Roast 10 minutes.
2. Turn the chicken over; drizzle with maple syrup and sprinkle with salt and pepper. Roast 25-30 minutes longer or until a thermometer inserted in chicken reads 170°-175° and the vegetables are tender.
1 SERVING: 363 cal., 14g fat (4g sat. fat), 81mg chol., 497mg sod., 36g carb. (23g sugars, 3g fiber), 24g pro. **DIABETIC EXCHANGES:** 3 lean meat, 2 starch, 1 vegetable.

WALNUT-CRUSTED SALMON

Whenever I see salmon for a good price, I turn to this simple and delicious recipe. I serve it up with mashed potatoes and fresh green beans.
—*Edie DeSpain, Logan, UT*

- -

Takes: 25 min. • **Makes:** 4 servings

4   **salmon fillets (4 oz. each)**
4   **tsp. Dijon mustard**
4   **tsp. honey**
2   **slices whole wheat bread, torn into pieces**
3   **Tbsp. finely chopped walnuts**
2   **tsp. canola oil**
½   **tsp. dried thyme**

1. Preheat oven to 400°. Place salmon on a baking sheet coated with cooking spray. Mix mustard and honey; brush over salmon. Place bread in a food processor; pulse until coarse crumbs form. Transfer to a small bowl. Stir in walnuts, oil and thyme; press onto salmon.
2. Bake 12-15 minutes or until topping is lightly browned and fish just begins to flake easily with a fork.
1 FILLET: 295 cal., 17g fat (3g sat. fat), 57mg chol., 243mg sod., 13g carb. (7g sugars, 1g fiber), 22g pro. **DIABETIC EXCHANGES:** 3 lean meat, 1 starch, ½ fat.

5i

CAESAR ORANGE ROUGHY

I'm so thankful that my mother taught me the ropes in the kitchen when I was young. Mom won several cooking contests over the years, and this is one of my favorite recipes of hers.
—*Mary Lou Boyce, Wilmington, DE*

- -

Takes: 25 min. • **Makes:** 8 servings

8   **orange roughy fillets (4 oz. each)**
1   **cup creamy Caesar salad dressing**
2   **cups crushed butter-flavored crackers (about 50 crackers)**
1   **cup shredded cheddar cheese**

1. Preheat oven to 400°. Place fillets in an ungreased 13x9-in. baking dish. Drizzle with salad dressing; sprinkle with crushed crackers.
2. Bake, uncovered, 10 minutes. Sprinkle with cheese. Bake 3-5 minutes longer or until fish flakes easily with a fork and cheese is melted.
1 FILLET: 421 cal., 28g fat (6g sat. fat), 93mg chol., 716mg sod., 17g carb. (3g sugars, 1g fiber), 24g pro.

LINDA SCHEND
Kenosha, WI

CRISPY FISH & CHIPS

A British pub classic turns into a crown jewel when you add horseradish, panko bread crumbs and Worcestershire. You can also try this recipe with a white fish like cod or haddock.

—*Linda Schend, Kenosha, WI*

- -

Takes: 30 min. • **Makes:** 4 servings

- 4 cups frozen steak fries
- 4 salmon fillets (6 oz. each)
- 1 to 2 Tbsp. prepared horseradish
- 1 Tbsp. grated Parmesan cheese
- 1 Tbsp. Worcestershire sauce
- 1 tsp. Dijon mustard
- ¼ tsp. salt
- ½ cup panko (Japanese) bread crumbs
  Cooking spray

1. Preheat oven to 450°. Arrange steak fries in a single layer on a baking sheet. Bake on the lowest oven rack for 18-20 minutes or until light golden brown.

2. Meanwhile, place salmon on a foil-lined baking sheet coated with cooking spray. In a small bowl, mix the horseradish, Parmesan cheese, Worcestershire sauce, mustard and salt; stir in panko. Press mixture onto fillets. Spritz tops with cooking spray.

3. Bake the salmon on middle oven rack for 8-10 minutes or until the fish just begins to flake easily with a fork. Serve with fries.

1 FILLET WITH ¾ CUP FRIES: 416 cal., 19g fat (4g sat. fat), 86mg chol., 698mg sod., 26g carb. (2g sugars, 2g fiber), 32g pro. **DIABETIC EXCHANGES:** 5 lean meat, 1½ starch.

TEST KITCHEN TIP
When buying fresh fish fillets, search for firm flesh with a moist look. Don't purchase fish that looks dried out. Fresh fish should have a mild smell, not a strong odor.

TACO LASAGNA

If you like foods with southwestern flair, this just might become a new favorite. Loaded with cheese, meat and beans, the layered casserole comes together in a snap. There are never any leftovers when I take this dish to potlucks.
—Terri Keenan, Tuscaloosa, AL

- -

Prep: 20 min. • **Bake:** 25 min.
Makes: 9 servings

- 1 lb. ground beef
- ½ cup chopped green pepper
- ½ cup chopped onion
- ⅔ cup water
- 1 envelope taco seasoning
- 1 can (15 oz.) black beans, rinsed and drained
- 1 can (14½ oz.) Mexican diced tomatoes, undrained
- 6 flour tortillas (8 in.)
- 1 can (16 oz.) refried beans
- 3 cups shredded Mexican cheese blend

1. Preheat oven to 350°. In a large skillet, cook beef, green pepper and onion over medium heat until the meat is no longer pink; drain. Add water and taco seasoning; bring to a boil. Reduce the heat; simmer, uncovered, for 2 minutes. Stir in black beans and tomatoes. Simmer, uncovered, for 10 minutes.

2. Place 2 tortillas in a greased 13x9-in. baking dish. Spread with half of the refried beans and half of the beef mixture; sprinkle with 1 cup cheese. Repeat layers. Top with the remaining tortillas and cheese.

3. Cover and bake for 25-30 minutes or until heated through and the cheese is melted.

1 PIECE: 448 cal., 21g fat (11g sat. fat), 69mg chol., 1152mg sod., 39g carb. (3g sugars, 5g fiber), 25g pro.

> **HEALTH TIP**
> To shave off a few calories from this recipe, substitute ground turkey or chicken for ground beef and use reduced-fat cheese.

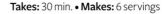

PARMESAN CHICKEN BREASTS

A rich, cheesy breading locks in this chicken's natural juices, making it moist and tempting every time. Because it can be made in advance, I rely on it often during the week.
—Kathie Landmann, Lexington Park, MD

- -

Takes: 30 min. • **Makes:** 6 servings

- 1 cup grated Parmesan cheese
- 2 cups soft bread crumbs
- ½ cup butter, melted
- 6 boneless skinless chicken breast halves (6 oz. each)
- ½ cup Dijon, yellow or country-style mustard

Preheat oven to 425°. Combine cheese, bread crumbs and butter. Coat chicken breasts with mustard, then dip into crumb mixture. Place breaded chicken in a 13x9-in. baking pan. Bake until a thermometer inserted in the chicken reads 165°, about 15 minutes.

1 CHICKEN BREAST HALF: 391 cal., 24g fat (13g sat. fat), 119mg chol., 1047mg sod., 10g carb. (1g sugars, 1g fiber), 33g pro.

BAKED CHICKEN FAJITAS

I can't remember when or where I found this recipe, but I've used it nearly every week since. We like to add some hot sauce for added spice.
—*Amy Trinkle, Milwaukee, WI*

Prep: 15 min. • **Bake:** 20 min.
Makes: 6 servings

- 1 lb. boneless skinless chicken breasts, cut into thin strips
- 1 can (14½ oz.) diced tomatoes and green chiles, drained
- 1 medium onion, cut into thin strips
- 1 medium green pepper, cut into thin strips
- 1 medium sweet red pepper, cut into thin strips
- 2 Tbsp. canola oil
- 2 tsp. chili powder
- 2 tsp. ground cumin
- ¼ tsp. salt
- 12 flour tortillas (6 in.), warmed

1. Preheat oven to 400°. In a 13x9-in. baking dish coated with cooking spray, combine the chicken, tomatoes, onion and peppers. Combine oil, chili powder, cumin and salt. Drizzle over the chicken mixture; toss to coat.
2. Bake, uncovered, 20-25 minutes or until chicken is no longer pink and vegetables are tender. Spoon onto the tortillas; fold or roll tortillas as desired.
2 FAJITAS: 375 cal., 14g fat (3g sat. fat), 42mg chol., 838mg sod., 40g carb. (3g sugars, 5g fiber), 22g pro.

READER REVIEW
"Absolutely delicious— I appreciate being able to throw this in the oven so I can do other things without having to stand watch over a skillet!"
MOM2LAUREN, TASTEOFHOME.COM

PORK CHOPS WITH BLUE CHEESE SAUCE

Sometimes a sauce is just a sauce, but with these juicy chops, it really makes the dish. If you like a little spice, mix a small pinch of nutmeg with the black pepper before you sprinkle it on the meat.
—*Kathy Specht, Clinton, MT*

Takes: 25 min. • **Makes:** 4 servings

- 4 bone-in pork loin chops (7 oz. each)
- 1 tsp. coarsely ground pepper
- 1 tsp. butter
- 1 green onion, finely chopped
- 1 garlic clove, minced
- 1 Tbsp. all-purpose flour
- ⅔ cup fat-free milk
- 3 Tbsp. crumbled blue cheese
- 1 Tbsp. white wine or reduced-sodium chicken broth

1. Preheat broiler. Sprinkle pork chops on both sides with pepper; place on a broiler pan coated with cooking spray. Broil 4-5 in. from heat 4-5 minutes on each side or until a thermometer reads 145°. Let stand 5 minutes before serving.
2. Meanwhile, in a small saucepan, heat butter over medium-high heat. Add green onion and garlic; cook and stir until tender. Stir in flour until blended; gradually whisk in milk. Bring to a boil, stirring constantly; cook and stir until thickened, 1-2 minutes. Add cheese and wine; heat through. Serve chops with sauce.
1 PORK CHOP WITH 3 TBSP. SAUCE: 263 cal., 11g fat (5g sat. fat), 94mg chol., 176mg sod., 5g carb. (2g sugars, 0 fiber), 33g pro.
DIABETIC EXCHANGES: 5 lean meat, ½ fat.

CHEESEBURGER CUPS

A terrific recipe for moms with young kids and busy lives, this simple, inexpensive dish is made with handy ingredients and takes just a short time. Best of all, kids will go absolutely crazy for these darling dinner bites!
—*Jeri Millhouse, Ashland, OH*

Takes: 30 min. • **Makes:** 5 servings

1	lb. ground beef
½	cup ketchup
2	Tbsp. brown sugar
1	Tbsp. prepared mustard
1½	tsp. Worcestershire sauce
1	tube (12 oz.) refrigerated buttermilk biscuits
½	cup cubed Velveeta

1. Preheat oven to 400°. In a large skillet, cook beef over medium heat until no longer pink; drain. Stir in ketchup, brown sugar, mustard and Worcestershire sauce. Remove from the heat; set aside.

2. Press a biscuit onto the bottom and up the sides of a greased muffin cup. Spoon beef mixture into cups; top with cheese cubes. Bake 14-16 minutes or until golden brown.

FREEZE OPTION: Freeze cooled pastries in a freezer container, separating layers with waxed paper. To use, thaw pastries in the refrigerator for 8 hours. Reheat on a baking sheet in a preheated 375° oven until heated through.

2 CHEESEBURGER CUPS: 440 cal., 16g fat (7g sat. fat), 78mg chol., 1142mg sod., 45g carb. (13g sugars, 0 fiber), 27g pro.

PARMESAN CHICKEN NUGGETS

My 3-year-old went through a chicken-nuggets-and-French-fries-only stage, so I made these golden nuggets for him. Even the grown-ups liked them!
—*Amanda Livesay, Mobile, AL*

Takes: 30 min. • **Makes:** 8 servings

¼	cup butter, melted
1	cup panko (Japanese) bread crumbs
½	cup grated Parmesan cheese
½	tsp. kosher salt
1½	lbs. boneless skinless chicken breasts, cut into 1-in. cubes
	Marinara sauce, optional

1. Preheat oven to 375°. Place the butter in a shallow bowl. Combine bread crumbs, cheese and salt in another shallow bowl. Dip chicken in the butter, then roll in the crumbs.

2. Place the chicken in a single layer on two 15x10x1-in. baking pans. Bake until no longer pink, 15-18 minutes, turning once. Serve with marinara sauce if desired.

FREEZE OPTION: Cool chicken nuggets. Freeze in freezer containers. To use, partially thaw in refrigerator overnight. Place on a baking sheet and reheat in a preheated 375° oven 7-12 minutes or until heated through.

6 NUGGETS: 191 cal., 9g fat (5g sat. fat), 67mg chol., 309mg sod., 5g carb. (0 sugars, 0 fiber), 20g pro.

SPICY CHICKEN NUGGETS: Add ¼ to ½ tsp. ground chipotle pepper to the bread crumb mixture.

ITALIAN SEASONED CHICKEN NUGGETS: Add 2 tsp. Italian seasoning to the bread crumb mixture.

RANCH CHICKEN NUGGETS: Substitute crushed cornflakes for bread crumbs. Toss the chicken cubes with ⅓ cup ranch salad dressing, then roll in the cornflake mixture. Serve with additional ranch dressing.

PARMESAN-BROILED TILAPIA

I love that simple Parmesan cheese brings such richness to an otherwise mild-tasting fish. It's one dish where leftovers are never a problem!
—*Tracy Locken, Gillette, WY*

Takes: 15 min. • **Makes:** 4 servings

- ½ cup grated Parmesan cheese
- 3 Tbsp. butter, softened
- 2 Tbsp. mayonnaise
- ¼ tsp. dried basil
- ¼ tsp. pepper
- ⅛ tsp. onion powder
- ⅛ tsp. celery salt
- 4 tilapia fillets (6 oz. each)
- 4 lemon wedges

1. In a small bowl, mix the first 7 ingredients. Arrange the fillets in a 15x10x1-in. baking pan coated with cooking spray. Spread the cheese mixture over the fish.

2. Broil 4 in. from heat for 4-5 minutes or until the topping is lightly browned and the fish flakes easily with a fork. Rotate pan halfway through cooking time for more even browning. Serve with lemon wedges.

1 FILLET: 306 cal., 18g fat (9g sat. fat), 115mg chol., 381mg sod., 2g carb. (0 sugars, 0 fiber), 35g pro.

SPICY SHEPHERD'S PIE

Taco seasoning adds zip to this hearty main dish. It's easy to top with instant mashed potatoes, which I stir up while browning the beef.
—*Mary Malchow, Neenah, WI*

Takes: 30 min. • **Makes:** 6 servings

- 3 cups mashed potato flakes
- 1 lb. ground beef
- 1 medium onion, chopped
- 1 can (14½ oz.) diced tomatoes, undrained
- 1 can (11 oz.) Mexicorn, drained
- 1 can (2¼ oz.) sliced ripe olives, drained
- 1 envelope taco seasoning
- 1½ tsp. chili powder
- ½ tsp. salt
- ⅛ tsp. garlic powder
- 1 cup shredded cheddar cheese, divided

1. Preheat oven to 350°. Prepare the mashed potatoes according to package directions. Meanwhile, in a large skillet, cook beef and onion over medium heat until the meat is no longer pink; drain. Add the tomatoes, corn, olives, taco seasoning, chili powder, salt and garlic powder. Bring to a boil; cook and stir for 1-2 minutes.

2. Transfer beef mixture to a greased 2½-qt. baking dish. Top with ¾ cup of the cheese. Spread the mashed potatoes over top; sprinkle with the remaining cheese. Bake, uncovered, 12-15 minutes or until the cheese is melted.

NOTE: You may substitute 4½ cups hot homemade mashed potatoes for the instant potatoes if desired.

1 SERVING: 516 cal., 25g fat (13g sat. fat), 90mg chol., 1337mg sod., 49g carb. (10g sugars, 5g fiber), 24g pro.

OVEN-BAKED SHRIMP & GRITS

On chilly days, I doctor up grits and top them with shrimp for a comforting meal. If you're not a seafood lover, add chicken, ham or both.
—*Jerri Gradert, Lincoln, NE*

- -

Prep: 20 min. • **Bake:** 45 min.
Makes: 6 servings

- 1 carton (32 oz.) chicken broth
- 1 cup quick-cooking grits
- 1 can (10 oz.) diced tomatoes and green chiles, drained
- 1 cup shredded Monterey Jack cheese
- 1 cup shredded cheddar cheese, divided
    Freshly ground pepper
- 2 Tbsp. butter
- 1 medium green pepper, chopped
- 1 medium onion, chopped
- 1 lb. uncooked shrimp (31-40 per lb.), peeled and deveined
- 2 garlic cloves, minced

1. Preheat the oven to 350°. In a 13x9-in. or 2½-qt. baking dish, combine broth and grits. Bake, uncovered, until the liquid is absorbed and grits are tender, 30-35 minutes.
2. Stir in tomatoes, Monterey Jack cheese and ½ cup cheddar cheese. Bake, uncovered, until heated through, about 10 minutes. Sprinkle with pepper and the remaining cheese; let stand 5 minutes.
3. In a large skillet, heat butter over medium-high heat; saute green pepper and onion until tender, 6-8 minutes. Add shrimp and garlic; cook and stir until the shrimp turn pink, 2-3 minutes. Spoon over the grits.
1⅔ CUPS: 360 cal., 18g fat (10g sat. fat), 141mg chol., 1199mg sod., 26g carb. (2g sugars, 2g fiber), 25g pro.

> **HEALTH TIP**
> Switching to reduced-sodium broth will save almost 300 milligrams of sodium per serving.

🦃 TURKEY & DRESSING BAKE

Folks will be amazed that just four ingredients can produce such a delicious dinner. You're certain to rely on this recipe as a standby for years to come!
—*Taste of Home Test Kitchen*

- -

Prep: 15 min. + standing • **Bake:** 25 min.
Makes: 4 servings

- 4 cups leftover cooked stuffing
- 2 Tbsp. minced fresh parsley
- 1½ cups cubed cooked turkey
- ⅔ cup condensed cream of chicken soup, undiluted
- 3 Tbsp. water

1. Preheat oven to 350°. In a bowl, combine stuffing and parsley. Transfer to a greased 8-in. square baking dish. Top with turkey. Combine soup and water; spoon over top.
2. Bake, uncovered, for 25-30 minutes or until heated through.
1 CUP: 484 cal., 22g fat (5g sat. fat), 43mg chol., 1414mg sod., 47g carb. (5g sugars, 6g fiber), 23g pro.

NUTTY OVEN-FRIED CHICKEN

Pecans are plentiful in the South, and so is fried chicken! I love to prepare and serve this easy dish because the chicken comes out moist and crispy.
—*Diane Hixon, Niceville, FL*

Prep: 10 min. • **Bake:** 1 hour
Makes: 6 servings

- ½ cup evaporated milk
- 1 cup biscuit/baking mix
- ⅓ cup finely chopped pecans
- 2 tsp. paprika
- ½ tsp. salt
- ½ tsp. poultry seasoning
- ½ tsp. rubbed sage
- 1 broiler/fryer chicken (3 to 4 lbs.), cut up
- ⅓ cup butter, melted

1. Preheat oven to 350°. Place milk in a shallow bowl. In another shallow bowl, combine the baking mix, pecans and seasonings. Dip the chicken pieces in milk, then coat generously with the pecan mixture.

2. Place in a lightly greased 13x9-in. baking dish. Drizzle with butter. Bake, uncovered, until the chicken is golden brown and crispy and the juices run clear, about 1 hour.

6 OZ. COOKED CHICKEN: 530 cal., 35g fat (13g sat. fat), 138mg chol., 595mg sod., 17g carb. (3g sugars, 1g fiber), 37g pro.

TEST KITCHEN TIP
Pecans have a higher fat content than other nuts, so they're more prone to going rancid. They'll stay fresh for twice as long in the freezer as they would at room temperature.

MONTEREY SAUSAGE PIE

It's so easy to make this dish using baking mix. I got the idea from a similar recipe that featured beef and cheddar cheese. That version was too bland for my family's tastes, so I made a few changes and this was the result.
—*Bonnie Marlow, Ottoville, OH*

Prep: 15 min. • **Bake:** 25 min. + standing
Makes: 8 servings

- 1 lb. bulk pork sausage
- 1 cup chopped onion
- 1 cup chopped sweet red pepper
- ½ cup chopped fresh mushrooms
- 3 tsp. minced garlic
- 2½ cups shredded Monterey Jack cheese, divided
- 1⅓ cups whole milk
- 3 large eggs
- ¾ cup biscuit/baking mix
- ¾ tsp. rubbed sage
- ¼ tsp. pepper

1. Preheat oven to 400°. In a large skillet, cook the sausage, onion, red pepper and mushrooms over medium heat until the meat is no longer pink. Add garlic; cook 1 minute longer. Drain. Stir in 2 cups cheese. Transfer to a greased 9-in. deep-dish pie plate.

2. In a small bowl, combine the milk, eggs, biscuit mix, sage and pepper. Pour over the sausage mixture.

3. Bake 20-25 minutes or until a knife inserted in the center comes out clean. Sprinkle with the remaining cheese; bake 1-2 minutes longer or until the cheese is melted. Let stand for 10 minutes before cutting.

1 PIECE: 361 cal., 26g fat (12g sat. fat), 137mg chol., 609mg sod., 14g carb. (5g sugars, 1g fiber), 18g pro.

ROADSIDE DINER CHEESEBURGER QUICHE

This unforgettable quiche tastes just like its burger counterpart. Easy and appealing, it's perfect for guests and fun for the whole family.
—*Barbara J. Miller, Oakdale, MN*

- -

Prep: 20 min. • **Bake:** 50 min. + standing
Makes: 8 servings

- 1 **sheet refrigerated pie crust**
- ¾ **lb. ground beef**
- 2 **plum tomatoes, seeded and chopped**
- 1 **medium onion, chopped**
- ½ **cup dill pickle relish**
- ½ **cup crumbled cooked bacon**
- 5 **large eggs**
- 1 **cup heavy whipping cream**
- ½ **cup 2% milk**
- 2 **tsp. prepared mustard**
- 1 **tsp. hot pepper sauce**
- ½ **tsp. salt**
- ¼ **tsp. pepper**
- 1½ **cups shredded cheddar cheese**
- ½ **cup shredded Parmesan cheese**
  Optional garnishes: Mayonnaise, additional pickle relish, crumbled cooked bacon, and chopped onion and tomato

1. Preheat oven to 375°. Unroll crust into a 9-in. deep-dish pie plate; flute edges and set aside. In a large skillet, cook beef over medium heat, crumbling the meat, until no longer pink; drain. Stir the tomatoes, onion, relish and bacon. Transfer to the prepared crust.
2. In a large bowl, whisk eggs, cream, milk, mustard, pepper sauce, salt and pepper. Pour over the beef mixture. Sprinkle with cheeses.
3. Bake until a knife inserted in the center comes out clean, 50-60 minutes. Cover edges with foil during the last 15 minutes to prevent overbrowning if necessary. Let stand for 10 minutes before cutting. Garnish with optional ingredients as desired.
1 PIECE: 502 cal., 35g fat (19g sat. fat), 236mg chol., 954mg sod., 24g carb. (8g sugars, 1g fiber), 23g pro.

BAKED MUSHROOM CHICKEN

Here's a way to dress up chicken using fresh mushrooms, green onions and two kinds of cheese. It's a recipe I can count on to yield tender and flavorful chicken every time.
—*Barbara McCalley, Allison Park, PA*

- -

Prep: 20 min. • **Bake:** 20 min.
Makes: 4 servings

- 4 **boneless skinless chicken breast halves (1 lb.)**
- ¼ **cup all-purpose flour**
- 3 **Tbsp. butter, divided**
- 1 **cup sliced fresh mushrooms**
- ½ **cup chicken broth**
- ¼ **tsp. salt**
- ⅛ **tsp. pepper**
- ⅓ **cup shredded part-skim mozzarella cheese**
- ⅓ **cup grated Parmesan cheese**
- ¼ **cup sliced green onions**

1. Preheat oven to 375°. Flatten each chicken breast half to ¼-in. thickness. Place flour in a shallow bowl. Dip chicken in flour to coat both sides; shake off excess.
2. In a large skillet, brown chicken in 2 Tbsp. butter on both sides. Transfer to a greased 11x7-in. baking dish. In the same skillet, saute the mushrooms in the remaining butter until tender. Add the broth, salt and pepper. Bring to a boil; cook until liquid is reduced to ½ cup, about 5 minutes. Spoon over the chicken.
3. Bake, uncovered, until chicken is no longer pink, about 15 minutes. Sprinkle with cheeses and green onions. Bake until the cheese is melted, about 5 minutes longer.
1 CHICKEN BREAST HALF : 311 cal., 16g fat (9g sat. fat), 109mg chol., 575mg sod., 8g carb. (1g sugars, 1g fiber), 33g pro.

JAMAICAN SALMON WITH COCONUT CREAM SAUCE

We eat salmon a lot because it's so healthy, and I love thinking of ways to make it different and delicious. It's easy, but this dazzler is my go-to meal for company.
—*Joni Hilton, Rocklin, CA*

Takes: 30 min. • **Makes:** 4 servings

4	**salmon fillets (6 oz. each)**
3	**Tbsp. mayonnaise**
4	**tsp. Caribbean jerk seasoning**
⅓	**cup sour cream**
¼	**cup cream of coconut**
1	**tsp. grated lime zest**
¼	**cup lime juice**
½	**cup sweetened shredded coconut, toasted**

1. Preheat oven to 350°. Place the fillets in a greased 13x9-in. baking dish. Spread the mayonnaise over fillets; sprinkle with the jerk seasoning.

2. Bake until fish just begins to flake easily with a fork, 18-22 minutes. Meanwhile, for sauce, in a small saucepan, combine sour cream, cream of coconut, lime zest and juice; cook and stir over medium-low heat until blended.

3. Drizzle the fillets with sauce; sprinkle with toasted coconut.

NOTE: To toast coconut, bake in a shallow pan in a 350° oven for 5-10 minutes or cook in a skillet over low heat until golden brown, stirring occasionally.

1 FILLET WITH 3 TBSP. SAUCE AND 2 TBSP. COCONUT: 497 cal., 34g fat (12g sat. fat), 102mg chol., 467mg sod., 16g carb. (14g sugars, 1g fiber), 30g pro.

CHICKEN CORDON BLEU CRESCENT RING

A classic cordon bleu has chicken, cheese and ham. To change it up, roll up everything inside crescent dough for a speedy meal. Nobody can get enough of this dish!
—*Stella Culotta, Pasadena, MD*

Takes: 30 min. • **Makes:** 6 servings

1	**tube (8 oz.) refrigerated crescent rolls**
2	**cups shredded Swiss cheese**
2	**cups cubed cooked chicken**
¾	**cup mayonnaise**
½	**cup cubed fully cooked ham**
2	**Tbsp. honey mustard**

1. Preheat oven to 375°. Unroll crescent dough and separate into triangles. On an ungreased 12-in. pizza pan, arrange the triangles in a ring with their points toward the outside and their wide ends overlapping. Press the overlapping dough to seal.

2. In a large bowl, mix the remaining ingredients. Spoon across the wide ends of the triangles. Fold the pointed ends of the triangles over the filling, tucking points under to form a ring (the filling will be visible).

3. Bake for 15-20 minutes or until golden brown and heated through.

1 SLICE: 603 cal., 45g fat (13g sat. fat), 91mg chol., 772mg sod., 19g carb. (6g sugars, 0 fiber), 29g pro.

JONI HILTON
Rocklin, CA

CONTEST-WINNING CHICKEN & WILD RICE CASSEROLE

While this special dish is perfect for a company dinner, it's also just too good not to make for everyday family meals. It is so nice served with rolls or French bread.
—*Elizabeth Tokariuk, Lethbridge, AB*

Prep: 20 min. • **Bake:** 30 min.
Makes: 8 servings

- 1   small onion, chopped
- ⅓ cup butter
- ⅓ cup all-purpose flour
- 1½ tsp. salt
- ½ tsp. pepper
- 1   can (14½ oz.) chicken broth
- 1   cup half-and-half cream
- 4   cups cubed cooked chicken
- 4   cups cooked wild rice
- 2   jars (4½ oz. each) sliced mushrooms, drained
- 1   jar (4 oz.) diced pimientos, drained
- 1   Tbsp. minced fresh parsley
- ⅓ cup slivered almonds

1. Preheat oven to 350°. In a large saucepan, saute onion in butter until tender. Stir in the flour, salt and pepper until blended. Gradually stir in broth; bring to a boil. Boil and stir for 2 minutes or until thickened and bubbly. Stir in the cream, chicken, rice, mushrooms, pimientos and parsley; heat through.

2. Transfer to a greased 2½-qt. baking dish. Sprinkle with almonds. Bake, uncovered, for 30-35 minutes or until bubbly.

1 CUP: 382 cal., 19g fat (8g sat. fat), 98mg chol., 878mg sod., 26g carb. (3g sugars, 3g fiber), 27g pro.

READER REVIEW

"A keeper! My family doesn't like mushrooms so I didn't add them, and I used a wild rice mixed blend. Forget seconds, we're going for thirds!"

NANCYC15, TASTEOFHOME.COM

SLOW COOKER & INSTANT POT

For savory dishes with a heavenly infusion of flavors, look no further! From classic roasts and ribs to tacos, pasta and even pizza, everyone will want a helping or two of these robust meals.

AMY LENTS
Grand Forks, ND

PRESSURE-COOKER BEEF TIPS

These beef tips remind me of a favorite childhood meal. I like to cook them with mushrooms and serve them over brown rice, noodles or mashed potatoes.
—*Amy Lents, Grand Forks, ND*

- -

Prep: 20 min. • **Cook:** 15 min.
Makes: 4 servings

3	tsp. olive oil
1	beef top sirloin steak (1 lb.), cubed
½	tsp. salt
¼	tsp. pepper
⅓	cup dry red wine or beef broth
½	lb. sliced baby portobello mushrooms
1	small onion, halved and sliced
2	cups beef broth
1	Tbsp. Worcestershire sauce
3	to 4 Tbsp. cornstarch
¼	cup cold water
	Hot cooked mashed potatoes

1. Select saute setting on a 6-qt. electric pressure cooker and adjust for medium heat. Add 2 tsp. oil. Sprinkle beef with salt and pepper. Brown meat in batches, adding oil as needed. Transfer the meat to a bowl.
2. Add wine to cooker, stirring to loosen browned bits. Return beef to cooker; add the mushrooms, onion, broth and Worcestershire sauce. Lock lid; close the pressure-release valve. Adjust to pressure-cook on high for 15 minutes. Quick-release cooker pressure.
3. Select saute setting and adjust for low heat; bring the liquid to a boil. In a small bowl, mix cornstarch and water until smooth; gradually stir into the beef mixture. Cook and stir until sauce is thickened, 1-2 minutes. Serve with mashed potatoes.

1 CUP: 212 cal., 7g fat (2g sat. fat), 46mg chol., 836mg sod., 8g carb. (2g sugars, 1g fiber), 27g pro. **DIABETIC EXCHANGES:** 3 lean meat, ½ starch, ½ fat.

TEST KITCHEN TIP
To make the most of the leftovers (if you have any leftovers!), stir heavy cream or sour cream into the remaining sauce and serve it over pasta as a second-night meal.

BEEF & BLACK BEAN SPAGHETTI SQUASH

I've been working on developing healthier recipes that still taste fabulous—and keep me satisfied. This squash tossed with beef, beans and kale has so much flavor it's easy to forget it's good for you!
—*Charlotte Cravins, Opelousas, LA*

Takes: 30 min. • **Makes:** 4 servings

- 1 medium spaghetti squash
- ¾ lb. lean ground beef (90% lean)
- ½ cup chopped red onion
- 2 Tbsp. yellow mustard
- 2 to 3 tsp. Louisiana-style hot sauce
- 4 small garlic cloves, minced
- 1 can (15 oz.) no-salt-added black beans, rinsed and drained
- 2 cups chopped fresh kale
- ¼ cup plain Greek yogurt

1. Trim ends of squash and halve lengthwise; discard seeds. Place squash, cut side down, on a trivet insert in a 6-qt. electric pressure cooker. Add 1 cup water. Lock lid; close pressure-release valve. Adjust to pressure-cook on high for 7 minutes. Quick-release pressure. Set squash aside.

2. In a large skillet, crumble beef and cook with onion over medium heat until meat is no longer pink, 4-6 minutes; drain. Add mustard, hot sauce and garlic to skillet; cook 1 minute more. Stir in black beans and kale; cook just until wilted, 2-3 minutes.

3. Using a fork, separate the strands of the spaghetti squash; combine with the meat mixture. Dollop individual servings with Greek yogurt.

1½ CUPS: 401 cal., 12g fat (4g sat. fat), 57mg chol., 314mg sod., 51g carb. (2g sugars, 13g fiber), 26g pro.

> **TEST KITCHEN TIP**
> If you don't have a pressure cooker, pop the squash halves in the microwave on high for 15-20 minutes or roast them in the oven upside down until tender.

MOIST CRANBERRY PORK ROAST

I love to serve this tender, flavorful pork to guests. You don't have to toil away in the kitchen to prepare it, yet it tastes like a gourmet meal—so it always impresses!
—*Kimberley Scasny, Douglasville, GA*

Prep: 5 min. • **Cook:** 4 hours + standing
Makes: 8 servings

- 1 boneless rolled pork loin roast (2½ to 3 lbs.)
- ½ tsp. salt
- ¼ tsp. pepper
- 1 can (14 oz.) whole-berry cranberry sauce
- ¼ cup honey
- 1 tsp. grated orange zest
- ⅛ tsp. ground cloves
- ⅛ tsp. ground nutmeg

Cut pork roast in half and place in a 3-qt. slow cooker; sprinkle with salt and pepper. Combine the remaining ingredients; pour over meat. Cover and cook on low for 4-5 hours or until a thermometer reads 160°. Let stand for 10 minutes before slicing and serving.

4 OZ. COOKED PORK WITH ¼ CUP SAUCE: 289 cal., 7g fat (2g sat. fat), 70mg chol., 201mg sod., 30g carb. (22g sugars, 1g fiber), 27g pro.

CREAMY CELERY BEEF STROGANOFF

Cream of celery soup adds richness to a recipe that has become a family favorite in our house. It's so simple to prepare and, oh, that flavor!
—Kimberly Wallace, Dennison, OH

Prep: 20 min. • **Cook:** 8 hours
Makes: 6 servings

- 2 lbs. beef stew meat, cut into 1-in. cubes
- 1 can (10¾ oz.) condensed cream of celery soup, undiluted
- 1 can (10¾ oz.) condensed cream of mushroom soup, undiluted
- 1 medium onion, chopped
- 1 jar (6 oz.) sliced mushrooms, drained
- 1 envelope onion soup mix
- ½ tsp. pepper
- 1 cup sour cream
  Hot cooked noodles

In a 3-qt. slow cooker, combine the first 7 ingredients. Cover and cook on low for 8 hours or until the beef is tender. Stir in sour cream. Serve with noodles.

1 CUP: 405 cal., 22g fat (10g sat. fat), 125mg chol., 1340mg sod., 16g carb. (4g sugars, 2g fiber), 33g pro.

PRESSURE-COOKER CAJUN PORK & RICE

I created this recipe after returning home from a trip and finding little food in the house. I used ingredients already available in the refrigerator and pantry. My husband loves this dish because it's tasty—and I love it because it's easy!
—Allison Gapinski, Cary, NC

Prep: 20 min. • **Cook:** 20 min. + releasing
Makes: 4 servings

- 1 tsp. olive oil
- 1 medium green pepper, julienned
- 1½ tsp. ground cumin
- 1½ tsp. chili powder
- 1½ lbs. boneless pork loin chops
- 1 can (14½ oz.) petite diced tomatoes, undrained
- 1 small onion, finely chopped
- 1 celery rib, chopped
- 1 small carrot, julienned
- 1 garlic cloves, minced
- ½ tsp. Louisiana-style hot sauce
- ¼ tsp. salt
- ¾ cup reduced-sodium chicken broth
- 1½ cups uncooked instant rice

1. Select the saute setting on a 6-qt. electric pressure cooker and adjust for medium heat; add oil. Add green pepper; cook and stir until crisp-tender, 4-5 minutes. Remove pepper and set aside. Press cancel.

2. Mix cumin and chili powder; sprinkle pork chops with 2 tsp. spice mixture. Place the pork in the pressure cooker. In a small bowl, mix tomatoes, onion, celery, carrot, garlic, hot sauce, salt and the remaining spice mixture; pour over the pork. Lock lid; close pressure-release valve. Adjust to pressure-cook on high for 6 minutes. Let pressure naturally release for 5 minutes; quick-release any remaining pressure. Press cancel.

3. Stir in chicken broth, breaking up pork into pieces. Select saute setting and adjust for medium heat; bring to a boil. Add rice. Cook until the rice is tender, 5 minutes longer. Serve with sauteed green pepper.

1 SERVING: 423 cal., 12g fat (4g sat. fat), 82mg chol., 573mg sod., 40g carb. (6g sugars, 4g fiber), 38g pro. **DIABETIC EXCHANGES:** 5 lean meat, 2 starch, 1 vegetable.

PRESSURE-COOKER CHICKEN CACCIATORE

Loaded with flavor and color, this chicken dish proves fall-off-the-bone tender in quick pressure-cooker time...a top pick for busy families.
—*Mary Beth Jung, Hendersonville, NC*

Prep: 30 min. • **Cook:** 15 min.
Makes: 6 servings

¼ cup all-purpose flour
1 tsp. salt
1 tsp. paprika
¼ tsp. pepper
1 broiler/fryer chicken (3 to 4 lbs.), cut up
¼ cup canola oil
1 medium green pepper, cut into strips
1 medium onion, chopped
1 garlic clove, minced
1 can (14½ oz.) diced tomatoes, undrained
¾ cup water
1 can (6 oz.) tomato paste
1 jar (6 oz.) sliced mushrooms, drained
Hot pepper sauce to taste

1. In a bowl or dish, combine the flour, salt, paprika and pepper. Add the chicken, a few pieces at a time, and toss to coat.
2. Select saute setting on a 6-qt. electric pressure cooker. Adjust for medium heat; add oil. When oil is hot, brown the chicken in batches. Return all chicken to cooker; add green pepper, onion, garlic, tomatoes and water. Press cancel.
3. Lock lid; close pressure-release valve. Pressure-cook on high for 12 minutes. Let pressure release naturally. (A thermometer inserted in chicken should read at least 165°.)
4. Using a slotted spoon, remove chicken to a platter. If desired, skim fat from cooking juices. Add tomato paste and mushrooms to the pan juices. Select saute and adjust for low heat; cook and stir until heated through. Stir in hot pepper sauce and chicken.
1 SERVING: 410 cal., 24g fat (5g sat. fat), 88mg chol., 699mg sod., 18g carb. (9g sugars, 5g fiber), 31g pro.

MEATY SLOW-COOKED JAMBALAYA

This recipe makes a big batch of spicy, meaty stew. Stash some in the freezer for those days you don't feel like cooking.
—*Diane Smith, Pine Mountain, GA*

Prep: 25 min. • **Cook:** 7¼ hours
Makes: 12 servings (3 qt.)

1 can (28 oz.) diced tomatoes, undrained
1 cup reduced-sodium chicken broth
1 large green pepper, chopped
1 medium onion, chopped
2 celery ribs, sliced
½ cup white wine or additional reduced-sodium chicken broth
4 garlic cloves, minced
2 tsp. Cajun seasoning
2 tsp. dried parsley flakes
1 tsp. dried basil
1 tsp. dried oregano
¾ tsp. salt
½ to 1 tsp. cayenne pepper
2 lbs. boneless skinless chicken thighs, cut into 1-in. pieces
1 pkg. (12 oz.) fully cooked andouille or other spicy chicken sausage links
2 lbs. uncooked medium shrimp, peeled and deveined
8 cups hot cooked brown rice

1. In a large bowl, combine the first 13 ingredients. Place chicken and sausage in a 6-qt. slow cooker. Pour the tomato mixture over top. Cook, covered, on low until the chicken is tender, 7-9 hours.
2. Stir in shrimp. Cook, covered, until the shrimp turn pink, 15-20 minutes longer. Serve with rice.
1 CUP JAMBALAYA WITH ⅔ CUP COOKED RICE: 387 cal., 10g fat (3g sat. fat), 164mg chol., 674mg sod., 37g carb. (4g sugars, 4g fiber), 36g pro. **DIABETIC EXCHANGES:** 3 lean meat, 2½ starch.

MELT-IN-YOUR-MOUTH MEAT LOAF

When my husband and I were first married, he refused to eat meat loaf because he said it was bland and dry. Then I prepared this version, and it became his favorite meal.
—*Suzanne Codner, Starbuck, MN*

- -

Prep: 15 min. • **Cook:** 5¼ hours + standing
Makes: 6 servings

- 2 large eggs
- ¾ cup whole milk
- ⅔ cup seasoned bread crumbs
- 2 tsp. dried minced onion
- 1 tsp. salt
- ½ tsp. rubbed sage
- 1½ lbs. ground beef
- ¼ cup ketchup
- 2 Tbsp. brown sugar
- 1 tsp. ground mustard
- ½ tsp. Worcestershire sauce

1. Cut three 25x3-in. strips of heavy-duty foil; crisscross so they resemble spokes of a wheel. Place strips on bottom and up sides of a 5-qt. slow cooker. Coat strips with cooking spray.

2. Combine the first 6 ingredients. Crumble beef over the mixture and mix well. Shape into a round loaf; place in the center of the strips in the slow cooker. Cook, covered, until a thermometer reads at least 160°, 5-6 hours.

3. In a small bowl, whisk ketchup, brown sugar, mustard and Worcestershire sauce. Spoon over the meat loaf. Cook until heated through, about 15 minutes longer. Using the foil strips as handles, remove the meat loaf to a platter. Let stand for 10-15 minutes before slicing and serving.

1 PIECE: 346 cal., 17g fat (7g sat. fat), 150mg chol., 800mg sod., 18g carb. (8g sugars, 1g fiber), 28g pro.

SIMPLE SOUTHWEST CHICKEN

Tender chicken is combined with corn, beans, cheese, and salsa for a delicious meal with southwestern flair. The garnishes are optional but really complete the meal.
—*Maddymoo,*
Taste of Home *Online Community*

- -

Prep: 15 min. • **Cook:** 4 hours
Makes: 6 servings

- 1 can (15¼ oz.) whole kernel corn, drained
- 1 can (15 oz.) black beans, rinsed and drained
- 1 jar (16 oz.) mild salsa
- 4 boneless skinless chicken breast halves (5 oz. each)
  Optional toppings: Sweet red and yellow pepper strips, sour cream, shredded cheddar cheese and sliced green onions

1. In a 3-qt. slow cooker, layer three-fourths each of the corn and beans and half the salsa. Arrange chicken over the salsa; top with the remaining corn, beans and salsa. Cover and cook on low for 4-5 hours or until the chicken is tender.

2. Shred the chicken with 2 forks and return meat to the slow cooker; heat through. Serve topped with peppers, sour cream, cheese and onions, if desired.

1 CUP: 234 cal., 3g fat (1g sat. fat), 52mg chol., 678mg sod., 23g carb. (6g sugars, 4g fiber), 24g pro. **DIABETIC EXCHANGES:** 3 lean meat, 1 starch, 1 vegetable.

LIP SMACKIN' RIBS

No matter what time of year you serve them, these ribs taste like summer. They're the ultimate feel-good food!
—*Ron Bynaker, Lebanon, PA*

- -

Prep: 20 min. • **Cook:** 6 hours
Makes: 8 servings

- 3 Tbsp. butter
- 3 lbs. boneless country-style pork ribs
- 1 can (15 oz.) tomato sauce
- 1 cup packed brown sugar
- 1 cup ketchup
- ¼ cup prepared mustard
- 2 Tbsp. honey
- 3 tsp. pepper
- 2 tsp. dried savory
- 1 tsp. salt

In a large skillet, heat butter over medium heat. Brown ribs in batches; transfer to a 5-qt. slow cooker. Add the remaining ingredients. Cook, covered, on low 6-8 hours or until the meat is tender.

1 SERVING: 474 cal., 20g fat (8g sat. fat), 109mg chol., 1117mg sod., 43g carb. (40g sugars, 1g fiber), 31g pro.

PRESSURE-COOKER HERBED CHICKEN & SHRIMP

Tender chicken and shrimp make a flavorful combination that's easy to prepare, yet elegant enough to serve at a dinner party. It practically cooks itself while I clean the house. I serve it with crusty bread and a green salad.
—*Diana Knight, Reno, NV*

- -

Prep: 15 min. • **Cook:** 30 min. + releasing
Makes: 4 servings

- 1 tsp. salt
- 1 tsp. pepper
- 1 broiler/fryer chicken (3 to 4 lbs.), cut up and skin removed
- 1 Tbsp. canola oil
- 1 large onion, chopped
- 1 can (8 oz.) tomato sauce
- ½ cup white wine or chicken broth
- 1 garlic clove, minced
- 1 tsp. dried basil
- ¼ cup butter, softened
- 1 lb. uncooked shrimp (31-40 per lb.), peeled and deveined
  Hot cooked egg noodles, optional

1. Combine salt and pepper; rub over the chicken pieces. Select saute setting on a 6-qt. electric pressure cooker. Adjust for medium heat. When oil is hot, working in batches, brown chicken on all sides.

2. In a bowl, combine the next 5 ingredients; pour over the chicken pieces. Dot with butter. Lock lid and adjust to pressure-cook on high for 15 minutes. Let the pressure release naturally for 10 minutes, then quick-release any remaining pressure. (A thermometer inserted in chicken should read at least 165°.)

3. Select saute setting; adjust for medium heat. Stir in shrimp. Cook until the shrimp turn pink, about 5 minutes. Serve over egg noodles, if desired.

1 SERVING: 606 cal., 34g fat (13g sat. fat), 330mg chol., 1275mg sod., 7g carb. (3g sugars, 1g fiber), 61g pro.

TEST KITCHEN TIP
This dish goes well on a bed of egg noodles, but rice or longer noodles, such as fettucine or linguine, would do nicely, too.

SOY-GINGER POT ROAST

My husband really likes roast beef—and I really like my slow cooker! I brought in Asian influences to create this all-day pot roast with some oomph.
—*Lisa Varner, El Paso, TX*

- -

Prep: 25 min. • **Cook:** 7 hours
Makes: 6 servings

- 1   boneless beef chuck roast (3 to 4 lbs.)
- 1   tsp. salt
- ½   tsp. pepper
- 1   Tbsp. canola oil
- 1½   cups water
- ½   cup reduced-sodium soy sauce
- ¼   cup honey
- 3   Tbsp. cider vinegar
- 3   garlic cloves, minced
- 2   tsp. ground ginger
- 1   tsp. ground mustard
- 1   large onion, halved and sliced
- 2   Tbsp. cornstarch
- 2   Tbsp. cold water

1. Sprinkle roast with salt and pepper. In a large skillet, heat oil over medium-high heat. Brown roast on all sides. Transfer the meat to a 5- or 6-qt. slow cooker. In a small bowl, mix water, soy sauce, honey, vinegar, garlic, ginger and mustard; pour over meat. Top with onion. Cook, covered, on low until the meat is tender, 7-9 hours.

2. Remove the roast and onion to a serving platter; keep warm. Transfer cooking juices to a large saucepan; skim fat. Bring cooking juices to a boil. In a small bowl, mix cornstarch and cold water until smooth; stir into the cooking juices. Return to a boil; cook and stir until thickened, 1-2 minutes. Serve with roast.

6 OZ. COOKED BEEF WITH ½ CUP GRAVY: 489 cal., 24g fat (9g sat. fat), 147mg chol., 1256mg sod., 19g carb. (13g sugars, 1g fiber), 46g pro.

SLOW-COOKED SPAGHETTI SAUCE

I like to serve this homey dish to company and not just because it's easy and economical. I'd be lost without my slow cooker!
—*Shelley McKinney, New Castle, IN*

- -

Prep: 15 min. • **Cook:** 7 hours
Makes: 8 servings

- 1   lb. ground beef or bulk Italian sausage
- 1   medium onion, chopped
- 2   cans (14½ oz. each) diced tomatoes, undrained
- 1   can (8 oz.) tomato sauce
- 1   can (6 oz.) tomato paste
- 1   bay leaf
- 1   Tbsp. brown sugar
- 4   garlic cloves, minced
- 1   to 2 tsp. dried basil
- 1   to 2 tsp. dried oregano
- 1   tsp. salt
- ½   to 1 tsp. dried thyme
      Hot cooked spaghetti

1. In a large skillet, cook beef and onion over medium heat until the meat is no longer pink; drain.

2. Transfer the beef mixture to a 3-qt. slow cooker. Add next 10 ingredients. Cover and cook on low 7-8 hours or until heated through. Discard bay leaf. Serve with spaghetti.

1 SERVING: 142 cal., 5g fat (2g sat. fat), 28mg chol., 546mg sod., 13g carb. (8g sugars, 3g fiber), 12g pro.

PRESSURE-COOKER PORK TACOS WITH MANGO SALSA

I've made quite a few tacos in my day, but you can't beat the tender filling made in a pressure cooker. These are by far the best pork tacos we've had—and we've tried plenty. If you have time, make the mango salsa from scratch for an unbeatably fresh flavor!
—*Amber Massey, Argyle, TX*

- -

Prep: 25 min. • **Cook:** 5 min.
Makes: 12 servings

- 2 Tbsp. white vinegar
- 2 Tbsp. lime juice
- 3 cups cubed fresh pineapple
- 1 small red onion, coarsely chopped
- 3 Tbsp. chili powder
- 2 chipotle peppers in adobo sauce
- 2 tsp. ground cumin
- 1½ tsp. salt
- ½ tsp. pepper
- 1 bottle (12 oz.) dark Mexican beer
- 3 lbs. pork tenderloin, cut into 1-in. cubes
- ¼ cup chopped fresh cilantro
- 1 jar (16 oz.) mango salsa
- 24 corn tortillas (6 in.), warmed
  Optional toppings: Cubed fresh pineapple, cubed avocado and queso fresco

1. Puree the first 9 ingredients in a blender; stir in beer. In a 6-qt. electric pressure cooker, combine the pork and pineapple mixture. Lock lid; close pressure-release valve. Adjust to pressure-cook on high for 3 minutes. Quick-release pressure. (A thermometer inserted into pork should read at least 145°.) Stir to break up pork.
2. Stir cilantro into salsa. Using a slotted spoon, serve the pork mixture in tortillas; add salsa and toppings as desired.
FREEZE OPTION: Freeze the cooled meat mixture and cooking juices in airtight freezer containers. To use, partially thaw overnight in refrigerator. Heat through in a saucepan, stirring occasionally.
2 TACOS: 284 cal., 6g fat (2g sat. fat), 64mg chol., 678mg sod., 30g carb. (5g sugars, 5g fiber), 26g pro. **DIABETIC EXCHANGES:** 3 lean meat, 2 starch.

PRESSURE-COOKER BUFFALO SHRIMP MAC & CHEESE

Rich, creamy and slightly spicy, this shrimp and pasta dish does it all. It's a nice new twist on popular Buffalo chicken dishes.
—*Robin Haas, Cranston, RI*

- -

Prep: 15 min. • **Cook:** 10 min. + releasing
Makes: 6 servings

- 2 cups 2% milk
- 1 cup half-and-half cream
- 1 Tbsp. unsalted butter
- 1 tsp. ground mustard
- ½ tsp. onion powder
- ¼ tsp. white pepper
- ¼ tsp. ground nutmeg
- 1½ cups uncooked elbow macaroni
- 2 cups shredded cheddar cheese
- 1 cup shredded Gouda or Swiss cheese
- ¾ lb. frozen cooked salad shrimp, thawed
- 1 cup crumbled blue cheese
- 2 Tbsp. Louisiana-style hot sauce
- 2 Tbsp. minced fresh chives
- 2 Tbsp. minced fresh parsley
  Additional Louisiana-style hot sauce, optional

1. In a 6-qt. electric pressure cooker, combine the first 7 ingredients; stir in the macaroni. Lock lid; close pressure-release valve. Adjust to pressure-cook on high for 3 minutes. Let pressure naturally release for 4 minutes, then quick-release any remaining pressure.
2. Select saute setting and adjust for medium heat. Stir in shredded cheeses, shrimp, blue cheese and hot sauce. Cook mixture until heated through, 5-6 minutes. Just before serving, stir in chives, parsley and, if desired, additional hot sauce.
1 SERVING: 551 cal., 34g fat (20g sat. fat), 228mg chol., 1269mg sod., 22g carb. (7g sugars, 1g fiber), 38g pro.

> **TEST KITCHEN TIP**
> It couldn't be easier to make a Buffalo chicken version of this dish. Remember to start with cooked protein. Try rotisserie chicken or poached chicken breast in place of the shrimp.

EASY CHICKEN TAMALE PIE

All you need are simple ingredients from the pantry to put this slow-cooker meal together. I love that I can go fishing while it cooks!
—*Peter Halferty, Corpus Christi, TX*

Prep: 20 min. • **Cook:** 7 hours
Makes: 8 servings

- 1 lb. ground chicken
- 1 tsp. ground cumin
- 1 tsp. chili powder
- ½ tsp. salt
- ¼ tsp. pepper
- 1 can (15 oz.) black beans, rinsed and drained
- 1 can (14½ oz.) diced tomatoes, undrained
- 1 can (11 oz.) whole kernel corn, drained
- 1 can (10 oz.) enchilada sauce
- 2 green onions, chopped
- ¼ cup minced fresh cilantro
- 1 pkg. (8½ oz.) cornbread/muffin mix
- 2 large eggs, lightly beaten
- 1 cup shredded Mexican cheese blend
  Optional toppings: Sour cream, salsa and minced fresh cilantro

1. In a skillet, cook chicken over medium heat until no longer pink, 6-8 minutes, breaking into crumbles. Stir in cumin, chili powder, salt and pepper.
2. Transfer to a 4-qt. slow cooker. Stir in beans, tomatoes, corn, enchilada sauce, green onions and cilantro. Cook, covered, on low until heated through, 6-8 hours.
3. In a small bowl, combine muffin mix and eggs; spoon over the chicken mixture. Cook, covered, on low until a toothpick inserted in the cornbread layer comes out clean, 1-1½ hours longer.
4. Sprinkle with cheese; let stand, covered, 5 minutes. If desired, serve with toppings.
1 SERVING: 359 cal., 14g fat (5g sat. fat), 110mg chol., 1021mg sod., 40g carb. (11g sugars, 5g fiber), 20g pro.

SMOTHERED ROUND STEAK

Try less expensive round steak and gravy served over egg noodles for a most hearty meal. Meaty and loaded with veggies, this slow-cooker creation will take the worry out of what's-for-supper any weeknight.
—*Kathy Garrett, Camden, WV*

Prep: 15 min. • **Cook:** 6 hours
Makes: 4 servings

- 1½ lbs. beef top round steak, cut into strips
- ⅓ cup all-purpose flour
- ½ tsp. salt
- ¼ tsp. pepper
- 1 large onion, sliced
- 1 large green pepper, sliced
- 1 can (14½ oz.) diced tomatoes, undrained
- 1 jar (4 oz.) sliced mushrooms, drained
- 3 Tbsp. reduced-sodium soy sauce
- 2 Tbsp. molasses
  Hot cooked egg noodles, optional

1. In a 3-qt. slow cooker, toss the beef with flour, salt and pepper. Stir in all remaining ingredients except noodles.
2. Cook, covered, on low until meat is tender, 6-8 hours. If desired, serve with noodles.
1¼ CUPS BEEF MIXTURE: 335 cal., 6g fat (2g sat. fat), 95mg chol., 1064mg sod., 28g carb. (14g sugars, 4g fiber), 42g pro.

SLOW-SIMMERED MEAT RAGU

After a day spent simmering in the slow cooker, this ragu is not your typical spaghetti sauce. It's so hearty, it's almost like a stew.
—*Laurie LaClair, North Richland Hills, TX*

Prep: 30 min. • **Cook:** 6 hours
Makes: 10 servings

- 1 lb. Italian sausage links, cut into 1-in. pieces
- 1 medium onion, chopped
- 1 jar (24 oz.) tomato basil pasta sauce
- 1 can (14½ oz.) Italian diced tomatoes, undrained
- 2 jars (6 oz. each) sliced mushrooms, drained
- 1 can (8 oz.) tomato sauce
- 1 jar (3½ oz.) prepared pesto
- 1½ lbs. chicken tenderloins
- 1 medium sweet red pepper, chopped
- ½ cup chopped pepperoni
- ½ cup pitted ripe olives, halved
- 1 tsp. dried oregano
- ½ tsp. hot pepper sauce
   Hot cooked angel hair pasta

1. Heat a large skillet over medium heat. Add sausage and onion; cook and stir until the sausage is no longer pink and the onion is tender. Drain.

2. In a 5- or 6-qt. slow cooker, combine the next 11 ingredients. Add the sausage mixture.

3. Cook, covered, on low 6-8 hours or until chicken is tender. Serve with pasta.

FREEZE OPTION: Freeze the cooled sauce in freezer containers. To use, partially thaw in refrigerator overnight. Place in a large saucepan; heat through, stirring occasionally and adding a little water if necessary. Cook pasta according to package directions. Serve as directed.

1 CUP: 341 cal., 20g fat (5g sat. fat), 64mg chol., 1294mg sod., 18g carb. (10g sugars, 4g fiber), 26g pro.

MEXICAN BEEF-STUFFED PEPPERS

I grew up eating stuffed peppers and thought my husband would love them as well—but he didn't. Because he loves fajitas and tacos, I created this slow-cooked recipe for peppers and tucked all his favorite flavors inside. Now he loves them!
—*Nicole Sullivan, Arvada, CO*

Prep: 15 min. • **Cook:** 5 hours
Makes: 4 servings

- 4 medium green or sweet red peppers
- 1 lb. ground beef
- 1 pkg. (8.8 oz.) ready-to-serve Spanish rice
- 2 cups shredded Colby-Monterey Jack cheese, divided
- 1½ cups salsa
- 1 Tbsp. hot pepper sauce
- 1 cup water
- 2 Tbsp. minced fresh cilantro

1. Cut the tops off peppers and remove seeds; set aside.
2. In a large skillet, cook beef over medium heat until no longer pink; drain. Stir in rice, 1½ cups cheese, salsa and pepper sauce.
3. Spoon meat mixture into peppers. Transfer to a 5-qt. slow cooker. Pour water around peppers. Cover and cook on low for 5-6 hours or until peppers are tender and the filling is heated through. Top with the remaining cheese; sprinkle with cilantro.

1 STUFFED PEPPER: 646 cal., 37g fat (19g sat. fat), 133mg chol., 1241mg sod., 39g carb. (12g sugars, 5g fiber), 40g pro.

BAJA PORK TACOS

This delicious recipe is my copycat version of the most excellent Mexican food we ever had. The original recipe used beef, but this pork version comes mighty close to the same taste.
—*Ariella Winn, Mesquite, TX*

Prep: 10 min. • **Cook:** 8 hours
Makes: 12 servings

- 1 boneless pork sirloin roast (3 lbs.)
- 5 cans (4 oz. each) chopped green chiles
- 2 Tbsp. reduced-sodium taco seasoning
- 3 tsp. ground cumin
- 24 corn tortillas (6 in.), warmed
- 3 cups shredded lettuce
- 1½ cups shredded part-skim mozzarella cheese

1. Cut roast in half; place in a 3- or 4-qt. slow cooker. Mix chiles, taco seasoning and cumin; spoon over pork. Cook, covered, on low until the meat is tender, 8-10 hours.
2. Remove pork roast; cool slightly. Skim fat from cooking juices. Shred meat with 2 forks. Return to slow cooker; heat through. Serve in tortillas with lettuce and cheese.
FREEZE OPTION: Place cooled pork mixture in freezer containers; freeze up to 3 months. To use, partially thaw in refrigerator overnight. Heat through in a covered saucepan, stirring gently and adding a little broth if necessary.
2 TACOS: 320 cal., 11g fat (4g sat. fat), 77mg chol., 434mg sod., 26g carb. (1g sugars, 4g fiber), 30g pro. **DIABETIC EXCHANGES:** 3 medium-fat meat, 2 starch.

HEALTH TIP
Using reduced-sodium taco seasoning brings sodium down about 80 milligrams per serving.

SWEET & SAVORY BRISKET

This recipe makes such tender and flavorful beef. It's wonderful to come home from work and have this mouthwatering dish waiting for me!
—*Chris Snyder, Boulder, CO*

- -

Prep: 10 min. • **Cook:** 8 hours
Makes: 10 servings

- 1 beef brisket (3 to 3½ lbs.), cut in half
- 1 cup ketchup
- ¼ cup grape jelly
- 1 envelope onion soup mix
- ½ tsp. pepper

Place half the brisket in a 5-qt. slow cooker. In a small bowl, combine the ketchup, jelly, soup mix and pepper; spread half over the meat. Top with the remaining meat and ketchup mixture. Cover and cook on low for 8-10 hours or until the meat is tender. Slice brisket; serve with cooking juice.

NOTE: This uses a fresh beef brisket, not corned beef.

4 OZ. COOKED BEEF: 223 cal., 6g fat (2g sat. fat), 58mg chol., 596mg sod., 13g carb. (11g sugars, 0 fiber), 28g pro. **DIABETIC EXCHANGES:** 4 lean meat, 1 starch.

PRESSURE-COOKER CHICKEN THIGHS IN WINE SAUCE

I love this recipe for its incredible flavor—and it seems everyone who tries it does, too. For an easy pairing, try mashed potatoes and peas.
—*Heike Annucci, Hudson, NC*

- -

Prep: 15 min. • **Cook:** 20 min. + releasing
Makes: 4 servings

- 2 Tbsp. butter, divided
- 1 cup sliced fresh mushrooms
- 6 bone-in chicken thighs, skin removed (about 2¼ lbs.)
- ¼ tsp. salt
- ¼ tsp. pepper
- ¼ tsp. Italian seasoning
- ¼ tsp. paprika
- ⅓ cup all-purpose flour
- ½ cup chicken broth
- ½ cup white wine or additional chicken broth
- 3 green onions, thinly sliced

1. Select saute setting on a 6-qt. electric pressure cooker and adjust for medium heat; add 1 Tbsp. butter. When hot, add mushrooms; cook until tender, 3-4 minutes. Remove. Sprinkle chicken with salt, pepper, Italian seasoning and paprika. Place flour in a shallow bowl. Add chicken, a few pieces at a time, and toss to coat; shake off excess.

2. Heat the remaining butter in pressure cooker; brown chicken on both sides. Remove. Add the broth and wine to pressure cooker. Cook 2-3 minutes, stirring to loosen browned bits from pan. Press cancel.

3. Return chicken and mushrooms to cooker; add green onions. Lock lid and close pressure-release valve. Adjust to pressure-cook on high for 10 minutes. Let pressure naturally release for 10 minutes and quick-release any remaining pressure. (A thermometer inserted in chicken should read at least 165°.)

1 SERVING: 243 cal., 13g fat (5g sat. fat), 97mg chol., 284mg sod., 3g carb. (1g sugars, 0 fiber), 25g pro. **DIABETIC EXCHANGES:** 3 lean meat, 1½ fat.

SLOW-COOKED CARNITAS

Simmer up succulent pork the slow-cooker way. Sometimes I put the seasoned meat on top of shredded lettuce for a tasty salad, instead of using tortillas.
—*Lisa Glogow, Aliso Viejo, CA*

- -

Prep: 20 min. • **Cook:** 6 hours
Makes: 12 servings

- 1 boneless pork shoulder butt roast (3 to 4 lbs.)
- 3 garlic cloves, thinly sliced
- 2 tsp. olive oil
- ½ tsp. salt
- ½ tsp. pepper
- 1 bunch green onions, chopped
- 1½ cups minced fresh cilantro
- 1 cup salsa
- ½ cup chicken broth
- ½ cup tequila or additional chicken broth
- 2 cans (4 oz. each) chopped green chiles
- 12 flour tortillas (8 in.) or corn tortillas (6 in.), warmed

Optional toppings: Fresh cilantro leaves, sliced red onion and chopped tomatoes

1. Cut roast in half; place in a 5-qt. slow cooker. Sprinkle with the garlic, oil, salt and pepper. Add the onions, cilantro, salsa, broth, tequila and chiles. Cover and cook on low for 6-8 hours or until meat is tender.
2. Remove meat; cool slightly. Shred with 2 forks and return to the slow cooker; heat through. Spoon about ⅔ cup meat mixture onto each tortilla; serve with the toppings of your choice.
1 TACO: 363 cal., 15g fat (5g sat. fat), 67mg chol., 615mg sod., 28g carb. (1g sugars, 1g fiber), 24g pro.

GERMAN-STYLE SHORT RIBS

Our whole family is excited when I plug in the slow cooker to make these amazing ribs. We like them served over rice or egg noodles.
—*Bregitte Rugman, Shanty Bay, ON*

- -

Prep: 15 min. • **Cook:** 8 hours
Makes: 8 servings

- ¾ cup dry red wine or beef broth
- ½ cup mango chutney
- 3 Tbsp. quick-cooking tapioca
- ¼ cup water
- 3 Tbsp. brown sugar
- 3 Tbsp. cider vinegar
- 1 Tbsp. Worcestershire sauce
- ½ tsp. salt
- ½ tsp. ground mustard
- ½ tsp. chili powder
- ½ tsp. pepper
- 4 lbs. bone-in beef short ribs
- 2 medium onions, sliced
  Hot cooked egg noodles

1. In a 5-qt. slow cooker, combine the first 11 ingredients. Add ribs and turn to coat. Top with onions.
2. Cover and cook on low for 8-10 hours or until the meat is tender. Remove ribs from the slow cooker. Skim fat from the cooking juices; serve with ribs and noodles.
3 OZ. COOKED BEEF: 302 cal., 11g fat (5g sat. fat), 55mg chol., 378mg sod., 28g carb. (17g sugars, 1g fiber), 19g pro.

PRESSURE-COOKER BBQ CHICKEN & SMOKED SAUSAGE

My party-ready barbecue recipe is perfect on weeknights, too. With just a little prep time, you still get that low-and-slow flavor everybody craves (thanks, pressure cooker!). Throw in minced jalapenos for extra oomph.
—*Kimberly Young, Mesquite, TX*

- -

Prep: 10 min. • **Cook:** 25 min. + releasing
Makes: 8 servings

- 1   medium onion, chopped
- 1   large sweet red pepper, cut into 1-in. pieces
- 4   bone-in chicken thighs, skin removed
- 4   chicken drumsticks, skin removed
- 1   pkg. (12 oz.) smoked sausage links, cut into 1-in. pieces
- 1   cup chicken broth
- 1   cup barbecue sauce
     Sliced seeded jalapeno pepper, optional

1. Place the first 6 ingredients in a 6-qt. electric pressure cooker; top with barbecue sauce. Lock lid and close pressure-release valve. Adjust to pressure-cook on high for 12 minutes. Quick-release pressure. Remove chicken, sausage and vegetables from cooker (a thermometer inserted in chicken should read at least 170°) and keep warm.
2. Select saute setting and adjust for low heat; bring the liquid to a boil. Reduce heat; simmer until thickened, 12-15 minutes, stirring occasionally.
3. Serve chicken, sausage and vegetables with the sauce. If desired, top with jalapeno.
1 SERVING: 338 cal., 18g fat (7g sat. fat), 93mg chol., 1009mg sod., 18g carb. (14g sugars, 1g fiber), 25g pro.

PRESSURE-COOKER RISOTTO WITH SHRIMP & ASPARAGUS

Forget standing over the stove and constantly stirring—this speedy method of making risotto works every time!
—*Kim Gray, Davie, FL*

- -

Takes: 30 min • **Makes:** 8 servings

- 2   Tbsp. olive oil
- 9   garlic cloves, minced, divided
- 2   lbs. uncooked shrimp (26-30 per lb.), peeled and deveined
- 4   Tbsp. unsalted butter, divided
- ½   cup Italian salad dressing
- 1   lb. fresh asparagus, trimmed
- 1   small onion, finely diced
- 1⅔   cups uncooked arborio rice
- 1   cup white wine
- 4   cups reduced-sodium chicken broth
- ½   cup shredded Parmesan cheese, divided
       Salt and pepper to taste

1. Select the saute setting on a 6-qt. electric pressure cooker. Adjust for medium heat; add oil. When oil is hot, add 3 minced garlic cloves; cook 1 minute. Add shrimp; cook and stir until the shrimp begin to turn pink, about 5 minutes. Add 1 Tbsp. butter and Italian salad dressing; stir until butter melts. Add asparagus; cook until tender, 3-5 minutes. Remove and keep warm.
2. Warm the remaining 3 Tbsp. butter until melted. Add diced onion; cook until tender, 4-5 minutes. Add remaining 6 minced garlic cloves; cook 1 minute. Add rice; cook and stir for 2 minutes. Stir in ½ cup wine; cook and stir until absorbed. Add remaining ½ cup wine, broth and ¼ cup cheese. Press cancel.
3. Lock the lid; close pressure-release valve. Adjust to pressure-cook on high for 8 minutes; quick-release pressure.
4. Serve shrimp mixture over risotto. Season with salt and pepper. Sprinkle with remaining ¼ cup cheese.
1 SERVING: 424 cal., 15g fat (6g sat. fat), 157mg chol., 661mg sod., 39g carb. (3g sugars, 1g fiber), 26g pro.

PRESSURE-COOKER MUSHROOM PORK RAGOUT

Savory, quickly made pork is luscious served in a delightful tomato gravy over noodles. It's a nice change from regular pork roast. I serve it with broccoli or green beans on the side.
—*Connie McDowell, Greenwood, DE*

- -

Prep: 20 min. • **Cook:** 10 min.
Makes: 2 servings

1	pork tenderloin (¾ lb.)
⅛	tsp. salt
⅛	tsp. pepper
1½	cups sliced fresh mushrooms
¾	cup canned crushed tomatoes
¾	cup reduced-sodium chicken broth, divided
⅓	cup sliced onion
1	Tbsp. chopped sun-dried tomatoes (not packed in oil)
1¼	tsp. dried savory
1	Tbsp. cornstarch
1½	cups hot cooked egg noodles

1. Cut pork tenderloin in half; rub with salt and pepper; cut in half. Place in a 6-qt. electric pressure cooker. Top with sliced mushrooms, tomatoes, ½ cup broth, the onion, sun-dried tomatoes and savory.
2. Lock lid and close pressure-release valve. Adjust to pressure-cook on high for 6 minutes. Quick-release pressure. (A thermometer inserted in the pork should read at least 145°.) Remove pork; keep warm.
3. In a small bowl, mix cornstarch and remaining broth until smooth; stir into the pressure cooker. Select the saute setting and adjust for low heat. Simmer, stirring constantly, until thickened, 1-2 minutes. Slice pork; serve with sauce and noodles.
FREEZE OPTION: Place sliced pork and vegetables in freezer containers; top with sauce. Cool and freeze. To use, partially thaw in refrigerator overnight. Heat through in a covered saucepan, stirring gently and adding a little broth if necessary.
1 SERVING: 387 cal., 8g fat (2g sat. fat), 119mg chol., 613mg sod., 37g carb. (8g sugars, 4g fiber), 43g pro. **DIABETIC EXCHANGES:** 5 lean meat, 2 vegetable, 1 starch.

PRESSURE-COOKER BARBECUED BEEF RIBS

These tender, tangy ribs taste slow-cooked but are a cinch to make. They're great for picnics as well as a family dinner.
—*Erin Glass, White Hall, MD*

- -

Prep: 15 min. • **Cook:** 45 min. + releasing
Makes: 8 servings

2	Tbsp. canola oil
4	lbs. bone-in beef short ribs, trimmed
1	large sweet onion, halved and sliced
½	cup water
1	bottle (12 oz.) chili sauce
¾	cup plum preserves or preserves of your choice
2	Tbsp. packed brown sugar
2	Tbsp. red wine vinegar
2	Tbsp. Worcestershire sauce
2	Tbsp. Dijon mustard
¼	tsp. ground cloves

1. Select saute or browning setting on a 6-qt. electric pressure cooker and adjust for medium heat; add oil. Brown ribs in batches, adding additional oil as needed. Remove ribs. Brown onions. Add ribs back to the pressure cooker. Add water. Lock lid; close pressure-release valve. Adjust to pressure-cook on high for 40 minutes. Let pressure release naturally for 10 minutes and then quick-release any remaining pressure.
2. In a small saucepan, combine the remaining ingredients; cook and stir over medium heat until heated through. Remove ribs from pressure cooker; discard cooking juices. Return ribs to pressure cooker. Pour sauce over top. Lock lid; close pressure-release valve. Adjust to pressure-cook on low for 5 minutes. Allow pressure to naturally release for 5 minutes and then quick-release any remaining pressure. Serve ribs with sauce.
1 SERVING: 359 cal., 14g fat (5g sat. fat), 55mg chol., 860mg sod., 40g carb. (33g sugars, 0 fiber), 18g pro.

SWEET & TANGY CHICKEN

My slow cooker comes in so handy during the haying and harvest seasons. We're so busy that if supper isn't prepared before I serve lunch, it doesn't seem to get done on time. This recipe is fuss-free and ready when we are.
—*Joan Airey, Rivers, MB*

Prep: 15 min. • **Cook:** 4 hours
Makes: 4 servings

- 1 medium onion, chopped
- 1½ tsp. minced garlic
- 1 broiler/fryer chicken (3 lbs.), cut up, skin removed
- ⅔ cup ketchup
- ⅓ cup packed brown sugar
- 1 Tbsp. chili powder
- 1 Tbsp. lemon juice
- 1 tsp. dried basil
- ½ tsp. salt
- ¼ tsp. pepper
- ⅛ tsp. hot pepper sauce
- 2 Tbsp. cornstarch
- 3 Tbsp. cold water

1. In a 3-qt. slow cooker, combine onion and garlic; top with chicken. In a small bowl, combine ketchup, brown sugar, chili powder, lemon juice, basil, salt, pepper and hot pepper sauce; pour over chicken. Cover and cook on low for 4-5 hours or until the meat is tender. Remove the chicken to a serving platter; keep warm.
2. Skim fat from the cooking juices; transfer to a small saucepan. Bring liquid to a boil. Combine cornstarch and water until smooth. Gradually stir into the pan. Bring to a boil; cook and stir for 2 minutes or until thickened. Serve with chicken.
12 OZ. COOKED CHICKEN WITH SAUCE: 385 cal., 9g fat (3g sat. fat), 110mg chol., 892mg sod., 38g carb. (25g sugars, 2g fiber), 38g pro.

PRESSURE-COOKER TOMATO-POACHED HALIBUT

Simple halibut with a burst of lemon comes together easily. Serve it with bread or, even better, with polenta or angel hair pasta.
—*Danna Rogers, Westport, CT*

Prep: 15 min. • **Cook:** 5 min.
Makes: 4 servings

- 1 Tbsp. olive oil
- 2 poblano peppers, finely chopped
- 1 small onion, finely chopped
- 1 can (14½ oz.) fire-roasted diced tomatoes, undrained
- 1 can (14½ oz.) no-salt-added diced tomatoes, undrained
- ½ cup water
- ¼ cup chopped pitted green olives
- 3 garlic cloves, minced
- ¼ tsp. pepper
- ⅛ tsp. salt
- 4 halibut fillets (4 oz. each)
- ⅓ cup chopped fresh cilantro
- 4 lemon wedges
  Crusty whole grain bread, optional

1. Select the saute setting on a 6-qt. electric pressure cooker. Adjust for medium heat; add oil. When oil is hot, cook and stir peppers and onion until crisp-tender, 2-3 minutes. Press cancel. Stir in tomatoes, water, olives, garlic, pepper and salt. Top with fillets.
2. Lock the lid; close pressure-release valve. Adjust to pressure-cook on high for 3 minutes. Quick-release pressure. (A thermometer inserted in fish should read at least 145°.)
3. Sprinkle with cilantro. Serve with lemon wedges and, if desired, bread.
1 FILLET WITH 1 CUP SAUCE: 215 cal., 7g fat (1g sat. fat), 56mg chol., 614mg sod., 16g carb. (7g sugars, 3g fiber), 23g pro. **DIABETIC EXCHANGES:** 3 lean meat, 1 starch, ½ fat.

PRESSURE-COOKER SAUERBRATEN

One of my all-time favorite German dishes is sauerbraten, but I don't love that it normally takes five to 10 days to make! Using an electric pressure cooker, I've captured that same distinctive flavor in less than two hours.
—*James Schend, Pleasant Prairie, WI*

Prep: 20 min. + standing • **Cook:** 20 min.
Makes: 4 servings

- 4 whole cloves
- 4 whole peppercorns
- 1 bay leaf
- ½ cup water
- ½ cup white vinegar
- 2 tsp. sugar
- ½ tsp. salt
  Dash ground ginger
- 1 lb. boneless beef top round steak, cut into 1-in. cubes
- 3 medium carrots, cut into ½-in. slices
- 2 celery ribs, cut into ½-in. slices
- 1 small onion, chopped
- ⅓ cup crushed gingersnaps
  Hot cooked egg noodles
  Optional: Chopped fresh parsley and coarsely ground pepper

1. Place cloves, peppercorns and bay leaf on a double thickness of cheesecloth; bring up the corners of the cloth and tie with kitchen string to form a bag. In a large bowl, combine water, vinegar, sugar, salt, ginger. Add beef and the spice bag; let stand at room temperature for 30 minutes.
2. Transfer all to a 6-qt. electric pressure cooker. Add carrots, celery and onion. Lock the lid and close pressure-release valve. Adjust to pressure-cook on high for 10 minutes. Quick-release pressure. Select saute setting and adjust for medium heat; bring liquid to a boil. Discard the spice bag. Stir in gingersnaps; cook and stir until thickened, about 3 minutes. Serve with egg noodles. If desired, top with parsley and pepper.

FREEZE OPTION: Freeze cooled sauerbraten in freezer containers. To use, partially thaw in refrigerator overnight. Heat through in a saucepan, stirring occasionally and adding a little broth or water if necessary.
1 CUP: 228 cal., 5g fat (2g sat. fat), 63mg chol., 436mg sod., 18g carb. (8g sugars, 2g fiber), 27g pro. **DIABETIC EXCHANGES:** 3 lean meat, 1 starch, 1 vegetable.

READER REVIEW

"We're big fans of sauerbraten, and when I saw this, I had to try it. It's a great recipe, and it has as much flavor as the one that takes days to make!"

ANNRMS, TASTEOFHOME.COM

PRESSURE-COOKER RISOTTO WITH CHICKEN & MUSHROOMS

Portobello mushrooms add an earthy flavor to this creamy classic, while shredded rotisserie chicken makes it a snap to prepare. You'll savor every bite.
—*Charlene Chambers, Ormond Beach, FL*

- -

Takes: 30 min. • **Makes:** 4 servings

- 4 Tbsp. unsalted butter, divided
- 2 Tbsp. olive oil
- ½ lb. sliced baby portobello mushrooms
- 1 small onion, finely chopped
- 1½ cups uncooked arborio rice
- ½ cup white wine or chicken broth
- 1 Tbsp. lemon juice
- 1 carton (32 oz.) chicken broth
- 2 cups shredded rotisserie chicken
- 3 Tbsp. grated Parmesan cheese
- 2 Tbsp. minced fresh parsley
- ½ tsp. salt
- ¼ tsp. pepper

1. On a 6-qt. electric pressure cooker, select the saute setting; adjust for medium heat. Add 2 Tbsp. butter and oil. Add mushrooms and onion; cook and stir until tender, 6-8 minutes. Add rice; cook and stir until the rice is coated, 2-3 minutes.

2. Stir in wine and lemon juice; cook and stir until liquid is absorbed. Pour in broth. Lock lid; make sure vent is closed. Adjust to pressure-cook on low for 4 minutes. Quick-release pressure. Stir until combined; continue stirring until creamy.

3. Stir in the remaining ingredients and the remaining butter. Select saute setting and adjust for low heat; heat through. Serve immediately.

1½ CUPS: 636 cal., 26g fat (10g sat. fat), 101mg chol., 1411mg sod., 66g carb. (4g sugars, 2g fiber), 29g pro.

PRESSURE-COOKER GENERAL TSO'S STEW

I love Asian food and wanted a chili-style soup with flavors of General Tso. You can use any meat you like—chicken, turkey pork or ground meats.
—*Lori McLain, Denton, TX*

Prep: 10 min. • **Cook:** 10 min.
Makes: 6 servings

- 1 cup tomato juice
- ½ cup water
- ½ cup pickled cherry peppers, chopped
- 2 Tbsp. soy sauce
- 2 Tbsp. hoisin sauce
- 1 Tbsp. peanut oil
- 1 to 2 tsp. crushed red pepper flakes
- 1 lb. boneless skinless chicken breast halves
- 1½ cups chopped onion
- 1 cup chopped fresh broccoli
- ¼ cup chopped green onions
- 1 tsp. sesame seeds, toasted

In a 6-qt. electric pressure cooker, combine the first 7 ingredients. Top with chicken, onion and broccoli. Lock lid; close pressure-release valve. Adjust to pressure-cook on high for 6 minutes. Quick-release pressure. (A thermometer inserted in chicken should read at least 165°.) Remove chicken; shred with 2 forks. Return to pressure cooker; heat through. Top with green onions and sesame seeds to serve.

FREEZE OPTION: Freeze cooled stew in freezer containers. To use, partially thaw in refrigerator overnight. Heat through in a saucepan, stirring occasionally and adding a little water if necessary.

1 CUP: 159 cal., 5g fat (1g sat. fat), 42mg chol., 762mg sod., 10g carb. (5g sugars, 2g fiber), 18g pro. **DIABETIC EXCHANGES:** 2 lean meat, 2 vegetable, ½ fat.

FLAVORFUL POT ROAST

On hectic days, this is so quick and easy to prep! Convenient packages of dressing and gravy combine to create a sauce worthy of a fall-apart roast. For a filling meal-in-one, serve with mashed potatoes and ladle the juices over top.
—*Arlene Butler, Ogden, UT*

Prep: 10 min. • **Cook:** 7 hours
Makes: 15 servings

- 2 boneless beef chuck roasts (2½ lbs. each)
- 1 envelope ranch salad dressing mix
- 1 envelope Italian salad dressing mix
- 1 envelope brown gravy mix
- ½ cup water
  Chopped fresh parsley, optional

Place the chuck roasts in a 5-qt. slow cooker. In a small bowl, combine the salad dressings and gravy mix; stir in water. Pour over meat. Cover and cook on low for 7-8 hours or until tender. If desired, sprinkle with parsley and thicken cooking juices for gravy.

6 OZ. COOKED BEEF: 142 cal., 7g fat (3g sat. fat), 49mg chol., 496mg sod., 3g carb. (1g sugars, 0 fiber), 15g pro.

PRESSURE-COOKER COUNTRY CAPTAIN CHICKEN

Whether or not it was brought to the region by a British sailor, as popular legend has it, the recipe for Country Captain Chicken has been around Georgia since the 1800s. Traditionally served over rice, it's also delicious with noodles or mashed potatoes.
—*Suzanne Banfield, Basking Ridge, NJ*

Prep: 25 min. • **Cook:** 10 min.
Makes: 8 servings

- 1 large onion, chopped
- 1 medium sweet red pepper, chopped
- 2 garlic cloves, minced
- 3 lbs. boneless skinless chicken thighs
- ½ cup chicken broth
- 1 Tbsp. brown sugar
- 1 Tbsp. curry powder
- 1 tsp. ground ginger
- 1 tsp. ground cinnamon
- 1 tsp. dried thyme
- 1 can (14½ oz.) diced tomatoes, undrained
- ½ cup golden raisins or raisins
  Hot cooked rice
  Chopped fresh parsley, optional

Place onion, red pepper and garlic in a 6-qt. electric pressure cooker; top with chicken. In a small bowl, whisk broth, brown sugar and seasonings; pour over chicken. Top with tomatoes and raisins. Lock lid; close pressure-release valve. Adjust to pressure-cook on high for 6 minutes. Quick-release the pressure. A thermometer inserted in chicken should read at least 170°. Thicken cooking juices if desired. Serve with rice and if desired, parsley.

FREEZE OPTION: Place cooked chicken and vegetables in airtight freezer containers; top with cooking juices. Cool and freeze. To use, partially thaw in refrigerator overnight. Heat through in a covered saucepan, stirring gently and adding a little broth if necessary.

1 SERVING: 298 cal., 13g fat (3g sat. fat), 114mg chol., 159mg sod., 13g carb. (9g sugars, 2g fiber), 32g pro. **DIABETIC EXCHANGES:** 4 lean meat, 1 vegetable, ½ starch.

MEXICAN BUBBLE PIZZA

This tasty slow-cooked pizza offers a new way to experience Mexican cuisine. Serve it at your next party and watch it disappear! The meat mixture can be made in advance; just rewarm it before stirring in the biscuits.
—*Jackie Hannahs, Cedar Springs, MI*

Prep: 15 min. • **Cook:** 3 hours
Makes: 6 servings

- 1½ lbs. ground beef
- 1 can (10¾ oz.) condensed tomato soup, undiluted
- ¾ cup water
- 1 envelope taco seasoning
- 1 tube (16.3 oz.) large refrigerated buttermilk biscuits
- 2 cups shredded cheddar cheese
  Optional toppings: Shredded lettuce, chopped tomatoes, salsa, sliced ripe olives, sour cream and thinly sliced green onions

1. Line a 6-qt. slow cooker with a double thickness of heavy-duty foil. Coat with cooking spray.

2. In a large skillet, cook beef over medium heat until no longer pink, 6-8 minutes, breaking into crumbles; drain. Stir in soup, water and taco seasoning. Bring to a boil. Reduce heat; simmer, uncovered, until slightly thickened, 3-5 minutes.

3. Cut each biscuit into 4 pieces; gently stir into the beef mixture. Transfer to prepared slow cooker. Cook, covered, on low until the dough is cooked through, 3-4 hours. Sprinkle with cheese. Cook, covered, until the cheese is melted, about 5 minutes longer. Serve with toppings of your choice.

1 SERVING: 643 cal., 35g fat (15g sat. fat), 109mg chol., 1870mg sod., 46g carb. (8g sugars, 2g fiber), 35g pro.

PRESSURE-COOKER AUTUMN APPLE CHICKEN

Fill the whole house with the aroma of chicken with apples and barbecue sauce. This is a meal you won't want to wait to dig into.
—*Caitlyn Hauser, Brookline, NH*

Prep: 25 min. • **Cook:** 20 min.
Makes: 4 servings

- 4 bone-in chicken thighs (about 1½ lbs.), skin removed
- ¼ tsp. salt
- ¼ tsp. pepper
- 1 Tbsp. canola oil
- ½ cup apple cider or juice
- 1 medium onion, chopped
- ⅓ cup barbecue sauce
- 1 Tbsp. honey
- 1 garlic clove, minced
- 2 medium Fuji or Gala apples, coarsely chopped

1. Sprinkle chicken with salt and pepper. Select saute or browning setting on a 6-qt. electric pressure cooker. Adjust for medium heat; add oil. When oil is hot, brown the chicken; remove and keep warm.
2. Add cider, stirring to loosen browned bits from pan. Stir in onion, barbecue sauce, honey, garlic and the chicken. Press cancel. Lock lid; close pressure-release valve. Adjust to pressure-cook on high for 10 minutes. Let pressure release naturally for 5 minutes; quick-release any remaining pressure. (A thermometer inserted in the chicken should read at least 170°.) Press cancel.
3. Remove chicken; keep warm. Select saute setting and adjust for low heat. Add apples; simmer, stirring constantly, until apples are tender, about 10 minutes. Serve with chicken.
1 CHICKEN THIGH WITH ½ CUP APPLE MIXTURE: 340 cal., 13g fat (3g sat. fat), 87mg chol., 458mg sod., 31g carb. (24g sugars, 3g fiber), 25g pro. **DIABETIC EXCHANGES:** 4 lean meat, 1½ starch, ½ fruit.

POLYNESIAN ROAST BEEF

This marvelous recipe from my sister has been a family favorite for years. The pineapple and peppers add a perfect contrast to the rich and savory beef.
—*Annette Mosbarger, Peyton, CO*

Prep: 15 min. • **Cook:** 7 hours
Makes: 10 servings

- 1 beef top round roast (3¼ lbs.)
- 2 Tbsp. browning sauce, optional
- ¼ cup all-purpose flour
- 1 tsp. salt
- ¼ tsp. pepper
- 1 medium onion, sliced
- 1 can (8 oz.) unsweetened sliced pineapple
- ¼ cup packed brown sugar
- 2 Tbsp. cornstarch
- ¼ tsp. ground ginger
- ½ cup beef broth
- ¼ cup reduced-sodium soy sauce
- ½ tsp. minced garlic
- 1 medium green pepper, sliced

1. Cut roast in half; brush with browning sauce if desired. Combine the flour, salt and pepper; rub over the meat. Place onion in a 3-qt. slow cooker; top with the roast.
2. Drain pineapple, reserving juice; refrigerate pineapple. In a small bowl, combine the brown sugar, cornstarch and ginger; whisk in the broth, soy sauce, garlic and the reserved pineapple juice until smooth. Pour over the meat. Cover and cook on low for 6-8 hours.
3. Add pineapple and green pepper. Cook for 1 hour longer or until the meat is tender.
4 OZ. COOKED BEEF: 253cal., 5g fat (2g sat. fat), 82mg chol., 560mg sod., 16g carb. (10g sugars, 1 fiber), 34g pro.

CREAMY ONION PORK CHOPS

Wine adds delectable flavor to these pork chops, and the meat falls from the bone. This easy dish just might initiate every family member into the clean-plate club!
—*Kristina Wyatt, Catawba, VA*

Prep: 10 min. • **Cook:** 8 hours
Makes: 6 servings

- 6 bone-in pork loin chops (8 oz. each)
- ¼ tsp. pepper
- ⅛ tsp. salt
- 1¼ cups 2% milk
- 1 can (10¾ oz.) condensed cream of onion soup, undiluted
- 1 can (10¾ oz.) reduced-fat reduced-sodium condensed cream of mushroom soup, undiluted
- ⅔ cup white wine or chicken broth
- 1 envelope ranch salad dressing mix
- 3 Tbsp. cornstarch
- 2 Tbsp. water
- Minced fresh parsley, optional

1. Sprinkle pork chops with pepper and salt; transfer to a 4-qt slow cooker. Combine milk, soups, wine and dressing mix; pour over the pork. Cover and cook on low 8-10 hours or until the pork is tender.

2. Remove the pork to a serving platter and keep warm. Skim fat from cooking juices; transfer to a large saucepan and bring to a boil. Combine cornstarch and water until smooth; gradually stir into the pan. Bring to a boil; cook and stir for 2 minutes or until thickened. Serve with pork. Sprinkle with parsley if desired.

1 PORK CHOP WITH ⅔ CUP GRAVY: 446 cal., 22g fat (8g sat. fat), 123mg chol., 1105mg sod., 18g carb. (5g sugars, 1g fiber), 39g pro.

CORNED BEEF SUPPER

What better way to celebrate St. Patrick's Day than with this hearty one-pot meal. I often fix it for the holiday, but it's good all year.
—*Dawn Fagerstrom, Warren, MN*

Prep: 25 min. • **Cook:** 3½ hours
Makes: 2 servings

- 1 small onion, sliced
- 4 small carrots, cut into chunks
- 2 medium potatoes, cut into chunks
- 1 corned beef brisket with spice packet (1 lb.)
- ⅓ cup unsweetened apple juice
- 2 whole cloves
- 1 Tbsp. brown sugar
- ½ tsp. grated orange zest
- ½ tsp. prepared mustard
- 2 cabbage wedges

1. Place onion in a 3-qt. slow cooker. Top with carrots, potatoes and brisket. Combine the apple juice, cloves, brown sugar, orange zest, mustard and the contents of spice packet; pour over brisket. Cover and cook on high for 3-4 hours.

2. Add cabbage; cover and cook 30 minutes longer or until the meat and vegetables are tender. Strain and discard cloves; serve pan juices with corned beef and vegetables.

1 SERVING: 692 cal., 31g fat (10g sat. fat), 156mg chol., 1918mg sod., 69g carb. (23g sugars, 9g fiber), 36g pro.

PRESSURE-COOKER CAJUN-STYLE BEANS AND SAUSAGE

Beans and rice make the perfect meal because they're well-balanced, an excellent source of protein, and easy to prepare. Sausage adds full flavor to the recipe, and traditional pork sausage lovers won't even notice the switch to chicken sausage.
—Robin Haas, Cranston, RI

Prep: 25 min. • Cook: 5 min. + releasing
Makes: 8 servings

- 1 pkg. (12 oz.) fully cooked spicy chicken sausage links, halved lengthwise and cut into ½-in. slices
- ¾ cup reduced-sodium chicken broth
- 2 cans (16 oz. each) red beans, rinsed and drained
- 2 cans (14½ oz. each) diced tomatoes, undrained
- 3 medium carrots, chopped
- 1 large onion, chopped
- 1 large green pepper, chopped
- ½ cup chopped roasted sweet red peppers
- 3 garlic cloves, minced
- 1 tsp. Cajun seasoning
- 1 tsp. dried oregano
- ½ tsp. dried thyme
- ½ tsp. pepper
- 5⅓ cups cooked brown rice

Select the saute or browning setting on a 6-qt. electric pressure cooker. Adjust for medium heat; brown sausage. Add broth; cook 1 minute, stirring to loosen browned bits. Press cancel. Stir in beans, tomatoes, vegetables, garlic and seasonings. Lock lid; close pressure-release valve. Adjust to pressure-cook on high for 5 minutes. Let pressure release naturally for 10 minutes; quick-release any remaining pressure. Serve with rice.

ROBIN HAAS
Cranston, RI

FREEZE OPTION: Freeze cooled meat mixture in freezer containers. To use, partially thaw in refrigerator overnight. Microwave, covered, on high in a microwave-safe dish until heated through, stirring gently and adding a little water if necessary.

1 CUP SAUSAGE AND BEAN MIXTURE WITH ⅔ CUP RICE: 377 cal., 5g fat (1g sat. fat), 33mg chol., 826mg sod., 63g carb. (7g sugars, 10g fiber), 18g pro.

PRESSURE-COOKER ROUND STEAK ITALIANO

My mom used to make a similar version of this wonderful dish, and I've always enjoyed it. The gravy is especially dense and flavorful.
—Deanne Stephens, McMinnville, OR

Prep: 15 min. • Cook: 20 min.
Makes: 8 servings

- 2 lbs. beef top round steak
- 1 can (8 oz.) tomato sauce
- ½ cup reduced-sodium beef broth
- 2 Tbsp. onion soup mix
- 2 Tbsp. canola oil
- 2 Tbsp. red wine vinegar
- 1 tsp. ground oregano
- ½ tsp. garlic powder
- ¼ tsp. pepper
- 8 medium potatoes (7 to 8 oz. each)
- 1 Tbsp. cornstarch
- 1 Tbsp. cold water

1. Cut steak into serving-size pieces; place in a 6-qt. electric pressure cooker. In a large bowl, combine tomato sauce, broth, soup mix, oil, vinegar and seasonings; pour over meat. Scrub and pierce potatoes; place over meat.
2. Lock the lid and close pressure-release valve. Adjust to pressure-cook on high for 15 minutes. Quick-release the pressure. Press cancel. A thermometer inserted into beef should read at least 160°. Remove meat and potatoes; keep warm.
3. For gravy, skim fat from the cooking juices; return juices to pressure cooker. In a small bowl, mix cornstarch and water until smooth; stir into pressure cooker. Select saute setting and adjust for low heat. Simmer, stirring constantly, until thickened, 1-2 minutes. Serve with meat and potatoes.

4 OZ. COOKED BEEF WITH 1 POTATO: 353 cal., 7g fat (2g sat. fat), 64mg chol., 357mg sod., 41g carb. (2g sugars, 5g fiber), 31g pro. **DIABETIC EXCHANGES:** 4 lean meat, 3 starch, ½ fat.

EASY SIDES

Take it easy! Whether you're looking for vegetables, rice or potato dishes, with these scrumptious recipes at your fingertips, it won't take long to whip up the perfect companion to a hearty main course.

HERBED RICE PILAF

This savory side dish has been a family favorite for years. Our daughter, Jennifer, is an expert with this recipe, which is a great help for a busy working mom. We sure enjoy this rice dish in the summer with a grilled entree.
—*Jeri Dobrowski, Beach, ND*

Prep: 15 min. • **Cook:** 15 min. + standing
Makes: 6 servings

- 1 cup uncooked long grain rice
- 1 cup chopped celery
- ¾ cup chopped onion
- ¼ cup butter, cubed
- 2½ cups water
- 1 pkg. (2 to 2½ oz.) chicken noodle soup mix
- 1 tsp. dried thyme
- ¼ tsp. rubbed sage
- ¼ tsp. pepper
- 2 Tbsp. fresh minced parsley
- 1 Tbsp. chopped pimientos, optional

1. In a large skillet, cook the rice, celery and onion in butter, stirring constantly, until the rice is browned. Stir in the next 5 ingredients; bring to a boil. Reduce heat; cover and simmer for 15 minutes. Sprinkle with parsley; stir in pimientos if desired.
2. Remove from heat and let stand, covered, for 10 minutes. Fluff with a fork.
¾ CUP: 226 cal., 8g fat (5g sat. fat), 23mg chol., 426mg sod., 34g carb. (3g sugars, 2g fiber), 4g pro. **DIABETIC EXCHANGES:** 2 starch, 1½ fat.

READER REVIEW

"This recipe is incredibly good! We use it all the time and pair it with a lemon grilled salmon recipe."
CHAND002, TASTEOFHOME.COM

DOLLOPED SWEET POTATOES

A little microwave magic turns sweet potatoes into a speedy side dish that brings a touch of the holidays to any evening meal. Brown sugar and pumpkin pie spice flavor the simple but rich cream-cheese topping.

—Taste of Home *Test Kitchen*

Takes: 15 min. • **Makes:** 4 servings

4	small sweet potatoes
3	oz. cream cheese, softened
1	Tbsp. butter, softened
2	Tbsp. brown sugar
¼	tsp. pumpkin pie spice

1. Scrub and pierce sweet potatoes; place on a microwave-safe plate. Microwave, uncovered, on high 10-13 minutes or until tender, turning twice. Meanwhile, in a small bowl, beat the cream cheese, butter, brown sugar and pumpkin pie spice.

2. Cut an X in the top of each potato; fluff the pulp with a fork. Top each potato with a dollop of the cream cheese mixture.

1 SERVING: 166 cal., 7g fat (5g sat. fat), 23mg chol., 128mg sod., 22g carb. (13g sugars, 2g fiber), 3g pro. **DIABETIC EXCHANGES:** 1½ starch, 1½ fat.

OVEN-ROASTED ASPARAGUS

Asparagus never tasted so good! Simply seasoned with butter and green onions, it tastes fresh and keeps its bright green color, too. This dish is so good, you might just want to make extra.

—*Jody Fisher, Stewartstown, PA*

Takes: 20 min. • **Makes:** 6 servings

2	lbs. fresh asparagus, trimmed
¼	cup butter, melted
2	to 4 green onions, chopped
½	tsp. salt

Preheat oven to 425°. Place asparagus in a 15x10x1-in. pan. Toss with melted butter and green onions; spread evenly. Sprinkle with salt. Roast until crisp-tender, 10-15 minutes.

1 SERVING: 87 cal., 8g fat (5g sat. fat), 20mg chol., 266mg sod., 4g carb. (1g sugars, 1g fiber), 2g pro.

> **TEST KITCHEN TIP**
> If you washed, dried and chopped more green onions than you need, store the leftovers in a covered glass jar in the refrigerator. They'll last a couple of weeks.

CREAMY CARROT CASSEROLE

My mom and I developed this recipe to see if there was a carrot dish that even people who don't care for carrots would enjoy. So far, I haven't met anyone who hasn't liked this casserole.
—*Laurie Heward, Fillmore, UT*

Prep: 15 min. • **Bake:** 30 min.
Makes: 8 servings

- 1½ lbs. carrots, sliced or 1 pkg. (20 oz.) frozen sliced carrots, thawed
- 1 cup mayonnaise
- 1 Tbsp. grated onion
- 1 Tbsp. prepared horseradish
- ¼ cup shredded cheddar cheese
- 2 Tbsp. crushed Ritz crackers

1. Preheat oven to 350°. Place 1 in. of water in a large saucepan; add carrots. Bring to a boil. Reduce heat; cover and simmer until crisp-tender, 7-9 minutes. Drain, reserving ¼ cup cooking liquid. Transfer carrots to a 1½-qt. baking dish.
2. In a small bowl, combine mayonnaise, onion, horseradish and the reserved cooking liquid; spread evenly over the carrots. Sprinkle with cheese; top with cracker crumbs. Bake, uncovered, for 30 minutes.
¾ CUP: 238 cal., 22g fat (4g sat. fat), 6mg chol., 241mg sod., 10g carb. (4g sugars, 2g fiber), 2g pro.

QUINOA TABBOULEH

When my mom and sister developed several food allergies, we had to modify many recipes. I substituted quinoa for couscous in this tabbouleh, and now we make it all the time.
—*Jennifer Klann, Corbett, OR*

Prep: 35 min. + chilling • **Makes:** 8 servings

- 2 cups water
- 1 cup quinoa, rinsed
- 1 can (15 oz.) black beans, rinsed and drained
- 1 small cucumber, peeled and chopped
- 1 small sweet red pepper, chopped
- ⅓ cup minced fresh parsley
- ¼ cup lemon juice
- 2 Tbsp. olive oil
- ½ tsp. salt
- ½ tsp. pepper

1. In a large saucepan, bring water to a boil. Add quinoa. Reduce heat; cover and simmer until the liquid is absorbed, 12-15 minutes. Remove from heat; fluff with a fork. Transfer to a bowl; let cool completely.
2. Add the beans, cucumber, red pepper and parsley. In a small bowl, whisk the remaining ingredients; drizzle over the salad and toss to coat. Refrigerate until chilled.
¾ CUP: 159 cal., 5g fat (1g sat. fat), 0 chol., 255mg sod., 24g carb. (1g sugars, 4g fiber), 6g pro. **DIABETIC EXCHANGES:** 1½ starch, 1 fat.

SOUTHWESTERN SAUTEED CORN

My mother-in-law came up with this dish one night for dinner. The lime juice might sound like a wild card, but everyone who tries it asks for more!
—*Chandy Ward, Aumsville, OR*

Takes: 20 min. • **Makes:** 5 servings

1	Tbsp. butter
3⅓	cups fresh corn or 1 pkg. (16 oz.) frozen corn
1	plum tomato, chopped
1	Tbsp. lime juice
½	tsp. salt
½	tsp. ground cumin
⅓	cup minced fresh cilantro

In a large cast-iron or other heavy skillet, heat butter over medium-high heat. Add the corn; cook and stir until tender, 3-5 minutes. Reduce heat to medium-low; stir in tomato, lime juice, salt and cumin. Cook until heated through, 3-4 minutes. Remove from the heat; stir in the minced cilantro.

⅔ CUP: 104 cal., 3g fat (2g sat. fat), 6mg chol., 256mg sod., 20g carb. (2g sugars, 2g fiber), 3g pro. **DIABETIC EXCHANGES:** 1 starch, ½ fat.

CROUTON-TOPPED BROCCOLI

We love this easy, tasty microwave dish—it's warm, cheesy and the perfect way to get your vegetables in!
—*Kathy Fry, Brockville, ON*

Takes: 10 min. • **Makes:** 5 servings

1	pkg. (16 oz.) frozen chopped broccoli
2	Tbsp. water
1	can (10¾ oz.) condensed cream of mushroom soup, undiluted
½	cup shredded Swiss cheese
½	cup shredded cheddar cheese
¼	cup whole milk
1½	cups cheese and garlic croutons

1. Place broccoli and water in a microwave-safe 2-qt. dish. Cover and microwave on high for 6-8 minutes or until tender; drain.
2. Stir in the soup, cheeses and milk. Cover and microwave for 2 minutes or until cheeses are melted. Sprinkle with croutons.

¾ CUP: 217 cal., 13g fat (6g sat. fat), 26mg chol., 706mg sod., 18g carb. (3g sugars, 4g fiber), 10g pro.

SANDI PICHON
Memphis, TN

MOM'S SWEET POTATO BAKE

Mom loves sweet potatoes and fixed them often in this creamy, comforting casserole. With its nutty topping, this side dish could almost serve as a dessert. It's a yummy treat!
—*Sandi Pichon, Memphis, TN*

Prep: 10 min. • **Bake:** 45 min.
Makes: 8 servings

3	cups cold mashed sweet potatoes (prepared without milk or butter)
1	cup sugar
3	large eggs
½	cup 2% milk
¼	cup butter, softened
1	tsp. salt
1	tsp. vanilla extract

TOPPING

½	cup packed brown sugar
½	cup chopped pecans
¼	cup all-purpose flour
2	Tbsp. cold butter

1. Preheat oven to 325°. In a large bowl, beat the sweet potatoes, sugar, eggs, milk, butter, salt and vanilla until smooth. Transfer to a greased 2-qt. baking dish.
2. In a small bowl, combine the brown sugar, pecans and flour; cut in butter until crumbly. Sprinkle over the potato mixture. Bake, uncovered, for 45-50 minutes or until a thermometer reads 160°.

½ CUP: 417 cal., 16g fat (7g sat. fat), 94mg chol., 435mg sod., 65g carb. (47g sugars, 4g fiber), 6g pro.

TEST KITCHEN TIP
Store sweet potatoes just as you would regular potatoes—in a cool, dark place for up to two weeks.

SUPER SIMPLE SCALLOPED POTATOES

I've made many types of scalloped potatoes but I always come back to this rich, creamy, foolproof recipe. The dish gets scraped clean every time I make it.
—*Kallee Krong-McCreery, Escondido, CA*

- -

Prep: 20 min. • **Bake:** 45 min. + standing
Makes: 10 servings

- 3 cups heavy whipping cream
- 1½ tsp. salt
- ½ tsp. pepper
- 1 tsp. minced fresh thyme, optional
- 3 lbs. russet potatoes, thinly sliced (about 10 cups)

1. Preheat oven to 350°. In a large bowl, combine cream, salt, pepper and, if desired, thyme. Arrange potatoes in a greased 13x9-in. baking dish. Pour the cream mixture over top.

2. Bake, uncovered, until the potatoes are tender and the top is lightly browned, 45-55 minutes. Let stand for 10 minutes before serving.

¾ CUP: 353 cal., 27g fat (17g sat. fat), 99mg chol., 390mg sod., 26g carb. (3g sugars, 3g fiber), 4g pro.

CHEESE & GRITS CASSEROLE

Grits are a staple in southern cooking. Serve this as a brunch item with bacon and eggs or as a side dish for dinner.
—*Jennifer Wallis, Goldsboro, NC*

- -

Prep: 10 min. • **Bake:** 30 min. + standing
Makes: 8 servings

- 4 cups water
- 1 cup uncooked old-fashioned grits
- ½ tsp. salt
- ½ cup 2% milk
- ¼ cup butter, melted
- 2 large eggs, lightly beaten
- 1 cup shredded cheddar cheese
- 1 Tbsp. Worcestershire sauce
- ⅛ tsp. cayenne pepper
- ⅛ tsp. paprika

1. Preheat oven to 350°. In a large saucepan, bring water to a boil. Slowly stir in grits and salt. Reduce heat; cover and simmer until thickened, 5-7 minutes. Cool slightly. Gradually whisk in milk, butter and eggs. Stir in cheese, Worcestershire sauce and cayenne.

2. Transfer to a greased 2-qt. baking dish. Sprinkle with paprika. Bake, uncovered, until bubbly, 30-35 minutes. Let stand 10 minutes before serving.

¾ CUP: 202 cal., 12g fat (7g sat. fat), 86mg chol., 335mg sod., 17g carb. (1g sugars, 0 fiber), 7g pro.

CHILI CHEESE GRITS: Omit Worcestershire and cayenne. With the cheese, stir in 2 Tbsp. canned chopped green chiles.

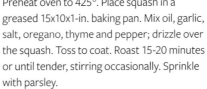

GARLIC-HERB PATTYPAN SQUASH

The first time I grew a garden, I harvested summer squash and cooked it with garlic and herbs. Using pattypan squash works beautifully, too.
—*Kaycee Mason, Siloam Springs, AR*

- -

Takes: 25 min. • **Makes:** 4 servings

- 5 cups halved small pattypan squash (about 1¼ lbs.)
- 1 Tbsp. olive oil
- 2 garlic cloves, minced
- ½ tsp. salt
- ¼ tsp. dried oregano
- ¼ tsp. dried thyme
- ¼ tsp. pepper
- 1 Tbsp. minced fresh parsley

Preheat oven to 425°. Place squash in a greased 15x10x1-in. baking pan. Mix oil, garlic, salt, oregano, thyme and pepper; drizzle over the squash. Toss to coat. Roast 15-20 minutes or until tender, stirring occasionally. Sprinkle with parsley.

⅔ CUP: 58 cal., 3g fat (0 sat. fat), 0 chol., 296mg sod., 6g carb. (3g sugars, 2g fiber), 2g pro. **DIABETIC EXCHANGES:** 1 vegetable, ½ fat.

READER REVIEW

"I love pattypan squash as it has mild flavor and is softer than other squashes. We served this dish with grilled chicken."

LPHJKITCHEN, TASTEOFHOME.COM

SPANAKOPITA MASHED POTATOES

I learned to cook by watching my mom in the kitchen. Most of the recipes I make use only five or six ingredients and have a healthier bent. I created this recipe after I tried a spinach-topped baked potato. By not peeling the potatoes, you not only keep some nutrients, you also save on prep time.
—*Ashley Laymon, Lititz, PA*

- -

Prep: 10 min. • **Cook:** 25 min.
Makes: 6 servings

- 6 medium red potatoes, quartered
- 1 pkg. (6 oz.) fresh baby spinach
- ¼ cup 2% milk
- 1 Tbsp. butter
- ½ tsp. salt
- ½ tsp. pepper
- ¾ cup crumbled feta cheese

1. Place the potatoes in a large saucepan and cover with water. Bring to a boil. Reduce heat; cover and cook for 15-20 minutes or until the potatoes are tender.

2. Meanwhile, in another large saucepan, bring ½ in. of water to a boil. Add spinach; cover and boil for 3-5 minutes or until wilted. Drain and coarsely chop; keep warm.

3. Drain potatoes and return to the saucepan. Add milk, butter, salt and pepper; mash until smooth. Fold in cheese and spinach.

¾ CUP: 145 cal., 5g fat (3g sat. fat), 13mg chol., 379mg sod., 20g carb. (2g sugars, 3g fiber), 6g pro. **DIABETIC EXCHANGES:** 1 starch, 1 fat.

PARMESAN ROASTED BROCCOLI

Sure, it's simple and healthy but, oh, is this roasted broccoli delicious. Cutting the stalks into tall trees turns this ordinary veggie into a standout side dish.

—*Holly Sander, Lake Mary, FL*

Takes: 30 min. • **Makes:** 4 servings

- 2 small broccoli crowns (about 8 oz. each)
- 3 Tbsp. olive oil
- ½ tsp. salt
- ½ tsp. pepper
- ¼ tsp. crushed red pepper flakes
- 4 garlic cloves, thinly sliced
- 2 Tbsp. grated Parmesan cheese
- 1 tsp. grated lemon zest

1. Preheat oven to 425°. Cut broccoli crowns into quarters from top to bottom. Drizzle with oil; sprinkle with salt, pepper and red pepper flakes. Place in a parchment-lined 15x10x1-in. pan.

2. Roast until crisp-tender, 10-12 minutes. Sprinkle with garlic; roast 5 minutes longer. Sprinkle with cheese; roast until the cheese is melted and the stalks of broccoli are tender, 2-4 minutes more. Sprinkle with lemon zest.

2 BROCCOLI PIECES: 144 cal., 11g fat (2g sat. fat), 2mg chol., 378mg sod., 9g carb. (2g sugars, 3g fiber), 4g pro. **DIABETIC EXCHANGES:** 2 fat, 1 vegetable.

RED ROASTED POTATOES

Fragrant rosemary, fresh or dried, gives these potatoes a distinctive and subtle taste. This dish is simple to prepare, yet elegant in color and flavor. It's a wonderful addition to any menu.

—*Margie Wampler, Butler, PA*

Takes: 30 min. • **Makes:** 8 servings

- 2 lbs. small unpeeled red potatoes, cut into wedges
- 2 to 3 Tbsp. olive oil
- 2 garlic cloves, minced
- 1 Tbsp. minced fresh rosemary or 1 tsp. dried rosemary, crushed
- ½ tsp. salt
- ¼ tsp. pepper

1. Preheat oven to 450°. Place potatoes in a 13x9-in. baking dish. Drizzle with oil. Sprinkle with the garlic, rosemary, salt and pepper; toss gently to coat.

2. Bake until potatoes are golden brown and tender, 20-30 minutes.

1 CUP: 114 cal., 4g fat (0 sat. fat), 0 chol., 155mg sod., 18g carb. (1g sugars, 2g fiber), 2g pro.

READER REVIEW

"I made these as a side with kielbasa. For a final glaze, I tumbled them through the skillet I'd cooked the sausage in. Delicious!"

LADY FINGERS, TASTEOFHOME.COM

BRUSSELS SPROUTS WITH BACON & GARLIC

When we have company, these sprouts are my go-to side dish because they look and taste fantastic. When you want a fancier version, use pancetta instead of bacon.
—*Mandy Rivers, Lexington, SC*

- -

Takes: 30 min. • **Makes:** 12 servings

2 lbs. fresh Brussels sprouts (about 10 cups)
8 bacon strips, coarsely chopped
3 garlic cloves, minced
¾ cup chicken broth
½ tsp. salt
¼ tsp. pepper

1. Trim the Brussels sprouts. Cut sprouts lengthwise in half; cut crosswise into thin slices. In a 6-qt. stockpot, cook bacon over medium heat until crisp, stirring occasionally. Add garlic; cook 30 seconds longer. Remove with a slotted spoon; drain on paper towels.
2. Add the Brussels sprouts to the bacon drippings; cook and stir until the sprouts begin to brown lightly, 4-6 minutes. Stir in broth, salt and pepper; cook, covered, until the Brussels sprouts are tender, 4-6 minutes longer. Stir in the bacon mixture.
¾ CUP: 109 cal., 8g fat (3g sat. fat), 13mg chol., 300mg sod., 7g carb. (2g sugars, 3g fiber), 5g pro. **DIABETIC EXCHANGES:** 1½ fat, 1 vegetable.

MANDY RIVERS
Lexington, SC

GARLIC PARMESAN ORZO

This buttery pasta dish calls for orzo, which cooks quickly and is a nice change from ordinary pasta shapes. This fantastic recipe was inspired by a similar dish I once tried, and it makes a superb side dish any time. The garlic and Parmesan cheese really stand out.
—*Stephanie Moon, Boise, ID*

- -

Takes: 15 min. • **Makes:** 8 servings

2 cups uncooked orzo pasta
3 tsp. minced garlic
½ cup butter, cubed
½ cup grated Parmesan cheese
¼ cup 2% milk
2 Tbsp. minced fresh parsley
1 tsp. salt
¼ tsp. pepper

Cook orzo according to package directions; drain. In a large skillet, saute garlic in butter until tender. Add the orzo, Parmesan cheese, milk, parsley, salt and pepper. Cook and stir until heated through.
1 CUP: 321 cal., 14g fat (8g sat. fat), 36mg chol., 513mg sod., 40g carb. (2g sugars, 2g fiber), 9g pro.

PEPPER PARMESAN BEANS

A colorful mixture of peppers and green beans gets an Italian treatment with basil and Parmesan cheese in this delightful vegetable dish.
—*Marian Platt, Sequim, WA*

Takes: 15 min. • **Makes:** 8 servings

- 1   large sweet red pepper, diced
- 1   small green pepper, diced
- ¼   cup chopped onion
- 1   garlic clove, minced
- ¼   cup olive oil
- 1½ lbs. fresh green beans, cut into 2-in. pieces
- 1   Tbsp. minced fresh basil or 1 tsp. dried basil
- 1   tsp. salt
- ⅓ to ½ cup shredded Parmesan cheese

In a large skillet, saute the peppers, onion and garlic in oil until the vegetables are tender, about 3 minutes. Add the beans, basil and salt; toss to coat. Cover and cook over medium-low heat for 7-8 minutes or until beans are crisp-tender. Stir in cheese; serve immediately.
¾ CUP: 107 cal., 8g fat (2g sat. fat), 2mg chol., 357mg sod., 8g carb. (3g sugars, 3g fiber), 3g pro.

BUTTERY GARLIC POTATOES

My husband and sons all love oven-roasted potatoes, but I usually don't have time to make them. I whipped up this quick and tasty microwave dish instead, and everyone likes it.
—*Heidi Iacovetto, Phippsburg, CO*

Takes: 15 min. • **Makes:** 4 servings

- 6   small red potatoes, quartered
- ¼   cup butter, melted
- 1   tsp. seasoned salt
- 1   tsp. paprika
- 1   tsp. dried parsley flakes
- 1   tsp. minced garlic

1. Place the potatoes in a 2-qt. microwave-safe dish. In a small bowl, combine the butter, seasoned salt, paprika, parsley and garlic; pour over potatoes and toss to coat.
2. Microwave, uncovered, on high until the potatoes are tender, 8-10 minutes, stirring the mixture frequently.
¾ CUP: 155 cal., 12g fat (7g sat. fat), 31mg chol., 477mg sod., 12g carb. (1g sugars, 1g fiber), 2g pro.

SPECIAL SCALLOPED CORN

The addition of carrots and green pepper makes this a colorful dish that grabs attention at a potluck. (For those occasions, I double the recipe.) It's also great when you need to prepare a dish ahead of time. Assemble the casserole the night before, and just bake it before serving.
—*J. Brown, Fort Dodge, IA*

Prep: 10 min. • **Bake:** 30 min.
Makes: 4 servings

- 1   can (14¾ oz.) cream-style corn
- 2   large eggs
- ½   cup crushed saltines (about 15 crackers)
- ¼   cup butter, melted
- ¼   cup evaporated milk
- ¼   cup shredded carrot
- ¼   cup chopped green pepper
- 1   Tbsp. chopped celery
- 1   tsp. chopped onion
- ½   tsp. sugar
- ½   tsp. salt
- ½   cup shredded cheddar cheese

1. Preheat oven to 350°. In a large bowl, combine the first 11 ingredients. Transfer to a greased 1-qt. baking dish. Sprinkle with shredded cheese.
2. Bake, uncovered, for 30-35 minutes or until a knife inserted in the center comes out clean.
1 SERVING: 322 cal., 20g fat (12g sat. fat), 157mg chol., 941mg sod., 29g carb. (7g sugars, 2g fiber), 10g pro.

SAUTEED RADISHES WITH GREEN BEANS

I'd been told radishes are the only vegetable you don't cook, but a cookbook from the 1950s disagrees. Green beans and wax beans round out this dish.
—*Pam Kaiser, Mansfield, MO*

Takes: 20 min. • **Makes:** 4 servings

- 1   Tbsp. butter
- ½   lb. fresh green or wax beans, trimmed
- 1   cup thinly sliced radishes
- ½   tsp. sugar
- ¼   tsp. salt
- 2   Tbsp. pine nuts, toasted

1. In a large skillet, heat butter over medium-high heat. Add the beans; cook and stir for 3-4 minutes or until crisp-tender.

2. Add radishes; cook 2-3 minutes longer or until the vegetables are tender, stirring occasionally. Stir in sugar and salt; sprinkle with nuts.

NOTE: To toast nuts, bake in a shallow pan in a 350° oven for 5-10 minutes or cook in a skillet over low heat until nuts are lightly browned, stirring occasionally.

½ CUP: 75 cal., 6g fat (2g sat. fat), 8mg chol., 177mg sod., 5g carb. (2g sugars, 2g fiber), 2g pro. **DIABETIC EXCHANGES:** 1 vegetable, 1 fat.

SALSA RICE

It's a snap to change the spice level in this popular rice side dish by choosing a milder or hotter salsa. It's a delicious way to round out burritos or tacos when the clock is ticking.
—*Molly Ingle, Canton, NC*

Takes: 15 min. • **Makes:** 5 servings

- 1½   cups water
- 1½   cups chunky salsa
- 2   cups uncooked instant rice
- 1   to 1½ cups shredded Colby-Monterey Jack cheese

In a saucepan, bring water and salsa to a boil. Stir in rice. Remove from the heat; cover and let stand for 5 minutes. Stir in cheese; cover and let stand for 30 seconds or until the cheese is melted.

1 SERVING: 232 cal., 4g fat (3g sat. fat), 12mg chol., 506mg sod., 35g carb. (3g sugars, 3g fiber), 9g pro. **DIABETIC EXCHANGES:** 2 starch, 1 lean meat.

EASY BAKED MUSHROOMS

Bet you've never had mushrooms like these! Skipping the deep fryer keeps them low in fat.
—*Denise DiPace, Medford, NJ*

Takes: 30 min. • **Makes:** 4 servings

- 1   lb. medium fresh mushrooms, halved
- 2   Tbsp. olive oil
- ¼   cup seasoned bread crumbs
- ¼   tsp. garlic powder
- ¼   tsp. pepper
    Fresh parsley, optional

1. Preheat oven to 425°. Place mushrooms on a baking sheet. Drizzle with olive oil; toss to coat. In a small bowl, combine seasoned bread crumbs, garlic powder and pepper; sprinkle over the mushrooms.

2. Bake, uncovered, for 18-20 minutes or until lightly browned. Garnish with parsley if desired.

¾ CUP: 116 cal., 8g fat (1g sat. fat), 0 chol., 112mg sod., 10g carb. (2g sugars, 2g fiber), 4g pro. **DIABETIC EXCHANGES:** 1½ fat, ½ starch.

LEMON ROASTED FINGERLINGS & BRUSSELS SPROUTS

I've used this recipe with other veggie combinations—the trick is choosing ones that roast in about the same amount of time. Try skinny green beans and thinly sliced onions, cauliflower florets and baby carrots, or okra and cherry tomatoes.
—*Courtney Gaylord, Columbus, IN*

- -

Prep: 15 min. • **Bake:** 20 min.
Makes: 8 servings

- 1 lb. fingerling potatoes, halved
- 1 lb. Brussels sprouts, trimmed and halved
- 6 Tbsp. olive oil, divided
- ¾ tsp. salt, divided
- ¼ tsp. pepper
- 3 Tbsp. lemon juice
- 1 garlic clove, minced
- 1 tsp. Dijon mustard
- 1 tsp. honey

1. Preheat oven to 425°. Place potatoes and Brussels sprouts in a greased 15x10x1-in. baking pan. Drizzle with 2 Tbsp. oil; sprinkle with ½ tsp. salt and pepper. Toss to coat. Roast for 20-25 minutes or until tender, stirring once.

2. In a small bowl, whisk lemon juice, garlic, mustard, honey and the remaining oil and salt until blended. Transfer the vegetables to a large bowl; drizzle with vinaigrette and toss to coat. Serve warm.

¾ CUP: 167 cal., 10g fat (1g sat. fat), 0 chol., 256mg sod., 17g carb. (3g sugars, 3g fiber), 3g pro. **DIABETIC EXCHANGES:** 2 fat, 1 starch, 1 vegetable.

THYME-ROASTED CARROTS

Cutting carrots lengthwise gives a simple side dish a special look. If you'd like, garnish with sprigs of fresh thyme or parsley.
—*Deirdre Cox, Kansas City, MO*

- -

Takes: 30 min. • **Makes:** about 12 servings

- 3 lbs. medium carrots, halved lengthwise
- 2 Tbsp. minced fresh thyme or 2 tsp. dried thyme
- 2 Tbsp. canola oil
- 1 Tbsp. honey
- 1 tsp. salt

Preheat oven to 400°. Divide carrots between 2 greased 15x10x1-in. baking pans. In a small bowl, mix thyme, oil, honey and salt; brush over the carrots. Roast for 20-25 minutes or until tender.

2 CARROT HALVES: 73 cal., 3g fat (0 sat. fat), 0 chol., 275mg sod., 12g carb. (7g sugars, 3g fiber), 1g pro. **DIABETIC EXCHANGES:** 1 vegetable, ½ starch, ½ fat.

> **TEST KITCHEN TIP**
> To strip thyme leaves, hold the top of the sprig and strip downward (against the grain) using your fingers to remove the leaves. This also works with rosemary.

SIMPLE LEMON PARSLEY POTATOES

For a simply delicious side dish, I often prepare these potatoes. I like that there are only a few ingredients and that it all goes from stove to table in so little time.
—*Dorothy Pritchett, Wills Point, TX*

- -

Takes: 20 min. • **Makes:** 12 servings

- 3   lbs. small red new potatoes, quartered
- ½   cup butter, melted
- 3   Tbsp. lemon juice
- 3   Tbsp. minced fresh parsley

Cook potatoes in boiling salted water until tender, about 15 minutes; drain. Combine butter, lemon juice and parsley; pour over the potatoes and stir gently to coat.

1 CUP: 150 cal., 8g fat (5g sat. fat), 20mg chol., 84mg sod., 18g carb. (1g sugars, 2g fiber), 2g pro.

BASIL GARLIC BREAD

This is a must-have accompaniment in my home. It goes well with anything from hearty Italian dishes to simple salad dishes.
—*Stephanie Moon, Boise, ID*

- -

Takes: 10 min. • **Makes:** 4 servings

- ¼   cup butter
- 2   Tbsp. minced fresh parsley
- 1½ tsp. minced fresh basil or
      ½ tsp. dried basil
- 1   garlic clove, minced
- ¼   cup grated Parmesan cheese
- 1   loaf (8 oz.) French bread

1. In a microwave-safe bowl, combine butter, parsley, basil and garlic. Cover and microwave until the butter is melted. Stir in cheese.
2. Cut the bread in half lengthwise; place cut side down on an uncovered grill over medium heat for 2 minutes or until lightly toasted. Brush cut side with the butter mixture. Grill or broil 1-2 minutes longer.

1 PIECE: 280 cal., 15g fat (8g sat. fat), 35mg chol., 555mg sod., 30g carb. (1g sugars, 2g fiber), 7g pro.

READER REVIEW

"Great garlic bread, and we eat some variety of garlic bread 3-4 times a week, so we know a good one when we try it!"

CYNANDTOM, TASTEOFHOME.COM

SNAPPY HERBED SPINACH

We have a small group that meets once a week for exercise and to share ideas on delicious lower-fat foods that are good for us but also quick. This is one of our favorite recipes.
—*Eva Brookman, Davis, IL*

Takes: 20 min. • **Makes:** 4 servings

- 1 tsp. butter
- 2 Tbsp. finely chopped onion
- 2 large eggs
- ⅓ cup fat-free milk
- ½ tsp. Worcestershire sauce
- ½ tsp. salt
- ¼ tsp. dried rosemary, crushed
- 1 pkg. (10 oz.) frozen chopped spinach, thawed and squeezed dry
- 1 cup cooked long grain rice
- ½ cup shredded cheddar cheese, divided

1. In a small microwave-safe bowl, melt butter. Add onion; cover and microwave at 50% power 1 minute, stirring after 30 seconds. Set aside.

2. In a large bowl, whisk eggs, milk, Worcestershire sauce, salt and rosemary. Stir in spinach, rice, onion mixture and ¼ cup of cheese. Transfer to an 8x4-in. microwave-safe dish coated with cooking spray.

3. Microwave, uncovered, on high for 6-8 minutes. Sprinkle with the remaining cheese; microwave 1-2 minutes or until firm and a thermometer reads 160°. Cover and let stand for 5 minutes before cutting.

1 PIECE: 174 cal., 8g fat (4g sat. fat), 124mg chol., 492mg sod., 16g carb. (2g sugars, 2g fiber), 10g pro.

PARMESAN BUTTERNUT SQUASH

Butternut squash sprinkled with Parmesan and bread crumbs makes a superb side dish we love to share. Using the microwave cuts down on long roasting time.
—*Jacqueline O'Callaghan, Troy, MI*

Takes: 25 min. • **Makes:** 8 servings

- 1 medium butternut squash (about 3 lbs.), peeled and cut into 1-in. cubes
- 2 Tbsp. water
- ½ cup panko (Japanese) bread crumbs
- ½ cup grated Parmesan cheese
- ¼ tsp. salt
- ⅛ tsp. pepper

1. Preheat the broiler. Place the squash and water in a large microwave-safe bowl. Microwave, covered, on high 15-17 minutes or until tender; drain.

2. Transfer squash to a greased 15x10x1-in. baking pan. Toss bread crumbs with cheese, salt and pepper; sprinkle over squash. Broil 3-4 in. from heat 1-2 minutes or until the topping is golden brown.

¾ CUP: 112 cal., 2g fat (1g sat. fat), 4mg chol., 168mg sod., 23g carb. (5g sugars, 6g fiber), 4g pro. **DIABETIC EXCHANGES:** 1½ starch.

JACQUELINE O'CALLAGHAN
Troy, MI

CHEESY SUMMER SQUASH CASSEROLE

Onion and cheddar cheese perk up the rich flavor of summer squash in this comforting casserole. A crispy cornflake-crumb topping adds a little crunch.
—*Katherine Metz, Jacksonville, FL*

Prep: 10 min. • **Bake:** 25 min.
Makes: 2 servings

- 2   small yellow summer squash, sliced
- ¼   cup chopped onion
- ½   tsp. salt, divided
- 1   large egg
- ¼   cup mayonnaise
- 2   tsp. sugar
-     Pepper to taste
- ¼   cup shredded cheddar cheese
- 2   Tbsp. crushed cornflakes
- 1½   tsp. butter, melted

1. Preheat oven to 350°. In a small saucepan, combine squash, onion and ¼ tsp. salt. Cover with water. Bring to a boil. Reduce heat; simmer, uncovered, until the squash is crisp-tender, about 2 minutes. Drain.
2. In a small bowl, whisk the egg, mayonnaise, sugar, pepper and the remaining salt until blended. Stir in the cheddar cheese and squash mixture. Transfer to a greased 2-cup baking dish. Toss the cornflakes and butter; sprinkle over top.
3. Bake, uncovered, until golden brown and bubbly, 25-30 minutes.
¾ CUP: 376 cal., 31g fat (8g sat. fat), 117mg chol., 937mg sod., 18g carb. (10g sugars, 2g fiber), 9g pro.

SOUTHWESTERN RICE

I created this colorful side dish after eating something similar at a restaurant. It is a wonderful complement to any Tex-Mex main. Sometimes I add cubes of grilled chicken breast to the rice to make it a whole meal.
—*Michelle Dennis, Clarks Hill, IN*

Takes: 30 min. • **Makes:** 8 servings

- 1   Tbsp. olive oil
- 1   medium green pepper, diced
- 1   medium onion, chopped
- 2   garlic cloves, minced
- 1   cup uncooked long grain rice
- ½   tsp. ground cumin
- ⅛   tsp. ground turmeric
- 1   can (14½ oz.) reduced-sodium chicken broth
- 2   cups frozen corn (about 10 oz.), thawed
- 1   can (15 oz.) black beans, rinsed and drained
- 1   can (10 oz.) diced tomatoes and green chiles, undrained

1. In a large nonstick skillet, heat oil over medium-high heat; saute pepper and onion 3 minutes. Add garlic; cook and stir 1 minute.
2. Stir in rice, spices and broth; bring to a boil. Reduce heat; simmer, covered, until the rice is tender, about 15 minutes. Stir in the remaining ingredients; cook, covered, until heated through.
¾ CUP: 198 cal., 3g fat (1g sat. fat), 1mg chol., 339mg sod., 37g carb. (0 sugars, 5g fiber), 7g pro.

PARMESAN SWEET POTATO WEDGES

I roast these sweet potato fries when I want a fun and different side. We use mustard, but they're also great dipped in garlic aioli, barbecue sauce or even ketchup.
—*Amy Green, Carrollton, TX*

Prep: 15 min. • **Bake:** 25 min.
Makes: 6 servings

- 3 large sweet potatoes (about 2½ to 3 lbs.)
- 4 large egg whites
- ¾ tsp. salt
- ¼ tsp. coarsely ground pepper
- 2 cups grated Parmesan cheese
  Prepared mustard, optional

1. Preheat oven to 425°. Peel and cut sweet potatoes lengthwise into ½-in. wedges. In a shallow bowl, whisk egg whites, salt and pepper until foamy. Place Parmesan cheese in another shallow bowl. Dip potatoes in egg white mixture, then in Parmesan cheese, patting to help coating adhere.
2. Transfer to 2 foil-lined 15x10x1-in. baking pans coated with cooking spray. Roast until potatoes are tender and cheese is golden brown, 25-30 minutes. If desired, serve with prepared mustard.
1 SERVING: 300 cal., 8g fat (4g sat. fat), 23mg chol., 830mg sod., 46g carb. (17g sugars, 5g fiber), 13g pro.

BUTTERMILK SMASHED POTATOES

You can also make this luscious and decadent recipe of buttermilk, potatoes and butter using reduced-fat ingredients—our family loves it that way.
—*Marla Clark, Albuquerque, NM*

Takes: 30 min. • **Makes:** 8 servings

- 4 lbs. Yukon Gold potatoes, peeled and cubed (about 8 cups)
- ½ cup butter, softened
- 1¼ tsp. salt
- ¼ tsp. pepper
- ¾ to 1 cup buttermilk
  Optional toppings: Crumbled cooked bacon, sour cream and thinly sliced green onions

1. Place potatoes in a 6-qt. stockpot; add water to cover. Bring to a boil. Reduce heat; cook, uncovered, until tender, 10-15 minutes.
2. Drain; return to pan. Mash potatoes, gradually adding butter, salt, pepper and enough buttermilk to reach the desired consistency. Serve with toppings as desired.
¾ CUP: 313 cal., 12g fat (7g sat. fat), 31mg chol., 531mg sod., 46g carb. (4g sugars, 4g fiber), 6g pro.

BROCCOLI-PASTA SIDE DISH

I love to fix new recipes for my husband and our children. With garlic and cheese, this is a tasty way to get kids to eat broccoli.
—*Judi Lacourse, Mesa, AZ*

Takes: 25 min. • **Makes:** 6 servings

- 2½ lbs. fresh broccoli
- 2 garlic cloves, minced
- ⅓ cup olive oil
- 1 Tbsp. butter
- 1 tsp. salt
- ¼ tsp. pepper
  Pinch cayenne pepper
- 8 oz. linguine or thin spaghetti, cooked and drained
  Grated Romano or Parmesan cheese

Cut florets and tender parts of the broccoli stems into bite-sized pieces. In a large skillet, saute the broccoli with garlic, oil, butter, salt, pepper and cayenne over medium heat for about 10 minutes or until just tender, stirring frequently. Place hot pasta in a serving dish; top with the broccoli mixture. Sprinkle with grated cheese.

1 SERVING: 313 cal., 15g fat (3g sat. fat), 5mg chol., 464mg sod., 37g carb. (5g sugars, 7g fiber), 11g pro.

SPINACH-PARM CASSEROLE

For those who ignore Popeye and won't eat their spinach, I find that spinach with garlicky butter and Parmesan helps change their minds.
—*Judy Batson, Tampa, FL*

Takes: 25 min. • **Makes:** 6 servings

- 2 lbs. fresh baby spinach
- 5 Tbsp. butter
- 3 Tbsp. olive oil
- 3 garlic cloves, minced
- 1 Tbsp. Italian seasoning
- ¾ tsp. salt
- 1 cup grated Parmesan cheese

1. Preheat oven to 400°. In a stockpot, bring 5 cups of water to a boil. Add the spinach; cook, covered, 1 minute or just until wilted. Drain well.

2. In a small skillet, heat butter and oil over medium-low heat. Add garlic, Italian seasoning and salt; cook and stir until the garlic is tender, 1-2 minutes.

3. Spread the spinach into a greased 1½-qt. or 8-in. square baking dish. Drizzle with the butter mixture; sprinkle with cheese. Bake, uncovered, until the cheese is lightly browned, 10-15 minutes.

⅔ CUP: 239 cal., 21g fat (9g sat. fat), 37mg chol., 703mg sod., 7g carb. (1g sugars, 3g fiber), 10g pro.

TEST KITCHEN TIP
Grating your own Parmesan cheese gives the freshest flavor. Use the finest section on your grater. You can also cut the cheese into 1-inch cubes and process 1 cup of cubes at a time in a blender or food processor on high until the cheese is finely grated.

ROASTED SUGAR SNAP PEAS

This is a super fast and fresh way to dress up crisp sugar snap peas. It's a bright complement to so many spring dishes, and is pretty enough for company.
—Taste of Home *Test Kitchen*

Takes: 15 min. • **Makes:** 2 servings

- 1 pkg. (8 oz.) fresh sugar snap peas, trimmed
- 1 Tbsp. chopped shallot
- 2 tsp. olive oil
- ½ tsp. Italian seasoning
- ⅛ tsp. salt

Preheat oven to 400°. Toss together all the ingredients; spread in a 15x10x1-in. pan. Roast until the peas are crisp-tender, 8-10 minutes, stirring once.

⅔ CUP: 91 cal., 5g fat (1g sat. fat), 0 chol., 153mg sod., 9g carb. (4g sugars, 3g fiber), 4g pro. **DIABETIC EXCHANGES:** 2 vegetable, 1 fat.

SESAME GREEN BEANS

For me, the most time-consuming part of preparing this light side dish is picking the green beans in the garden. My family loves their fresh taste, and I love that they're fast to fix!
—*Jeanne Bennett, North Richland Hills, TX*

Takes: 15 min. • **Makes:** 6 servings

- ¾ lb. fresh green beans
- ½ cup water
- 1 Tbsp. butter
- 1 Tbsp. soy sauce
- 2 tsp. sesame seeds, toasted

In a large saucepan, bring beans and water to a boil; reduce heat to medium. Cover and cook for 10-15 minutes or until the beans are crisp-tender; drain. Add butter, soy sauce and sesame seeds; toss to coat.

½ CUP: 39 cal., 2g fat (1g sat. fat), 5mg chol., 181mg sod., 4g carb. (1g sugars, 2g fiber), 1g pro.

MINTY PEAS & ONIONS

Mother always relied on peas and onions when she was in a hurry and needed a quick side dish. Besides being easy to prepare, this dish was loved by everyone in our family. It was handed down to my mother by my grandmother. This recipe is easy to cut in half to serve four.
—*Santa D'Addario, Jacksonville, FL*

Takes: 20 min. • **Makes:** 8 servings

- 2   large onions, cut into ½-in. wedges
- ½   cup chopped sweet red pepper
- 2   Tbsp. vegetable oil
- 2   pkgs. (16 oz. each) frozen peas
- 2   Tbsp. minced fresh mint
     or 2 tsp. dried mint

In a large skillet, saute onions and red pepper in oil until the onions just begin to soften. Add peas; cook, uncovered, stirring occasionally, for 10 minutes or until heated through. Stir in mint and cook for 1 minute.

1 SERVING: 134 cal., 4g fat (1g sat. fat), 0 chol., 128mg sod., 19g carb. (9g sugars, 6g fiber), 6g pro. **DIABETIC EXCHANGES:** 1 starch, 1 fat.

BAKED BROCCOLINI

Broccoli is my favorite vegetable, but I heard about broccolini and wanted to try it out. This is really tasty and I think kids will love it.
—*Katie Helliwell, Hinsdale, IL*

Takes: 15 min. • **Makes:** 4 servings

- ¾   lb. Broccolini or broccoli spears
- 2   Tbsp. lemon juice
- 2   Tbsp. olive oil
- ½   tsp. salt
- ⅛   tsp. pepper

Preheat oven to 425°. Place broccolini in a greased 15x10x1-in. baking pan. Combine lemon juice, oil, salt and pepper; drizzle over broccolini and toss to coat. Bake, uncovered, 10-15 minutes or until broccolini is tender, stirring occasionally.

1 SERVING: 97 cal., 7g fat (1g sat. fat), 0 chol., 320mg sod., 7g carb. (2g sugars, 1g fiber), 3g pro. **DIABETIC EXCHANGES:** 1 vegetable, 1 fat.

SMOKY CAULIFLOWER

Smoked Spanish paprika gives this simple side of roasted cauliflower extra depth. This is definitely a favorite with us!
—*Juliette Mulholland, Corvallis, OR*

Takes: 30 min. • **Makes:** 8 servings

- 1   large head cauliflower, broken into 1-in. florets (about 9 cups)
- 2   Tbsp. olive oil
- 1   tsp. smoked paprika
- ¾   tsp. salt
- 2   garlic cloves, minced
- 2   Tbsp. minced fresh parsley

1. Preheat oven to 450°. Place cauliflower in a large bowl. Combine oil, paprika and salt. Drizzle over the cauliflower; toss to coat. Transfer to a 15x10x1-in. baking pan. Bake, uncovered, for 10 minutes.

2. Stir in garlic. Bake 10-15 minutes longer or until cauliflower is tender and lightly browned, stirring occasionally. Sprinkle with parsley.

¾ CUP: 58 cal., 4g fat (0 sat. fat), 0 chol., 254mg sod., 6g carb. (3g sugars, 3g fiber), 2g pro. **DIABETIC EXCHANGES:** 1 vegetable, ½ fat.

READER REVIEW

"By far the best cauliflower I've ever had. We got raves from all our dinner guests, including my two young grandsons. The 5-year-old said, 'I love the white broccoli!'"

HAPPYGMA, TASTEOFHOME.COM

SNACKS & SWEETS

You may not have hours to spend when you need to satisfy a salt craving or a sweet tooth. Never fear! From delectable dips and finger foods to divine cakes and pies, these recipes will make mouths water—and leave you with time and energy to spare.

GRASSHOPPER PIE

You'll need only six ingredients to whip up this fluffy and refreshing treat. I usually make two of these minty pies for our family, since we're never satisfied with just one slice.
—*LouCinda Zacharias, Spooner, WI*

Prep: 15 min. + freezing • **Makes:** 8 servings

- 6 oz. cream cheese, softened
- 1 can (14 oz.) sweetened condensed milk
- 15 drops green food coloring
- 24 chocolate-covered mint cookies, divided
- 2 cups whipped topping
- 1 chocolate crumb crust (8 in.)

In a large bowl, beat cream cheese until fluffy. Gradually beat in milk until smooth. Beat in food coloring. Coarsely crush 16 cookies; stir into the cream cheese mixture. Fold in whipped topping. Spoon into the crust. Cover and freeze overnight. Remove pie from the freezer 15 minutes before serving. Garnish with the remaining cookies.

1 PIECE: 357 cal., 16g fat (11g sat. fat), 29mg chol., 151mg sod., 46g carb. (38g sugars, 1g fiber), 6g pro.

TEST KITCHEN TIP
Cut 6 oz. from an 8-oz. brick of cream cheese for this recipe. Use the leftover on a bagel or celery for a great snack.

RHUBARB-BLUEBERRY CRUMBLE

Rhubarb and strawberry often go together, but blueberries give rhubarb a fresh and summery touch.

—*Mike Schulz, Tawas City, MI*

Prep: 15 min. • **Bake:** 40 min.
Makes: 8 servings

- ⅔ cup sugar
- 2 Tbsp. cornstarch
- ¼ tsp. salt
- 3 cups fresh blueberries
- 3 cups sliced fresh or frozen rhubarb, thawed

TOPPING

- ¾ cup biscuit/baking mix
- ⅓ cup sugar
- ⅛ tsp. salt
- ⅓ cup cold unsalted butter, cubed
- ½ cup old-fashioned oats
- ½ cup chopped almonds

1. Preheat oven to 375°. In a bowl, mix sugar, cornstarch and salt. Add the blueberries and rhubarb; toss to coat. Transfer to a greased 8-in. square baking dish.

2. For topping, in a small bowl, mix baking mix, sugar and salt. Cut in butter until crumbly; stir in oats and almonds. Sprinkle over filling. Bake until filling is bubbly and the topping is golden brown, 40-45 minutes.

NOTE: If using frozen rhubarb, measure it while it's still frozen, then thaw completely. Drain in a colander, but do not press the liquid out.

1 SERVING: 324 cal., 14g fat (6g sat. fat), 20mg chol., 255mg sod., 49g carb. (32g sugars, 4g fiber), 4g pro.

HOMEMADE CHOCOLATE PUDDING

This delightful pudding is always a treat and easy to whip up using common pantry ingredients. I usually top my pudding with M&M's, my husband likes whipped topping on his and our daughter loves to dip fresh strawberries in hers.

—*Carrina Cooper, McAlpin, FL*

Prep: 10 min. + chilling • **Makes:** 8 servings

- 1 cup sugar
- ½ cup baking cocoa
- ¼ cup cornstarch
- ½ tsp. salt
- 4 cups whole milk
- 2 Tbsp. butter
- 2 tsp. vanilla extract
  M&M's, optional

In a heavy saucepan, combine sugar, cocoa, cornstarch and salt. Gradually add milk. Bring to a boil over medium heat; boil and stir for 2 minutes. Remove from the heat; stir in butter and vanilla. Spoon into individual serving dishes. Chill until serving. Sprinkle with M&M's if desired.

½ CUP: 196 cal., 4g fat (0 sat. fat), 2mg chol., 244mg sod., 38g carb. (0 sugars, 0 fiber), 5g pro. **DIABETIC EXCHANGES:** 2 starch, 1 fat, ½ milk.

JAYE BEELER
Grand Rapids, MI

5i PESTO TWISTS

Use pesto made with basil from your kitchen garden or purchase it prepared from the grocery store to fill these easy appetizers. They're also great as a quick snack any time.
—*Jaye Beeler, Grand Rapids, MI*

Takes: 25 min. • **Makes:** 12 servings

- 1   **pkg. (17.3 oz.) frozen puff pastry, thawed**
- ½   **cup prepared pesto**
- ½   **cup shredded Parmesan cheese**

1. Preheat oven to 400°. Unfold puff pastry sheets on a lightly floured surface. Roll each sheet into a 12-in. square. Spread pesto onto 1 pastry sheet to within ¼ in. of the edges. Sprinkle with cheese. Top with the remaining pastry sheet, pressing lightly. Cut into twelve 1-in.-wide strips. Twist each strip 4 times. Place 2 in. apart on parchment-lined baking sheets; pressing down the ends.

2. Bake 12-15 minutes or until golden brown. Serve warm.

1 TWIST: 265 cal., 17g fat (4g sat. fat), 6mg chol., 270mg sod., 24g carb. (0 sugars, 3g fiber), 6g pro.

CHEDDAR TWISTS: Beat 1 egg and 1 Tbsp. water; brush over pastry sheets. Top 1 sheet with ¾ cup shredded cheddar cheese. Top with remaining pastry, egg wash side down. Cut and bake as directed.

SWEET ALMOND TWISTS: Beat 1 egg and 1 Tbsp. water; brush over pastry sheets. Top 1 sheet with ¼ cup almond pastry filling and 1 cup sliced almonds. Top with the remaining pastry sheet, egg wash side down. Cut and bake as directed.

PEACH COBBLER

I created this recipe with a few tips from my mom and grandma. This cobbler can be made in minutes to suit any occasion.
—*Martha Betten, North Manchester, IN*

Prep: 15 min. • **Bake:** 25 min.
Makes: 8 servings

- ½   **cup butter, melted**
- 1   **can (15¼ oz.) sliced peaches, drained**
- 1¼ **cups sugar, divided**
- 1   **cup all-purpose flour**
- 1   **cup whole milk**
- 2   **tsp. baking powder**
- ¼   **tsp. salt**

1. Preheat oven to 400°. Pour melted butter into a shallow 2-qt. baking dish; set aside. Drain the peaches, reserving ¼ cup juice. In a saucepan, bring the peaches and juice just to a boil.

2. Meanwhile, in a bowl, combine 1 cup sugar, flour, milk, baking powder and salt; mix well. Pour over butter in baking dish. Spoon hot peaches over batter. Sprinkle with remaining sugar. Bake 25 minutes or until cake tests done. Serve warm.

1 CUP: 328 cal., 13g fat (8g sat. fat), 34mg chol., 282mg sod., 52g carb. (40g sugars, 1g fiber), 3g pro.

CHICKEN CHILI NACHOS

Spicy nachos with plenty of chicken and two kinds of beans make a fun and filling snack.
—*Karen Horning, Rockford, IL*

Takes: 25 min. • **Makes:** 8 servings

- 1   lb. boneless skinless chicken breasts, cubed
- 1   can (10 oz.) diced tomatoes and green chiles, undrained
- 1   can (16 oz.) kidney beans, rinsed and drained
- 1   can (16 oz.) chili beans, undrained
- 1   tsp. paprika
- 1   tsp. ground cumin
- ½   tsp. cayenne pepper
- 1   pkg. (13½ oz.) tortilla chips
- 1½ cups shredded Mexican cheese blend

1. In a large skillet coated with cooking spray, saute chicken until no longer pink. Add the tomatoes; cook over medium-high heat for 3 minutes or until the tomato juice is reduced. Stir in the beans, paprika, cumin and cayenne; cook for 5 minutes or until heated through.
2. Arrange the tortilla chips on 2 large microwave-safe plates; sprinkle each with ¼ cup cheese. Top with the chicken mixture and the remaining cheese. Microwave, uncovered, on high for 25-30 seconds or until the cheese is melted.
½ CUP: 484 cal., 19g fat (7g sat. fat), 50mg chol., 754mg sod., 54g carb. (2g sugars, 8g fiber), 26g pro.

GRILLED HONEY BALSAMIC-GLAZED FRUIT

One summer my mother-in-law made us grilled peaches basted with a sweet and tangy sauce. These are so good I'm always tempted to eat the whole batch.
—*Kristin Van Dyken, Kennewick, WA*

Takes: 25 min.
Makes: 6 servings (½ cup glaze)

- ½   cup balsamic vinegar
- ½   cup honey
-      Dash salt
- 6   medium peaches or nectarines, halved and pitted
     Vanilla ice cream, optional

1. In a small saucepan, combine the vinegar, honey and salt; cook and stir over low heat until blended, 2-3 minutes. Reserve ⅓ cup mixture for brushing peaches.
2. Bring the remaining mixture to a boil over medium heat; cook and stir just until mixture begins to thicken slightly (do not overcook), 4-6 minutes. Remove from heat.
3. Brush peaches with some of the reserved balsamic mixture. Grill, covered, on an oiled rack over medium heat until caramelized, brushing occasionally with the remaining reserved balsamic mixture, 6-8 minutes on each side. Serve with glaze and, if desired, vanilla ice cream.
2 FRUIT HALVES WITH GLAZE: 164 cal., 0 fat (0 sat. fat), 0 chol., 26mg sod., 43g carb. (40g sugars, 2g fiber), 1g pro.

OLD-FASHIONED MOLASSES CAKE

This old-time spice cake is low in fat but big on flavor. Serve it warm for breakfast on a frosty morning, or have a square with hot cider on a snowy afternoon. It's a great cold-weather treat.
—*Deanne Bagley, Bath, NY*

Prep: 15 min. • **Bake:** 25 min. + cooling
Makes: 9 servings

2	Tbsp. reduced-fat butter, softened
¼	cup sugar
1	large egg, room temperature
½	cup molasses
1	cup all-purpose flour
1	tsp. baking soda
¼	tsp. ground ginger
¼	tsp. ground cinnamon
⅛	tsp. salt
½	cup hot water
9	Tbsp. fat-free whipped topping

1. Preheat oven to 350°. In a small bowl, beat butter and sugar until crumbly, about 2 minutes. Beat in egg. Beat in the molasses. Combine flour, baking soda, ginger, cinnamon and salt; add to the butter mixture alternately with water, mixing well after each addition.
2. Transfer to a 9-in. square baking pan coated with cooking spray. Bake for 25-30 minutes or until a toothpick inserted in the center comes out clean. Cool on a wire rack. Cut into squares; garnish with whipped topping.
1 SLICE: 148 cal., 2g fat (1g sat. fat), 28mg chol., 205mg sod., 30g carb. (17g sugars, 0 fiber), 2g pro. **DIABETIC EXCHANGES:** 2 starch, ½ fat.

OAT-RAGEOUS CHOCOLATE CHIP COOKIES

My aunt gave me this recipe, and my family thinks these cookies are delicious. We enjoy all different kinds of cookies, but with these, we can combine three of our favorites—oatmeal, peanut butter and chocolate chip—in one!
—*Jaymie Noble, Kalamazoo, MI*

Prep: 25 min. • **Bake:** 10 min./batch
Makes: about 3 dozen

½	cup butter, softened
½	cup creamy peanut butter
½	cup sugar
⅓	cup packed brown sugar
1	large egg, room temperature
½	tsp. vanilla extract
1	cup all-purpose flour
½	cup quick-cooking oats
1	tsp. baking soda
¼	tsp. salt
1	cup (6 oz.) semisweet chocolate chips

Preheat oven to 350°. In a bowl, cream butter, peanut butter and sugars; beat in the egg and vanilla. Combine flour, oats, baking soda and salt. Add to the creamed mixture and mix well. Stir in chocolate chips. Drop dough by rounded tablespoonfuls onto ungreased baking sheets. Bake 10-12 minutes or until lightly browned.
2 COOKIES: 207 cal., 12g fat (6g sat. fat), 25mg chol., 194mg sod., 24g carb. (15g sugars, 1g fiber), 4g pro.

FROZEN PEANUT PARFAIT PIES

People will think you went to a lot of trouble to make this luscious pie, but it's quite simple to create. The crowd-pleasing dessert will be the hit of any potluck or party.

—Anne Powers, Munford, AL

- -

Prep: 20 min. + freezing
Makes: 2 pies (8 servings each)

- 1 pkg. (8 oz.) cream cheese, softened
- 1 can (14 oz.) sweetened condensed milk
- 1 carton (16 oz.) frozen whipped topping, thawed
- 2 pastry shells (9 in.), baked
- 1 jar (11¾ oz.) hot fudge ice cream topping, warmed
- 2 cups dry roasted peanuts

1. In a large bowl, beat the cream cheese and condensed milk until smooth; fold in whipped topping. Spread a fourth of the mixture into each pie shell. Drizzle each with a fourth of the fudge topping; sprinkle each with ½ cup peanuts. Repeat layers.

2. Cover and freeze for 4 hours or overnight. Remove pies from the freezer 5 minutes before cutting.

1 PIECE: 492 cal., 28g fat (13g sat. fat), 29mg chol., 336mg sod., 51g carb. (29g sugars, 2g fiber), 9g pro.

DIANNE VAN DER VEEN
Plymouth, MA

🔵 APPLE SNACK WEDGES

Break out these easy, fun apple wedges before you head out the door. The protein in the peanut butter will help fill you up.

—Jacquie Berg, St. Cloud, WI

- -

Takes: 10 min. • **Makes:** 1 dozen

- 2 medium apples
- 1 cup Rice Chex, crushed
- 1½ tsp. packed brown sugar
- 2 Tbsp. reduced-fat creamy peanut butter

1. Core apples; cut each into 6 wedges. Pat dry with paper towels.

2. In a small shallow bowl, combine the cereal and brown sugar. Spread cut sides of apples with peanut butter; roll in cereal mixture. Serve immediately.

1 PIECE: 36 cal., 1g fat (0 sat. fat), 0 chol., 33mg sod., 6g carb. (3g sugars, 1g fiber), 1g pro. **DIABETIC EXCHANGES:** ½ starch.

DOWN EAST BLUEBERRY BUCKLE

This buckle won a contest at my daughter's college. They shipped us four lobsters as a prize, but the real reward was seeing the smile on our daughter's face.

—Dianne van der Veen, Plymouth, MA

- -

Prep: 15 min. • **Bake:** 30 min.
Makes: 9 servings

- 2 cups all-purpose flour
- ¾ cup sugar
- 2½ tsp. baking powder
- ¼ tsp. salt
- 1 large egg, room temperature
- ¾ cup 2% milk
- ¼ cup butter, melted
- 2 cups fresh or frozen blueberries

TOPPING

- ½ cup sugar
- ⅓ cup all-purpose flour
- ½ tsp. ground cinnamon
- ¼ cup butter, softened

1. Preheat oven to 375°. In a large bowl, whisk flour, sugar, baking powder and salt. In another bowl, whisk egg, milk and melted butter until blended. Add to flour mixture; stir just until moistened. Fold in blueberries. Transfer to a greased 9-in. square baking pan.

2. For topping, in a small bowl, mix sugar, flour and cinnamon. Using a fork, stir in softened butter until the mixture is crumbly. Sprinkle over the batter.

3. Bake 30-35 minutes or until a toothpick inserted in the center comes out clean (do not overbake). Cool in pan on a wire rack. Serve warm or at room temperature.

NOTE: If using frozen blueberries, use without thawing to avoid discoloring the batter.

1 PIECE: 354 cal., 12g fat (7g sat. fat), 49mg chol., 277mg sod., 59g carb. (32g sugars, 2g fiber), 5g pro.

PAY DIRT CAKE

With its layers of crushed chocolate sandwich cookies and creamy filling, this is a rich dessert. You can decorate the top with a few wrapped chocolate coins.

—*Betty Jean Jordan, Monticello, GA*

Takes: 15 min. • **Makes:** 10 servings

28 Oreo cookies
1 pkg. (8 oz.) cream cheese, softened
¼ cup butter, softened
1 cup confectioners' sugar
3⅓ cups cold whole milk
2 pkg. (3.4 oz. each) instant French vanilla pudding mix
1 carton (8 oz.) frozen whipped topping, thawed

1. In a food processor or blender, process the cookies until finely crushed. Set aside 2 Tbsp. of crumbs for topping.

2. In a large bowl, beat the cream cheese, butter and sugar. In a bowl, whisk the milk and pudding mix for 2 minutes. Add to the cream cheese mixture; mix well. Fold in the whipped topping.

3. Place half the cookie crumbs in 2½-qt. container or bowl; top with half the pudding mixture. Repeat layers. Sprinkle with the reserved crumbs. Refrigerate until serving.

1 SERVING: 463 cal., 25g fat (15g sat. fat), 48mg chol., 494mg sod., 52g carb. (37g sugars, 1g fiber), 6g pro.

5i

DREAMY FRUIT DIP

Everyone will love this thick, buttery sensation. It's offered alongside apple wedges, pineapple chunks and grapes.

—*Anna Beiler, Strasburg, PA*

Takes: 10 min. • **Makes:** about 4 cups

1 pkg. (8 oz.) cream cheese, softened
½ cup butter, softened
½ cup marshmallow creme
1 carton (8 oz.) frozen whipped topping, thawed
Assorted fresh fruit

In a small bowl, beat cream cheese and butter until smooth. Beat in the marshmallow creme. Fold in the whipped topping. Serve with fruit. Store in the refrigerator.

2 TBSP.: 75 cal., 6g fat (5g sat. fat), 15mg chol., 51mg sod., 3g carb. (2g sugars, 0 fiber), 1g pro.

TEST KITCHEN TIP
You can chill any leftover dip for a tasty topping for toast the next morning.

PEANUT BUTTER PINWHEELS

I came across this easy and tasty snack while searching online for healthy munchies for kids. They're quick and easy to make—and filling enough to hold the kids until dinner. Once you've got the idea, it's easy to make these wraps with different combinations of ingredients, too.
—Mary Haluch, Ludlow, MA

- -

Takes: 5 min. • **Makes:** 16 appetizers

- 4   Tbsp. creamy peanut butter
- 2   flour tortillas (8 in.)
- 2   tsp. honey
- ½   cup granola without raisins

Spread peanut butter over each tortilla; drizzle with honey and sprinkle with granola. Roll up each tortilla; cut into slices.

1 PINWHEEL: 60 cal., 3g fat (1g sat. fat), 0 chol., 48mg sod., 7g carb. (2g sugars, 1g fiber), 2g pro.

VEGGIE DILL PINWHEELS: Mix 3 oz. softened cream cheese with 1 Tbsp. each minced dill and chives. Spread over tortillas; top with baby spinach and thinly sliced tomato. Roll up; slice.

SALAMI PINWHEELS: Mix 4 oz. whipped cream cheese, 2 oz. diced hard salami and 1 Tbsp. dill pickle relish. Spread over tortillas; roll up and slice.

SALMON PINWHEELS: Mix 4 oz. softened cream cheese, ½ cup flaked cooked salmon, 1 Tbsp. salsa, 2 tsp. minced parsley and a dash of cumin. Spread over tortillas; roll up and slice.

ORANGE BUNDT CAKE

This pretty cake comes together quickly with a boxed mix. Fat-free mayonnaise replaces the heavy oils, and the citrus glaze finishes it nicely.
—Deborah Williams, Peoria, AZ

- -

Prep: 15 min. • **Bake:** 40 min. + cooling
Makes: 14 servings

- 1   pkg. yellow cake mix (regular size)
- 1   envelope whipped topping mix (Dream Whip)
- ¾   cup orange juice
- ¾   cup fat-free mayonnaise
- 3   large eggs, room temperature
- 1   Tbsp. grated orange zest

GLAZE
- 1½   cups confectioners' sugar
- 2   Tbsp. orange juice

1. Preheat oven to 350°. In a large bowl, combine the first 6 ingredients; beat on low speed for 30 seconds. Beat on medium for 2 minutes. Coat a 10-in. fluted tube pan with cooking spray and dust with flour. Pour the batter into pan.

2. Bake 40-45 minutes or until a toothpick inserted in the center comes out clean. Cool for 10 minutes before removing from pan to a wire rack to cool completely. Combine the glaze ingredients; drizzle over cake.

1 PIECE: 257 cal., 5g fat (2g sat. fat), 46mg chol., 353mg sod., 48g carb. (34g sugars, 1g fiber), 3g pro.

HONEY-PEANUT BUTTER COOKIES

It's not unusual for my husband to request these cookies by name. You'll love 'em.
—*Lucile Proctor, Panguitch, UT*

Prep: 15 min. • **Bake:** 10 min./batch
Makes: 5 dozen

- ½ cup shortening
- 1 cup creamy peanut butter
- 1 cup honey
- 2 large eggs, room temperature, lightly beaten
- 3 cups all-purpose flour
- 1 cup sugar
- 1½ tsp. baking soda
- 1 tsp. baking powder
- ½ tsp. salt

1. Preheat oven to 350°. In a bowl, mix the shortening, peanut butter and honey. Add eggs; mix well. Combine dry ingredients; add to peanut butter mixture and mix well.
2. Roll into 1- to 1½-in. balls and place on ungreased baking sheets. Flatten with a fork dipped in flour. Bake 8-10 minutes or until set. Remove to wire racks to cool.
2 COOKIES: 191 cal., 8g fat (2g sat. fat), 14mg chol., 160mg sod., 27g carb. (16g sugars, 1g fiber), 4g pro.

LITTLE PIGS IN A HAMMOCK

Pigs in a blanket aren't just for kids anymore! Dijon and Camembert transform this children's favorite into a version that's perfect for grown-ups, too.
—*Crystal Schlueter, Northglenn, CO*

Takes: 30 min. • **Makes:** 1½ dozen

- 1 pkg. (17.3 oz.) frozen puff pastry, thawed
- 3 Tbsp. seedless raspberry jam
- 1 Tbsp. Dijon mustard
- 1 round (8 oz.) Camembert cheese
- 18 miniature smoked sausages
- 1 large egg
- 1 Tbsp. water

1. Preheat oven to 425°. Unfold puff pastry. Cut each pastry into 9 squares. Cut each square into 2 triangles. In a small bowl, mix jam and mustard; spread over triangles. Cut cheese in half crosswise; cut each half into 9 wedges.
2. Top each triangle with a wedge of cheese and a sausage. Fold pastry over sausage and cheese; press to seal. Place on a parchment-lined baking sheet. In a small bowl, whisk egg with water. Brush over the pastries. Bake for 15-17 minutes or until golden brown.
1 APPETIZER: 211 cal., 13g fat (5g sat. fat), 25mg chol., 312mg sod., 18g carb. (2g sugars, 2g fiber), 6g pro.

ONE-BOWL CHOCOLATE CAKE

This cake mixes up quickly and bakes while we enjoy our dinner.
—*Coleen Martin, Brookfield, WI*

Prep: 15 min. • **Bake:** 35 min. + cooling
Makes: 15 servings

- 2 cups all-purpose flour
- 2 cups sugar
- ½ cup baking cocoa
- 2 tsp. baking soda
- 1 tsp. baking powder
- ½ tsp. salt
- 2 large eggs, room temperature, lightly beaten
- 1 cup canola oil
- 1 cup buttermilk
- 1 cup hot water
  Frosting of your choice
  Colored sprinkles, optional

1. Preheat oven to 350°. Grease a 13x9-in. baking pan. In a large bowl, whisk the first 6 ingredients. Stir in eggs, oil and buttermilk. Add water; stir until combined.

2. Transfer batter to prepared pan. Bake for 35-40 minutes or until a toothpick inserted in center comes out clean. Cool completely in pan on a wire rack. Frost the cake. If desired, decorate with sprinkles.

1 PIECE: 297 cal., 15g fat (2g sat. fat), 27mg chol., 281mg sod., 39g carb. (25g sugars, 1g fiber), 3g pro.

CHOCOLATE BUTTERCREAM FROSTING: In a large bowl, beat ½ cup softened butter until creamy. Beat in 2 cups confectioners' sugar, ¼ cup baking cocoa, 1½ tsp. vanilla and 3-4 Tbsp. 2% milk until reaching the desired consistency.

TOMATILLO SALSA

Dare to deviate from tomato salsa and try this tomatillo-based version for a deliciously addictive change of pace. It's fantastic on its own, with tortilla chips or served as a condiment alongside a variety of meats.
—*Lori Kostecki, Wausau, WI*

Takes: 20 min. • **Makes:** 2¼ cups

- 8 tomatillos, husked
- 1 medium tomato, quartered
- 1 small onion, cut into chunks
- 1 jalapeno pepper, seeded
- 3 Tbsp. fresh cilantro leaves
- 3 garlic cloves, peeled
- 1 Tbsp. lime juice
- ½ tsp. salt
- ¼ tsp. ground cumin
- ⅛ tsp. pepper
  Tortilla chips

1. In a large saucepan, bring 4 cups of water to a boil. Add tomatillos. Reduce heat; simmer, uncovered, for 5 minutes. Drain.

2. Place tomatillos, tomato, onion, jalapeno, cilantro, garlic, lime juice and seasonings in a food processor. Cover and process until blended. Serve with chips.

NOTE: Wear disposable gloves when cutting the hot peppers; the oils can burn skin. Avoid touching your face.

¼ CUP: 19 cal., 0 fat (0 sat. fat), 0 chol., 133mg sod., 4g carb. (2g sugars, 1g fiber), 1g pro.

STRAWBERRY CHEESECAKE TRIFLE

For a dessert that looks as great as it tastes, this one can't be beat! Layers of rich pound cake, luscious cream and sweet strawberries make this treat very inviting.

—Marnie Stoughton, Glenburnie, ON

Prep: 20 min. + chilling • **Makes:** 16 servings

- 2 pints fresh strawberries, sliced
- 1 cup sugar, divided
- 2 pkg. (8 oz. each) cream cheese, softened
- 3 Tbsp. orange juice
- 3 cups heavy whipping cream, whipped
- 1 loaf (10¾ oz.) frozen pound cake, thawed and cut into ½-in. cubes
- 3 oz. semisweet chocolate, grated
  Optional toppings: Chocolate curls and additional strawberries

1. In a bowl, toss the strawberries with ½ cup sugar; set aside.
2. In a bowl, beat cream cheese, orange juice and the remaining sugar until smooth. Fold in whipped cream; set aside.
3. Drain strawberries, reserving the juice; set the berries aside. Gently toss cake cubes with the reserved juice. Place half of the cake in a 4-qt. trifle dish or serving bowl. Top with a third of the cream cheese mixture, half of the strawberries and half of the grated chocolate. Repeat layers. Top with the remaining cream cheese mixture. Garnish with chocolate curls and strawberries if desired. Cover and refrigerate for at least 4 hours.
1 CUP: 344 cal., 25g fat (15g sat. fat), 104mg chol., 129mg sod., 28g carb. (22g sugars, 1g fiber), 4g pro.

TOASTED RAVIOLI PUFFS

I call toasted ravioli a fan favorite because it disappears faster than I can make it. With just five ingredients, this is how you start the party.

—Kathy Morgan, Temecula, CA

Takes: 30 min. • **Makes:** 2 dozen

- 24 refrigerated cheese ravioli
- 1 Tbsp. reduced-fat Italian salad dressing
- 1 Tbsp. Italian-style panko (Japanese) bread crumbs
- 1 Tbsp. grated Parmesan cheese
  Warm marinara sauce

1. Preheat oven to 400°. Cook the ravioli according to the package directions; drain. Transfer to a greased baking sheet. Brush with salad dressing. In a small bowl, mix bread crumbs and cheese; sprinkle over ravioli.
2. Bake 12-15 minutes or until golden brown. Serve with marinara sauce.
1 RAVIOLI: 21 cal., 1g fat (0 sat. fat), 3mg chol., 43mg sod., 3g carb. (0 sugars, 0 fiber), 1g pro.

GOLDEN POUND CAKE

The surprise ingredient in this cake is a can of Mountain Dew. I sometimes substitute orange cake mix and orange soda for a flavorful variation.
—*Vicki Boyd, Mechanicsville, VA*

Prep: 10 min. • **Bake:** 45 min. + cooling
Makes: 12 servings

- 1   pkg. lemon cake mix (regular size)
- 1   pkg. (3.4 oz.) instant vanilla pudding mix
- 4   large eggs, room temperature
- ¾   cup canola oil
- 1   can (12 oz.) Mountain Dew
     Confectioners' sugar, optional

1. Preheat the oven to 350°. In a large bowl, combine cake mix, pudding mix, eggs, oil and soda; beat on low speed for 30 seconds. Beat on medium for 2 minutes.
2. Pour the batter into a greased and floured 10-in. fluted tube pan. Bake 45-50 minutes or until a toothpick inserted in the center comes out clean. Cool 10 minutes before removing from pan to a wire rack to cool completely. Dust with confectioners' sugar if desired.
1 SLICE: 363 cal., 19g fat (4g sat. fat), 71mg chol., 413mg sod., 46g carb. (29g sugars, 1g fiber), 4g pro.

READER REVIEW

"This is my go-to pound cake recipe when I want dessert with dinner. It's quick, moist and delicious and one of my husband's favorite cakes."

JAZZYINJAPAN, TASTEOFHOME.COM

CHOCOLATE COBBLER

Talk about comfort food! This ultra moist dessert makes a decadent end to any meal. Best of all, it comes together in no time with just a few ingredients.
—*Margaret McNeil, Germantown, TN*

Prep: 10 min. • **Bake:** 40 min.
Makes: 8 servings

- 1   cup self-rising flour
- ½   cup sugar
- 2   Tbsp. plus ¼ cup baking cocoa, divided
- ½   cup whole milk
- 3   Tbsp. vegetable oil
- 1   cup packed brown sugar
- 1¾ cups hot water
      Vanilla ice cream, optional

Preheat oven to 350°. In a bowl, combine the flour, sugar and 2 Tbsp. cocoa. Stir in the milk and oil until smooth. Pour into a greased 8-in. square baking pan. Combine brown sugar and remaining cocoa; sprinkle over batter. Pour hot water over top (do not stir). Bake until the top of the cake springs back when lightly touched, 40-45 minutes. Serve warm, with ice cream if desired.
NOTE: As a substitute for 1 cup of self-rising flour, place 1½ tsp. baking powder and ½ tsp. salt in a measuring cup. Add all-purpose flour to measure 1 cup.
1 SERVING: 267 cal., 6g fat (1g sat. fat), 2mg chol., 198mg sod., 53g carb. (40g sugars, 1g fiber), 3g pro.

3 large eggs, room temperature
1 tsp. vanilla extract
4½ cups quick-cooking oats
2 tsp. baking soda
1 cup miniature semisweet chocolate chips
1 cup M&M's miniature baking bits

1. Preheat oven to 350°. In a large bowl, cream peanut butter, butter and sugars until blended. Beat in eggs and vanilla. In another bowl, whisk oats and baking soda; gradually beat into the creamed mixture. Stir in the chocolate chips and baking bits.

2. Drop dough by heaping tablespoonfuls 2 in. apart onto ungreased baking sheets. Bake 12-14 minutes or until the edges are browned. Remove from pans to wire racks to cool. Store in airtight containers.

NOTE: Reduced-fat or generic brands of peanut butter are not recommended for this recipe. This recipe does not use flour.

1 COOKIE: 153 cal., 8g fat (3g sat. fat), 18mg chol., 106mg sod., 18g carb. (13g sugars, 1g fiber), 4g pro. **DIABETIC EXCHANGES:** 1 fat, ½ starch.

MARINATED MOZZARELLA

I always come home with an empty container when I take this dish to a party. It can be made ahead to free up time later. I serve it with pretty party picks for a festive look.

—*Peggy Cairo, Kenosha, WI*

- -

Prep: 15 min. + marinating
Makes: 10 servings

⅓ cup olive oil
1 Tbsp. chopped oil-packed sun-dried tomatoes
1 Tbsp. minced fresh parsley
1 tsp. crushed red pepper flakes
1 tsp. dried basil
1 tsp. minced chives
¼ tsp. garlic powder
1 lb. cubed part-skim mozzarella cheese

In a large bowl, combine first 7 ingredients; add the cheese cubes. Stir to coat. Cover; refrigerate at least 30 minutes.

¼ CUP: 203 cal., 16g fat (7g sat. fat), 24mg chol., 242mg sod., 2g carb. (trace sugars, trace fiber), 12g pro.

DATE PUDDING COBBLER

There were eight children in my family when I was a girl, and all of us enjoyed this cobbler. I now serve it for everyday and special occasions alike.

—*Carolyn Miller, Guys Mills, PA*

- -

Prep: 15 min. • **Bake:** 25 min.
Makes: 8 servings

1 cup all-purpose flour
1½ cups packed brown sugar, divided
2 tsp. baking powder
1 Tbsp. cold butter
½ cup whole milk
¾ cup chopped dates
¾ cup chopped walnuts
1 cup water
Optional toppings: Whipped cream and ground cinnamon

1. Preheat oven to 350°. In a large bowl, combine flour, ½ cup brown sugar and the baking powder. Cut in butter until crumbly. Gradually add milk, dates and walnuts.

2. In a large saucepan, combine water and the remaining brown sugar; bring to a boil. Remove from heat; add the date mixture and mix well.

3. Transfer to a greased 10-in. cast-iron skillet or an 8-in. square baking pan. Bake for 25-30 minutes or until the top is golden brown and the fruit is tender. Serve warm, with whipped cream and cinnamon if desired.

1 SERVING: 347 cal., 9g fat (2g sat. fat), 5mg chol., 150mg sod., 65g carb. (50g sugars, 2g fiber), 4g pro.

PEANUT BUTTER JUMBOS

M&M's baking bits, chocolate chips, peanut butter, oats—they're all here!

—*Deborah Huffer, Staunton, VA*

- -

Prep: 15 min. • **Bake:** 15 min./batch
Makes: 9 dozen

1½ cups peanut butter
½ cup butter, softened
1 cup sugar
1 cup packed brown sugar

SPEEDY BROWNIES

Since you dump all the ingredients together for these brownies, they don't take long to make. There's no mistaking the homemade goodness of a freshly baked batch—rich and fudgy!
—*Diane Heier, Harwood, ND*

Prep: 15 min. • **Bake:** 30 min.
Makes: about 3 dozen

- 2 cups sugar
- 1¾ cups all-purpose flour
- ½ cup baking cocoa
- 1 tsp. salt
- 5 large eggs, room temperature
- 1 cup canola oil
- 1 tsp. vanilla extract
- 1 cup (6 oz.) semisweet chocolate chips

1. Preheat oven to 350°. In a large bowl, beat the first 7 ingredients. Pour batter into a greased 13x9-in. baking pan. Sprinkle with chocolate chips.
2. Bake for 30 minutes or until a toothpick inserted in the center comes out clean. Cool in pan on a wire rack.
1 BROWNIE: 155 cal., 8g fat (2g sat. fat), 30mg chol., 75mg sod., 19g carb. (14g sugars, 1g fiber), 2g pro.

MARINA CASTLE KELLEY
Canyon Country, CA

CANNELLINI BEAN HUMMUS

Hummus features a delightful nuttiness from tahini, a peanut butter-like paste made from ground sesame seeds. My version is made with cannellini beans, which pack a lot of protein, so it's a healthy snack for kids.
—*Marina Castle Kelley, Canyon Country, CA*

Takes: 5 min. • **Makes:** 10 servings (1¼ cups)

- 2 garlic cloves, peeled
- 1 can (15 oz.) cannellini beans, rinsed and drained
- ¼ cup tahini
- 3 Tbsp. lemon juice
- 1½ tsp. ground cumin
- ¼ tsp. salt
- ¼ tsp. crushed red pepper flakes
- 2 Tbsp. minced fresh parsley
  Pita breads, cut into wedges
  Assorted fresh vegetables

1. Place garlic in a food processor; cover and process until minced. Add the beans, tahini, lemon juice, cumin, salt and pepper flakes; cover and process until smooth.
2. Transfer to a small bowl; stir in parsley. Refrigerate until serving. Serve with pita wedges and assorted fresh vegetables.
2 TBSP.: 78 cal., 4g fat (1g sat. fat), 0 chol., 114mg sod., 8g carb. (0 sugars, 2g fiber), 3g pro. **DIABETIC EXCHANGES:** 1 fat, ½ starch.

READER REVIEW

"This is a delicious hummus. I especially like it because, to me, it's much creamier than one using chickpeas (though I like that kind, too)."

ANNRMS, TASTEOFHOME.COM

CHERRY CREAM CHEESE DESSERT

Cherries, graham crackers and a creamy filling make a festive parfait-style dessert. We sometimes substitute blueberry pie filling or other fruits for the cherry.
—*Melody Mellinger, Myerstown, PA*

Takes: 15 min. • **Makes:** 8 servings

- ¾ cup graham cracker crumbs (about 12 squares)
- 2 Tbsp. sugar
- 2 Tbsp. butter, melted

FILLING
- 1 pkg. (8 oz.) cream cheese, softened
- 1 can (14 oz.) sweetened condensed milk
- ⅓ cup lemon juice
- 1 tsp. vanilla extract
- 1 can (21 oz.) cherry pie filling

1. In a small bowl, combine the cracker crumbs, sugar and butter. Divide crumb mixture among 8 dessert dishes, about 4 rounded teaspoonfuls in each.

2. In a small bowl, beat cream cheese until smooth. Gradually add milk until blended. Beat in lemon juice and vanilla. Spoon ¼ cup into each dish. Top with pie filling, about ¼ cup in each.

1 PARFAIT: 418 cal., 18g fat (11g sat. fat), 56mg chol., 228mg sod., 59g carb. (51g sugars, 1g fiber), 7g pro.

WAFFLED PIZZA BITES

The whole family will love this playful twist on waffles. Mozzarella and Parmesan cheeses are sandwiched between layers of dough and cooked up in the waffle iron. It's like a pizza grilled cheese waffle!
—*Deirdre Cox, Kansas City, MO*

Takes: 20 min. • **Makes:** 8 appetizers

- 1¼ cups shredded part-skim mozzarella cheese
- ¼ cup shredded Parmesan cheese
- ½ tsp. dried basil
- ½ tsp. dried oregano
- 2 tubes (8 oz. each) refrigerated crescent rolls
- 32 slices pepperoni (about 2 oz.)
- 1 jar (14 oz.) pizza sauce, warmed
  Optional toppings: sliced pepperoni, shredded mozzarella cheese and basil

1. In a small bowl, combine the cheeses, basil and oregano. Separate each roll of crescent dough into two 7x6-in. rectangles; seal the perforations.

2. Place 1 rectangle on a preheated greased 8-in. square waffle maker (the dough will not cover the entire surface). Layer with half the cheese mixture and half the pepperoni to ½ in. of edges; top with another rectangle. Bake until golden brown, 4-5 minutes. Repeat.

3. Remove to a cutting board and cool slightly. Cut each rectangle into 4 triangles; serve pizza bites warm with pizza sauce and, if desired, optional toppings.

1 APPETIZER: 329 cal., 19g fat (4g sat. fat), 21mg chol., 909mg sod., 29g carb. (9g sugars, 1g fiber), 12g pro.

BLUEBERRY SLUMP

My mother-in-law used to make slump with wild blueberries and serve it warm with a pitcher of cream on the table. My husband and I have been eating it for over 65 years, but the recipe is even older!
—*Eleanore Ebeling, Brewster, MN*

Takes: 30 min. • **Makes:** 6 servings

- 3 cups fresh or frozen blueberries
- ½ cup sugar
- 1¼ cups water
- 1 tsp. finely grated lemon zest
- 1 Tbsp. lemon juice
- 1 cup all-purpose flour
- 2 Tbsp. sugar
- 2 tsp. baking powder
- ½ tsp. salt
- 1 Tbsp. butter
- ½ cup whole milk
  Cream or whipped cream, optional

1. In a large heavy saucepan, combine the blueberries, sugar, water, lemon zest and juice; bring to a boil. Reduce heat and simmer, uncovered, for 5 minutes.
2. Meanwhile, in a large bowl, combine the flour, sugar, baking powder and salt; cut in butter until the mixture resembles coarse crumbs. Add milk quickly; stir until moistened.
3. Drop dough by spoonfuls onto berries (makes 6 dumplings). Cover and cook over low heat for 10 minutes. Do not lift lid while simmering. Spoon dumplings into individual serving bowls; top with sauce. Serve warm with cream or whipped cream if desired.
1 SERVING: 228 cal., 3g fat (2g sat. fat), 8mg chol., 361mg sod., 48g carb. (29g sugars, 2g fiber), 3g pro.

> **TEST KITCHEN TIP**
> Lemon and lime juice or zest can be used interchangeably in equal amounts in most recipes. Add a little of both for a refreshing lemon-lime flavor.

OLD-FASHIONED BANANA CREAM PIE

This fluffy no-bake pie is full of old-fashioned flavor, with only a fraction of the work. Because the recipe uses instant pudding , the pie is ready in just minutes.
—*Perlene Hoekema, Lynden, WA*

Takes: 10 min. • **Makes:** 8 servings

- 1 cup cold 2% milk
- ½ tsp. vanilla extract
- 1 pkg. (3.4 oz.) instant vanilla pudding mix
- 1 carton (12 oz.) frozen whipped topping, thawed, divided
- 1 graham cracker crust (9 in.)
- 2 medium firm bananas, sliced
  Additional banana slices, optional

1. In a large bowl, whisk milk, vanilla and pudding mix for 2 minutes (the mixture will be thick). Fold in 3 cups whipped topping.

2. Pour 1⅓ cups of the pudding mixture into pie crust. Layer with banana slices and the remaining pudding mixture. Top with the remaining whipped topping. Garnish with additional banana slices if desired. Refrigerate until serving.
1 PIECE: 311 cal., 13g fat (9g sat. fat), 2mg chol., 213mg sod., 43g carb. (29g sugars, 1g fiber), 2g pro.

CHOCOLATE & PEANUT BUTTER BANANA CREAM PIE: Substitute 1 (9 in.) chocolate crumb crust for the graham cracker crust. Arrange banana slices on the crust. In a microwave-safe bowl, mix ¾ cup peanut butter and 2 oz. chopped chocolate; microwave on high for 1-1½ minutes or until blended and smooth, stirring every 30 seconds. Spoon over bananas. Pour the pudding mixture over top. Garnish with the remaining whipped topping. Just before serving, garnish with 2 Tbsp. chopped salted peanuts or chopped peanut butter cups.

ALMOND TOFFEE SANDIES

I knew after sampling these cookies from a friend that I had to add them to my bulging recipe files! If you prefer, you can make these into pecan sandies by using 2 cups of coarsely chopped pecans instead of the almonds.
—*Vicki Crowley, Monticello, IA*

Prep: 15 min. • **Bake:** 10 min./batch
Makes: 9 dozen

- 1 cup butter, softened
- 1 cup sugar
- 1 cup confectioners' sugar
- 2 large eggs, room temperature
- 1 cup canola oil
- 1 tsp. almond extract
- 4½ cups all-purpose flour
- 1 tsp. baking soda
- 1 tsp. cream of tartar
- 1 tsp. salt
- 2 cups sliced almonds
- 1 pkg. (8 oz.) toffee bits

1. Preheat oven to 350°. In a large bowl, cream butter and sugars until blended. Add 1 egg at a time, beating well after each addition. Gradually beat in oil and extract. Combine the flour, baking soda, cream of tartar and salt; gradually add to the creamed mixture and mix well. Stir in almonds and toffee bits.
2. Drop dough by teaspoonfuls 2 in. apart onto ungreased baking sheets. Bake until golden brown, 10-12 minutes. Remove to wire racks to cool.
2 COOKIES: 178 cal., 11g fat (4g sat. fat), 19mg chol., 134mg sod., 18g carb. (9g sugars, 1g fiber), 2g pro.

⑤ CARAMEL APPLE & BRIE SKEWERS

I'm a caterer, and these sweet treats rank among my best-sellers. Using prepared caramel makes them a snap to assemble. Who doesn't love a shortcut?
—*Camille Ellis, Tampa, FL*

Takes: 10 min. • **Makes:** 6 skewers

- 2 medium apples, cubed
- 1 log (6 oz.) Brie cheese, cubed
- ½ cup hot caramel ice cream topping
- ½ cup finely chopped macadamia nuts
- 2 Tbsp. dried cranberries

On each of 6 appetizer skewers, alternately thread apple and cheese cubes; place on a serving plate. Drizzle with caramel topping; sprinkle with macadamia nuts and cranberries.
1 SKEWER: 272 cal., 16g fat (6g sat. fat), 29mg chol., 303mg sod., 27g carb. (7g sugars, 2g fiber), 7g pro.

CLASSIC APPLE CRANBERRY CRISP

For a little old-fashioned goodness, treat your clan to this divine dish that bakes up warm and bubbly.
—*Billie Moss, Walnut Creek, CA*

Prep: 10 min. • **Bake:** 25 min.
Makes: 4 servings

- 3 cups chopped peeled tart apples
- 1½ cups fresh or frozen cranberries, thawed
- ¾ cup packed brown sugar, divided
- 1 Tbsp. lemon juice
- ½ tsp. ground cinnamon
- ½ cup all-purpose flour
- ⅓ cup cold butter, cubed
  Vanilla ice cream, optional

1. Preheat oven to 375°. In a large bowl, combine apples, cranberries, ¼ cup brown sugar, lemon juice and cinnamon. Pour into a greased 8-in. square baking dish. In a small bowl, mix flour and remaining brown sugar. Cut in butter until crumbly. Sprinkle over fruit.
2. Bake, uncovered, 25-30 minutes or until topping is golden brown and filling is bubbly. If desired, serve with ice cream.
1 SERVING: 408 cal., 16g fat (10g sat.fat), 41mg chol., 134mg sod., 68g carb.(50g sugars, 3g fiber), 2g pro.

PUMPKIN MOUSSE

Guests savor every creamy, smooth spoonful of this spiced autumn dessert. It tastes so good, no one guesses that it's actually low in fat.

—*Patricia Sidloskas, Anniston, AL*

Takes: 15 min. • **Makes:** 4 servings

1½ cups cold fat-free milk
1 pkg. (1 oz.) sugar-free instant butterscotch pudding mix
½ cup canned pumpkin
½ tsp. ground cinnamon
¼ tsp. ground ginger
¼ tsp. ground allspice
1 cup fat-free whipped topping, divided
    Coarse sugar, optional

1. In a large bowl, whisk milk and pudding mix for 2 minutes. Let stand for 2 minutes or until soft-set. Combine the pumpkin, cinnamon, ginger and allspice; fold into the pudding. Fold in ½ cup of whipped topping.
2. Transfer to individual serving dishes. Refrigerate until serving. Garnish with the remaining whipped topping. Sprinkle with coarse sugar if desired.
⅔ CUP: 95 cal., 0 fat (0 sat. fat), 2mg chol., 351mg sod., 19g carb. (8g sugars, 1g fiber), 4g pro. **DIABETIC EXCHANGES:** ½ starch, ½ fat-free milk.

NUTTY BERRY TRAIL MIX

This recipe, my son's favorite, earned me an A in my early-childhood nutrition course. It lets you take control of what your children snack on!

—*Cheri Majors, Claremont, CA*

Takes: 5 min. • **Makes:** 10 cups

1 can (15 oz.) mixed nuts
2 cups (12 oz.) semisweet chocolate chips
1 pkg. (9 oz.) raisins
1 pkg. (6 oz.) chopped dried pineapple
1 jar (5.85 oz.) sunflower kernels
1 pkg. (5 oz.) dried cranberries

In a large bowl, combine all the ingredients; mix well. Store in an airtight container.
⅓ CUP: 283 cal., 17g fat (5g sat. fat), 0 chol., 106mg sod., 34g carb. (25g sugars, 4g fiber), 5g pro.

GINGER DROP COOKIES

My mother shared the recipe for her soft spice cookies—I'm so grateful to have it!
—*Bethel Walters, Willow River, MN*

Prep: 15 min. + chilling • **Bake:** 10 min./batch
Makes: about 5½ dozen

- 1 cup shortening
- 1 cup packed brown sugar
- 1 cup molasses
- 2 large eggs, room temperature
- 4 cups all-purpose flour
- 2 tsp. baking soda
- 2 tsp. ground cinnamon
- 2 tsp. ground ginger
- 1 tsp. salt
- ½ cup water

1. In a large bowl, cream shortening and brown sugar until light and fluffy. Beat in the molasses and eggs. Combine the dry ingredients; add to the creamed mixture alternately with water. Refrigerate for at least 8 hours.

2. Preheat oven to 350°. Drop the dough by tablespoonfuls 2 in. apart onto greased baking sheets. Bake 10-12 minutes or until lightly browned. Remove to wire racks to cool.

2 COOKIES: 165 cal., 6g fat (2g sat. fat), 13mg chol., 158mg sod., 25g carb. (13g sugars, 0 fiber), 2g pro.

CHERRY PUDDING CAKE

A cross between a cake and a cobbler, this cherry dessert is awesome. Add it to your list of trusty potluck recipes, because this one is sure to go fast.
—*Brenda Parker, Kalamazoo, MI*

Prep: 10 min. • **Bake:** 40 min.
Makes: 12 servings

- 2 cups all-purpose flour
- 2½ cups sugar, divided
- 4 tsp. baking powder
- 1 cup whole milk
- 2 Tbsp. canola oil
- 2 cans (14½ oz. each) water-packed pitted tart red cherries, well drained
- 2 to 3 drops red food coloring, optional
- ⅛ tsp. almond extract
  Optional: Whipped cream or ice cream

1. Preheat oven to 375°. In a bowl, combine flour, 1 cup of sugar, baking powder, milk and oil; pour into a greased shallow 3-qt. baking dish. In a bowl, combine cherries, food coloring if desired, extract and remaining sugar; spoon over batter.

2. Bake 40-45 minutes or until a toothpick inserted in the cake portion comes out clean. Serve warm, with whipped cream or ice cream if desired.

1 SERVING: 296 cal., 3g fat (1g sat. fat), 3mg chol., 147mg sod., 65g carb. (48g sugars, 1g fiber), 3g pro.

BAKED APPLE SURPRISE

This sweet-savory recipe is a favorite. Use Brie instead of blue cheese if you like things creamier. If you bake the apples in a muffin tin, they won't roll around.
—Jessica Levinson, Nyack, NY

Prep: 10 min. • **Bake:** 35 min.
Makes: 2 servings

- 2 medium apples
- 2 Tbsp. crumbled blue cheese, divided
- 2 Tbsp. quick-cooking oats
- 2 Tbsp. bran flakes
- 1 Tbsp. golden raisins
- 1 Tbsp. raisins
- 1 Tbsp. brown sugar

1. Preheat oven to 350°. Cut apples in half lengthwise; remove the cores. Place in an ungreased 8-in. square baking dish. Fill each apple half with 1 tsp. blue cheese.
2. In a small bowl, combine the oats, bran flakes, golden raisins, raisins and brown sugar; spoon into apples. Top with remaining cheese. Bake, uncovered, until tender, 35-40 minutes.
2 FILLED APPLE HALVES: 181 cal., 3g fat (2g sat. fat), 6mg chol., 141mg sod., 39g carb. (27g sugars, 5g fiber), 3g pro.

CHEWY HONEY GRANOLA BARS

There's sweetness from the honey, chewiness from the raisins, a hint of chocolate and cinnamon, and a bit of crunch. These bars also freeze beautifully, so you can snack anytime.
—Tasha Lehman, Williston, VT

Prep: 10 min. • **Bake:** 15 min. + cooling
Makes: 20 servings

- 3 cups old-fashioned oats
- 2 cups unsweetened puffed wheat cereal
- 1 cup all-purpose flour
- ⅓ cup chopped walnuts
- ⅓ cup raisins
- ⅓ cup miniature semisweet chocolate chips
- 1 tsp. baking soda
- 1 tsp. ground cinnamon
- 1 cup honey
- ¼ cup butter, melted
- 1 tsp. vanilla extract

1. Preheat oven to 350°. In a large bowl, combine the first 8 ingredients. In a small bowl, combine the honey, butter and vanilla; pour over the oat mixture and mix well. (Mixture will be sticky.)
2. Press into a 13x9-in. baking pan coated with cooking spray. Bake for 14-18 minutes or until set and the edges are lightly browned. Cool on a wire rack. Cut into bars.
1 BAR: 178 cal., 5g fat (2g sat. fat), 6mg chol., 81mg sod., 32g carb. (17g sugars, 2g fiber), 3g pro. **DIABETIC EXCHANGES:** 2 starch, ½ fat.

COOKIES & CREAM BERRY DESSERTS

This sweet berry dessert makes an especially pretty final course. With berries, a creamy topping and a sprinkle of meringue cookies, it always earns rave reviews.

—*Lily Julow, Lawrenceville, GA*

- -

Prep: 10 min. + standing • **Makes:** 6 servings

- 2 cups quartered fresh strawberries
- 1¼ cups fresh raspberries
- 1¼ cups fresh blackberries
- ⅔ cup fresh blueberries
- 4 Tbsp. sugar, divided
- 2 tsp. lemon juice
- 4 oz. reduced-fat cream cheese
- 1½ cups fat-free whipped topping
  Dash ground cinnamon
- 6 meringue cookies

1. In a large bowl, combine the berries, 2 Tbsp. of sugar and the lemon juice; let stand at room temperature for 30 minutes.

2. In a small bowl, beat cream cheese until smooth. Beat in whipped topping, cinnamon and the remaining sugar until combined.

3. Just before serving, divide the berry mixture among 6 dessert dishes. Dollop with topping and add a cookie.

1 SERVING: 170 cal., 5g fat (3g sat. fat), 13mg chol., 93mg sod., 26g carb. (20g sugars, 5g fiber), 3g pro. **DIABETIC EXCHANGES:** 1 starch, 1 fruit, 1 fat.

LILY JULOW
Lawrenceville, GA

MINI WHITE PIZZAS

I make these savory pizzas in advance and freeze them. Then I can bake them whenever I need a quick appetizer or snack. They are so delicious!

—*Jocelyn Hook, Swoyersville, PA*

- -

Takes: 20 min. • **Makes:** 8 mini pizzas

- 1⅓ cups shredded part-skim mozzarella cheese
- ½ cup mayonnaise
- 1½ tsp. dried oregano
- ½ tsp. garlic powder
- ¼ tsp. salt
- ¼ tsp. pepper
- 4 English muffins, split

In a small bowl, combine first 6 ingredients. Spread over muffin halves; place on a baking sheet. Broil 3-4 in. from the heat until bubbly and golden brown, 5-8 minutes.

1 MINI PIZZA: 214 cal., 14g fat (4g sat. fat), 16mg chol., 358mg sod., 13g carb. (2g sugars, 1g fiber), 7g pro.

READER REVIEW

"These are so tasty and yet so simple to prepare and with so few ingredients— we loved them! You could also just bake up the cheese/mayo mixture and serve as a dip with crackers as an alternative snack."

JSANTULLO, TASTEOFHOME.COM

ALPHABETICAL INDEX

SUBSTITUTIONS & EQUIVALENTS

EQUIVALENT MEASURES

3 teaspoons	= 1 tablespoon	16 tablespoons	= 1 cup
4 tablespoons	= ¼ cup	2 cups	= 1 pint
5⅓ tablespoons	= ⅓ cup	4 cups	= 1 quart
8 tablespoons	= ½ cup	4 quarts	= 1 gallon

FOOD EQUIVALENTS

Macaroni	1 cup (3½ ounces) uncooked	= 2½ cups cooked
Noodles, medium	3 cups (4 ounces) uncooked	= 4 cups cooked
Popcorn	⅓-½ cup unpopped	= 8 cups popped
Rice, long grain	1 cup uncooked	= 3 cups cooked
Rice, quick-cooking	1 cup uncooked	= 2 cups cooked
Spaghetti	8 ounces uncooked	= 4 cups cooked

Bread	1 slice	= ¾ cup soft crumbs, ¼ cup fine dry crumbs
Graham crackers	7 squares	= ½ cup finely crushed
Buttery round crackers	12 crackers	= ½ cup finely crushed
Saltine crackers	14 crackers	= ½ cup finely crushed

Bananas	1 medium	= ⅓ cup mashed
Lemons	1 medium	= 3 tablespoons juice, 2 teaspoons grated zest
Limes	1 medium	= 2 tablespoons juice, 1½ teaspoons grated zest
Oranges	1 medium	= ¼-⅓ cup juice, 4 teaspoons grated zest

Cabbage	1 head = 5 cups shredded	Green pepper	1 large = 1 cup chopped
Carrots	1 pound = 3 cups shredded	Mushrooms	½ pound = 3 cups sliced
Celery	1 rib = ½ cup chopped	Onions	1 medium = ½ cup chopped
Corn	1 ear fresh = ⅔ cup kernels	Potatoes	3 medium = 2 cups cubed

Almonds	1 pound = 3 cups chopped	Pecan halves	1 pound = 4½ cups chopped
Ground nuts	3¾ ounces = 1 cup	Walnuts	1 pound = 3¾ cups chopped

EASY SUBSTITUTIONS

WHEN YOU NEED...		USE...
Baking powder	1 teaspoon	½ teaspoon cream of tartar + ¼ teaspoon baking soda
Buttermilk	1 cup	1 tablespoon lemon juice or vinegar + enough milk to measure 1 cup (let stand 5 minutes before using)
Cornstarch	1 tablespoon	2 tablespoons all-purpose flour
Honey	1 cup	1¼ cups sugar + ¼ cup water
Half-and-Half cream	1 cup	1 tablespoon melted butter + enough whole milk to measure 1 cup
Onion	1 small, chopped (⅓ cup)	1 teaspoon onion powder or 1 tablespoon dried minced onion
Tomato juice	1 cup	½ cup tomato sauce + ½ cup water
Tomato sauce	2 cups	¾ cup tomato paste + 1 cup water
Unsweetened chocolate	1 square (1 ounce)	3 tablespoons baking cocoa + 1 tablespoon shortening or oil
Whole milk	1 cup	½ cup evaporated milk + ½ cup water

GET COOKING WITH A WELL-STOCKED KITCHEN

In a perfect world, you plan weekly or even monthly menus and have the specific ingredients on hand to make each night's dinner. In reality, you may not have time to think about dinner until you walk through the door. With a thoughtfully stocked pantry, refrigerator and freezer, you'll still be able to serve a satisfying meal in short order. Having these basics on hand will keep your options wide open:

QUICK-COOKING MEATS—boneless chicken breasts and thighs, pork tenderloin and chops, ground meats, Italian sausage, sirloin and flank steaks, fish fillets or shrimp—should be stocked in the freezer. Wrap individual pieces and portions, so you can remove only the amount you need and defrost quickly.

FROZEN VEGETABLES are a real timesaver. Simply pour out the amount needed—no additional preparation is required.

PASTAS, RICE, RICE MIXES AND COUSCOUS are great staples to have in the pantry—and they generally have a long shelf life. Remember that thinner pastas, such as angel hair, cook more quickly than thicker pastas, and fresh (refrigerated) pasta cooks faster than dried.

DAIRY PRODUCTS like milk, sour cream, cheese, eggs, yogurt and butter are perishable, so be sure to check the package dates. Yogurt, sour cream or cream cheese can replace each other in most recipes.

CONDIMENTS like ketchup, mustard, mayonnaise, salad dressings, salsa, taco sauce, soy sauce, stir-fry sauce, hot sauce, lemon juice and lime juice add flavor to many dishes. Personalize the list to suit your family's tastes.

FRESH FRUITS AND VEGETABLES should be on your regular shopping list not only as recipe ingredients, but as a quick and satisfying pre-dinner snack. Bags of ready-to-use greens create instant salads.

SALAD DRESSINGS AND VINEGARS keep for months. They can be used on salads, of course, but also make flavorful marinades or recipe ingredients.

BROTH OR STOCK, CANNED OR DRIED SOUPS are pantry essentials. Stocks (or broths) are a basic building block; soups can be a quick meal on their own, or can be added to casseroles or other dishes.

PASTA SAUCE straight out of the jar on fresh pasta is a no-brainer dinner. But it also can be used in casseroles, skillet suppers and more.

CANNED TOMATOES, BEANS AND OTHER VEGETABLES are common recipe ingredients and can help add dimension to soups, sauces, and prepared rice and pasta dishes.

ONE FINAL TIP: Keep a running grocery list. When an item is almost gone, just add it to the list. You're less likely to run completely out of an item, and you'll save time when preparing your shopping list.

MAKE THE MOST OF YOUR TIME EVERY NIGHT

With recipes in hand and the kitchen stocked, you're well on the way to a relaxing family meal.
Here are some pointers to help get dinner on the table fast:

PREHEAT THE OVEN OR GRILL before starting on the recipe.

PULL OUT THE REQUIRED INGREDIENTS, mixing tools and cooking tools before beginning any prep work.

USE CONVENIENCE ITEMS whenever possible. Think pre-chopped garlic, onion and peppers, shredded or cubed cheese, seasoning mixes and jarred sauces.

MULTITASK! While the meat is simmering for a main dish, toss a salad, cook a side dish or start on dessert.

ENCOURAGE HELPERS. Younger children can set the table. Older ones can help with ingredient prep or assembling the recipes.

TAKE CARE OF TWO MEALS IN ONE NIGHT by planning main-dish leftovers or making a double batch of favorite sides.

TRICKS TO TAME HUNGER WHEN IT STRIKES

Are the kids begging for a pre-supper snack? Calm their rumbling tummies with nutritious, not-too-filling noshes.

START WITH A SMALL TOSSED SALAD. Try a ready-to-serve salad mix, and add their favorite salad dressing and a little protein, like cubed cheese or julienned slices of deli meat.

CUT UP AN APPLE and smear a little bit of peanut butter on each slice, or offer other fruits such as seedless grapes, cantaloupe, oranges or bananas. For variety, give kids vanilla yogurt as a dipper, or combine a little reduced-fat sour cream with a sprinkling of brown sugar. Too busy to cut up the fruit? A fruit snack cup will also do the trick!

DURING THE COLD MONTHS, a small mug of soup with a few oyster crackers on top can really hit the spot.

RAW VEGGIES such as carrots, cucumbers, mushrooms, broccoli and cauliflower are tasty treats, especially when served with a little hummus for dipping. Many vegetables can be purchased pre-cut.

OFFER CHEESE AND CRACKERS. Buy pre-sliced cheese, and cut the slices into smaller squares to fit the crackers. Choose crackers made from whole wheat, such as an all-natural seven-grain type.